658.4

Bankable
Leadership

Happy People, Bottom-Line Results,
and the Power to Deliver Both

DR. TASHA EURICH

GREENLEAF
BOOK GROUP PRESS

Published by Greenleaf Book Group Press
Austin, Texas
www.gbgpress.com

Distributed by Greenleaf Book Group LLC

For ordering information or special discounts for bulk purchases, please contact Greenleaf Book Group LLC at PO Box 91869, Austin, TX 78709, 512.891.6100.

Design and composition by Greenleaf Book Group LLC
Cover design by Greenleaf Book Group LLC
Cover image: ©Thinkstock/Zoonar Collection

Cataloging-in-Publication data
(Prepared by The Donohue Group, Inc.)
Eurich, Tasha.
  Bankable leadership : happy people, bottom-line results, and the power to deliver both / Tasha Eurich.—1st ed.
   p. : ill. ; cm.
  Issued also as an ebook.
  ISBN: 978-1-62634-019-0
  1. Leadership. 2. Personnel management. 3. Work environment. I. Title.
HD57.7 .E97 2013
658.4/092   2013941204

Part of the Tree Neutral® program, which offsets the number of trees consumed in the production and printing of this book by taking proactive steps, such as planting trees in direct proportion to the number of trees used: www.treeneutral.com

TreeNeutral®

Printed in the United States of America on acid-free paper

13 14 15 16 17 18   10 9 8 7 6 5 4 3 2 1

First Edition

CONTENTS

For my HB. ILYVVM

ACKNOWLEDGMENTS

They say that it takes a village to raise a child. Though I am sure that raising a child is pretty complicated, I believe that it takes a large town—a city, even—to transform a book from the mere seed of an idea into a reality. So please settle in—I need to thank a lot of people.

My journey to get here started in high school. When I was seventeen years old, I remember watching an episode of *Sex and the City* where the main character, Carrie Bradshaw, publishes her first book. The pang of jealousy I felt was a profound signal to me: We humans, and most especially teenage girls, tend to envy the things that we desperately want in our lives. So from then on, it's been my dream to publish a book. My first acknowledgement therefore goes to the fine writers of *Sex and the City* (and to Carrie Bradshaw for being so utterly fabulous—not related to the book but it needs to be said).

Flash forward fifteen years. One seemingly random day, I woke up and decided it was time to make my dream a reality. I knew absolutely nothing about writing or publishing a book, and therefore concluded that I needed professional help. I first turned to my mentor, Ray Vigil, to ask if I was delusional. He was confident I wasn't, though I had my doubts; luckily, I listened to Ray instead of the voices in my head. Ray, your unwavering support has helped me muster the courage to do things I never thought possible—this book is just one small part of that. I'm so lucky to have you in my life, as made possible by our mutual friend Bob Gonzales.

Thanks to the many authors who generously guided me throughout this process: Marshall Goldsmith, Chip Heath, Barbara Corcoran, Tony Schwartz, Debra Fine, Tommy Spaulding, Kim Cameron, David Nour, and Scott Halford: I am deeply humbled and grateful for your support. In return, as Marshall once requested, I vow to do the same for a budding future author—if and when I have anything helpful to tell her!

I'd like to reserve an extra measure of gratitude for Scott Halford. Scott, unquestionably, this amazing journey would not have happened without you. Early on in my quest for guidance, Scott took me up on a coffee invitation. After some witty and enjoyable repartee, he asked about my book. I told him my vague idea, and to my great amazement, he offered to introduce me to the CEO of his publisher. *That's so generous,* I thought, *What wonderful intentions—but this probably won't go anywhere. It won't be this easy.* Scott saw the disbelief in my eyes and promised, "I'll do it today."

I arrived home to Scott's e-mail to Clint Greenleaf and—gasp!—a response! I soon found myself pitching my half-formed idea to the CEO of one of the choosiest publishers in the business. I remember hovering above my body, listening to what I was saying, and thinking, *Stop talking! Get off the phone! Abort! You have never sounded so trite and simplistic—he'll never go for it!* Clint listened calmly. When I was finished, he thoughtfully replied, "Wow. If I had known any of that when I took on my first leadership role, it would have saved me about ten years of pain and suffering." I almost fainted.

I cannot say enough superlative things about the team at Greenleaf. Clint: Thank you for taking my meeting and for creating a publishing house where authors are supported and valued. Lari Bishop: You are an absolute treasure and I was lucky to have you as my editor. I don't typically relish phone calls, but our weekly conversations were always stimulating and enjoyable. Let's do this again sometime. Jonas Koffler: You helped me crystalize so many things about the book—and life in general—I appreciate your kind and creative nudging. Many thanks to the rest of the team who guided this book, including Justin Branch, Aaron Hierholzer (my favorite e-mail buddy!), Kim Lance, Abby Kitten, Steven Elizalde and Jessica Birenz Pflanz, for your commitment to this project—and your patience with my perfectionist, Type A personality. It's tough to handle, I know, and I thank you.

To all the Bankable Leaders whom I interviewed for this project: Your stories and insights have made the book what it is. Margaret Kelly, Kim Jordan, Natalie Roper, Elisa Speranza, Todd Habliston, Scott Page, Greg Herr, Morre Dean, Andrea Gwyn, Bob Chapman, Christy Martello, Samer Al-Faqih, Cathy Bernardino Bailey, Bud Ahearn, Jandel Allen-Davis, Jacob Wiesmann, Tom Horton, Courtney Harrison, Lynn Gangone, Mark Hughes, Patty Gage, Steve Gelman, Penni Key, Stephen Ladek, Jill McClure, Tracee Hendershott, Pat Lawrence, Ray Vigil, Carolyn De Rubertis, Terri Wanger, Mark Gasta, Andy Ziller, Jandel Allen-Davis, Ty Kasperbauer, Jerry Maglio, Emeka Ene, Betsy Hunsicker, Guadalupe Del Canto, Sheryl Benjamin, and Rajesh Setty, you're an inspiration to leaders everywhere—I'm truly in awe!

To my team at The Eurich Group: You are rock stars. First, my research team—Mike Jacobson, Uma Kedharnarth, and Kyle Sandell: You did a lovely job of translating my vague ideas into tangible, empirically supported arguments. An extra shout-out goes to Mike: You were there from the beginning and contributed so much—any PhD program will be lucky to have you. To Gretchen Anderson, my sassy and spectacular right-hand woman: I still cannot figure out how I functioned before I had you on my team. I am truly thankful and will try to be as bankable as possible every day, so I never have to live without you!

To those in my life who donated their time and brilliance and/or took pity on me at various stages of this process: Dana Bowler, Patty Gage, Bill Whalen, Lucy Miller, Sarah Gibson, Stephen Ladek, Mike Herron, Coles Whalen, Rachel Johnson, Scott Haskins, Erin Blackwell, Kristen Kenton, Jenn Fox Bell, and Elisa Speranza (especially our pivotal late-night phone call). To Lauren Choate, my friend, colleague, and spirit guide: Every step of the way, you've helped me see things clearly.

Thanks to my friends and family—who haven't seen me in the last year while I was writing this book—for being so understanding and (I think) continuing to love me anyway. I look forward to seeing you all again very soon.

To my grandparents, parents, and siblings, who teach me the value of hard work and character every day. I am standing on your shoulders and hope I've made you proud. And to Terri Wanger (aka Mama): You are more than just a mother to me in ways I am only beginning to understand. You're my proudest fan, my most fervent supporter, my fiercest protector, my smartest business development person, my most loving heart, and the only singular person who's been by my side through all of my thirty-two years. Thank you.

To my husband, Dave Ladek (aka HB). You are my soulmate. I knew this virtually immediately on our first date, when we comfortably held five simultaneous conversations, one of which was about show tunes. From the moment you walked into my life, you've supported me in every conceivable way—I have never met a person with a more generous heart or spirit. You put up with my constant obsession with my work, my unrelenting travel, and my general exhaustion and whininess from the aforementioned activities—and you do it with understanding and grace. You've contributed to the success of The Eurich Group and this book in more ways than I think you know. I will strive to show you how much I appreciate everything you do for me, big and small, every day. I hope to do this by selling a million books so you can become a man of leisure and we can travel the world together. ILY.

To Spike, Willow, and Cleo: Even though you're very smart dogs, I know you can't read this. But you have given me the most unconditional love and support I could ever ask for in my life—you're my fluffy children and my three other soulmates. Love you babies!

INTRODUCTION

"How could they think this about me?" muttered Todd Habliston, shaking his head dejectedly.

"It's not great news," I conceded, "but the problems are fixable."

In a corner office at company headquarters, Todd and I were poring over the results of my interviews with his team. He was a leader at a public oil and gas company, and we'd scheduled four hours together. We were going to need every second.

The head of human resources and Todd's boss had asked me to serve as his coach. The company was in the middle of a large-scale, top-to-bottom turnaround. To succeed, leaders at all levels would need to rise to the challenge, and Todd was poised to play a big role in the organization's future. Currently managing a $240 million budget in one of the most critical areas of the company, he had the perfect pedigree of technical skills and experience. In his thirty years in oil and gas, he'd done everything from field development to reservoir management. He had a track record of tremendous results; in a prior role, his operating assets reached production levels of more than twenty thousand barrels of oil per day. But Todd's ascension was in danger of being interrupted. Beneath the veneer of successful leadership lurked some serious issues. Most notably, two talented engineers had recently resigned from his team. Of course, it's not news that poor leadership is the number one reason people quit their jobs, but these two engineers had made it explicit: In their exit interviews, they indicated that Todd's leadership style was a significant factor in their decision to leave.

When I interviewed those who worked with Todd, most agreed that he was a hardworking professional who cared deeply about the company. But nearly everyone believed that he wasn't getting the most from his team, and many questioned his motives. One disquieting story I heard more than once occurred when Todd's boss, Glen, went on vacation and asked Todd to run the staff meeting. Todd entered the conference room and quipped, "Since I'm in charge, I'll take Glen's chair." What Todd had intended to be a joke was interpreted quite differently by his peers—they took it as overwhelming evidence of his nefarious intentions to climb over them in his quest for professional domination.

Put simply, Todd wasn't bankable. He was struggling to reliably produce the results expected of him. Why? The way he was coming across made it difficult for others to trust him. The general impression was that he didn't communicate and made unilateral decisions. His staff felt micromanaged, noting that Todd was often in the office until late in the evening looking over (or re-doing) the work they had done, and that he hardly ever took vacations. Instead of feeling supported, they felt like he didn't believe in their capabilities. Perhaps most tragically, they rarely received feedback on, or recognition for, their hard work.

This was the news I had to break to Todd when we met. In the ten-plus years I have worked with leaders, from the front line to the C-suite, I have had to break similar news many times. Usually the recipient is a highly technically competent professional who then realizes that the people skills needed to be a good leader are completely different from the skills he or she has relied on so far.

What's worse, most newly promoted leaders don't receive leadership training. They are left to their own devices from the beginning, and the myth that being a good leader is an inborn quality is perpetuated. "I don't understand it," one leader once confided in me. "Being a leader seems so easy for everyone else. Am I the only one who's missing something?"

Let's see if any of the following questions feel familiar to you:

- Whenever I walk into the room and all conversation halts, are they talking about me behind my back? Have I become Michael Scott from *The Office*?

- Why can't my employees just do what I tell them? Why do I have to have so many conversations with them just to get the work done?

- Why do I feel so uncomfortable when I have to make difficult decisions or hold people accountable? Why is it so hard for me to be the bad guy when I need to?

- Are my employees getting complacent? Are they perfectly happy with the status quo? And if I recognize them for their work, what will I do if they start to act entitled?

- Why is my team leaving the office at 4:00, leaving me to do the work on my own? Why are they so lazy when they could be more productive and keep me from being burnt out beyond belief?

These questions represent a fundamental tension—felt by every leader—between putting people first and delivering results:

$$\text{PEOPLE} \Longleftrightarrow \text{RESULTS}$$

On one hand, you must build relationships by connecting with your team, earning trust and motivating them to perform. On the other, you must drive top- and bottom-line results through your team's performance and productivity (Todd was certainly leaning heavily toward the results end of the spectrum). These two outcomes often feel like they are mutually exclusive. *I can drive my people to perform*, you think, *OR I can be their friend.*

But the belief that leaders can't learn to do both is the biggest leadership myth in business.

As it turned out, Todd would serve as living proof of this truth. Much to his credit, Todd accepted the feedback I shared that day with grace, humility, and curiosity. Clearly, it was time to do things differently. Todd wanted to create an environment known for long-term employment—a place where employees could be happy and fulfilled and perform at their best—all while delivering the results and continuous improvement the company needed.

So we rolled up our sleeves and crafted a plan. First, Todd came clean to his direct reports. He took each person to the restaurant of their choice. In these one-on-one meetings, he courageously shared his interview results and thanked the employee for their feedback. Then he explained his true intentions: to do the best thing for them and the company. He asked for their support in holding him to these goals, just as he would do with them. If he was misbehaving, he noted, they had permission to call him out. Todd ended each meeting by committing to continue these one-on-one meetings every month so his direct reports could receive regular coaching and feedback. Over a period of weeks, Todd and his team created a series of agreements for how they'd work together to make everyone successful.

The second part of Todd's plan was to find frequent opportunities to recognize and thank his team members for their hard work. As luck would have it, while Todd was implementing his coaching plan, the company was going through its annual budgeting process. Todd's team played a key role and threw itself into this challenging assignment. After the budgets were submitted, Todd sent a handwritten card to each person, thanking them for their contribution. He reported that this simple action was satisfying and heartwarming. And much to his surprise, he even received a thank-you card for his thank-you card! It came from a fresh-out-of-school engineer with her whole career ahead of her. Todd was truly touched by her message:

> Thank you so much for the gift card. I greatly appreciate the thought and words of encouragement; it means a lot to me. I will continue to try hard and do the best I can in hopes to further grow as a reservoir engineer. Thank you for all of your help, time, and efforts!

The third part of Todd's plan was to change his communication patterns. Before our coaching process, Todd would make a daily beeline from his morning leadership meetings to his office and fire off e-mails with work assignments to his team. This almost always led to groans from his employees. *What does he want now?* they'd think. Or, *What on earth is he asking us to do?* Now, he manages by walking around. Todd literally makes laps around the office, sitting down with his direct reports to check in individually. His team is no longer left wondering why his requests are important, or why they're being asked to do certain things. One week, Todd made three full laps and didn't return to his office until lunchtime!

In just three short months, Todd had made a 180-degree turn as a leader. He managed to transform a team that was merely functioning into one that excelled. He set high—and crystal clear—expectations, and the team was working more productively and collaboratively than ever. His team now trusted him and felt committed to the company. His boss was thrilled. And Todd was finally able to take a vacation.

Like Todd, effective leaders manage the universal tension between focusing on people and delivering results. The ability to do both is the essence of Bankable Leadership, a series of learnable behaviors that will allow you to develop a successful team, increase your own confidence and well-being, and deliver results that you—and your company—can take straight to the bank.

I have maintained for a long time that the field of leadership is unnecessarily complex. If you search for a leadership book on Amazon, you'll be overwhelmed with more than 100,000 options. Most of those books cover only one aspect of leadership, making the goal of learning how to lead feel complex and impossible. But I believe that effective leadership is quite simple. It's not always easy—in fact, it's really hard for many of us—but we've known for decades nearly everything we need to know about what it takes to be a good leader. We don't need new theories. We just need a straightforward model that builds on what already exists.

BANKABLE LEADERSHIP: MANAGING FOUR BASIC TENSIONS

You probably already know how to build a budget, negotiate a deal, read a financial statement, and build a capital expenditure case. But does that make you a good leader? You may be a top performer in sales, but do you know how to create a high-performing sales team? To get the most out of them? To feel fulfilled in your job beyond just meeting your quota? If you're like many leaders, these questions make you feel anxious, or maybe even slightly panicked. Why? Because most organizations spend a lot of time and money on technical training but invest precious little in teaching people to lead. The senior leaders in your organization may feel just as overwhelmed by the topic of leadership as you do, hoping that if they simply hire good leaders, everyone will magically follow their example.

For such an important factor in the success of an organization, this is a pretty passive approach. You've probably heard that employee engagement is strongly linked to financial success. One famous study conducted at Sears found that for every five-point increase in employee engagement, customer satisfaction increased 1.3 percent, which then increased revenue by 0.5 percent. In a company with $50 million in revenue, that means a $250,000 increase, which translates directly to the bottom line!

And what creates employee engagement? Leadership! In one study, researchers divided leaders at a Fortune 500 commercial bank into three groups: excellent leaders (the top 10 percent), average leaders (the middle 80 percent), and poor leaders (the bottom 10 percent). When they looked at the operating profit of each office, they found that leadership effectiveness had a clear effect on the bottom line: The poor leaders' departments had a net loss of $1.2 million, while the departments of the excellent leaders had a total net income of $4.5 million.[1]

When we put it that way, who *wouldn't* want to be a great leader? Good leaders create prosperity for all involved: themselves, their team, and their organization. Prosperity is certainly about financial viability, but not entirely. We've all had jobs where the money is great, but we're miserable. My definition of prosperity is more like this: *thriving through a combination of achievement, happiness, health, and wealth.* How do leaders achieve it? And how do they become bankable? By displaying behaviors that balance four basic tensions between taking care of people and driving results:

- **Be Human *and* Drive Performance**. Bankable Leaders balance caring for and understanding team members as people with the need to drive their individual performance.

- **Be Helpful *and* Drive Responsibility**. They balance helping team members succeed with ensuring that they feel responsibility for the results they produce, rather than abdicating or making excuses.

- **Be Thankful *and* Drive Improvement**. They balance showing appreciation for what team members contribute with driving a continuous improvement mindset that things can always be better.

- **Be Happy *and* Drive Productivity**. They balance enjoying (and not being overwhelmed by) work with ensuring that each team member is maximally contributing.

This balance between *people* and *results* lies at the heart of the Bankable Leadership model, which not only integrates current research on the best ways to lead but is based on a premise that was put forth almost seventy years ago. It's like the time you found your TV remote tucked under a couch cushion after hours of searching elsewhere in your house: The secrets to leadership have been here all along. We just didn't look in the most obvious place—the earliest research on the topic.

In 1945, a group of researchers at Ohio State University set out to disprove the notion that the ability to be a good leader was an inborn personality trait. With foremen at the International Harvester Company as their subjects, the researchers found that successful leadership was indeed *not* related to personality. Instead, it was related to the presence of two behaviors.

Bankable Leadership™ Model

PEOPLE ⟺ RESULTS
Be Human ⟺ Drive Performance
Be Helpful ⟺ Drive Responsibility
Be Thankful ⟺ Drive Improvement
Be Happy ⟺ Drive Productivity

First, effective leaders *initiated structure*. They clearly defined the role that each employee played and drove their performance so they could accomplish their goals. Second, they *showed consideration*, displaying support, compassion, and friendliness to their team. Does this sound familiar? It should: These two components of effective leadership map directly onto the *people* and *results* elements of the Bankable Leadership model. This was the first study that brought its core concepts to light.

Perhaps the most interesting finding of the study was that the abilities to initiate structure (*Results*) and show consideration (*People*) were independent of one another. That is, a leader could be strong in one, both, or neither. And as we'll see, Bankable Leaders are able to do both.

Not long ago, I received the ultimate validation of Bankable Leadership. I was presenting the model to a group of leaders in a workshop, and toward the end, I asked what they thought of it. One gentleman raised his hand and said, "This describes the best boss I ever had." In that moment, I realized that the same was true for me. Though I've had a string of amazing managers, I immediately thought of Shelie Gustafson. Shelie was the perfect example of a Bankable Leader—she took care of people and drove results by successfully managing the four tensions:

- Despite her soft-spoken demeanor, she set aggressive performance targets (*Drive Performance*). At the same time, I could always talk to her about my challenges and receive support (*Be Human*).

- She helped me perform by giving me coaching and clear goals (*Be Helpful*), but never let me shirk responsibility for my successes or failures (*Drive Responsibility*).

- Shelie regularly showed gratitude for my efforts and accomplishments (*Be Thankful*), but always pushed me to improve (*Drive Improvement*).

- And though she expected us to get our work done efficiently (*Drive Productivity*), she frequently found time and space for her team to celebrate and have fun together—I remember that one of the loveliest moments the week I got engaged to my husband was sharing the news with Shelie and our team (*Be Happy*).

In short, Shelie Gustafson was, and is, a Bankable Leader.

Shelie showed me that even though the behaviors in the model might initially feel mutually exclusive, the best leaders are able to do both at the same time. Most leaders' natural tendency is to lean more toward people or more toward results. The comfort position we find on the spectrum is usually based on a variety of factors, including personality, organizational culture, upbringing, and early role models. For a few, that comfort position is naturally in the middle; these individuals leverage each pole to support the other.

Other leaders, however, seem to exist all the way at one pole or the other. On the left side—*People*—is the "cool parent" leader, who doesn't create boundaries, set expectations, or make tough decisions. I once worked with a leader who was one of the kindest souls I have ever met. She cared so deeply about her people that she was afraid of upsetting them and therefore wasn't clear about what she expected. She would even reverse decisions if they appeared to distress anyone. But instead of making the team happy, this behavior was frustrating, confusing, and demoralizing. Despite her best intentions, she was not effective.

On the right side—*Results*—is the "It's not personal—it's just business" leader, who drives results so aggressively that the human side of the team is neglected and people suffer physically (burnout, stress, sickness) and psychologically (fear, dread, paranoia). I have also worked with this type of leader. He pushed his people so hard that they frequently broke into tears in his office. He rarely showed appreciation for his team's hard work and frequently said things like, "You need to work harder next time." He often achieved his business plan, but his team was demoralized and burnt out. His was not a sustainable leadership method. Few could work for him for long, so he experienced constant turnover, and his team wasted energy on being afraid of him that they could have used to produce results.

Even if you recognize aspects of your leadership approach in these descriptions, you can learn to *Move to the Middle*. The Bankable Leadership model can help you build on your natural tendencies and strengths to achieve guaranteed relationships and results by doing both.

ANYONE CAN LEARN TO BE AN EFFECTIVE LEADER

The drive to be better is an essential part of the equation of good leadership. You certainly wouldn't have picked up this book if you had no interest in being more effective. Luckily, there's good news: Researchers are becoming increasingly confident that leadership is largely learned. Richard Arvey, professor at the NUS Business School in Singapore, showed that a whopping 70 percent of the variability in leadership effectiveness is the result of experience.[2] This is very good news. It means that *virtually anyone can become an effective leader,* particularly if they are willing to learn from leadership research and the experience of others.

Throughout this book, you'll hear true stories of leaders—across industries and organizational levels—who have made powerful transformations. I'll also describe the core practices of effective leadership. What I *won't* do is provide a plethora of leadership generalities or platitudes. I believe that the science of leadership is strong, so you'll see decades of research findings put together in new ways to help you learn how the best leaders lead.

These stories and science are helpful, but you're probably also looking for specific advice to help you face your own daily leadership challenges. So for every idea we discuss, I'll present clear approaches and tools that you can use to improve in each area. Each chapter will end with a series of "Bankable Actions"—based on the content of the chapter—listing specific suggestions to improve that particular leadership behavior. And at the end of the book, you'll choose two specific behaviors to work on that will improve your leadership effectiveness in the next three months.

I also encourage you to visit BankableLeadership.com for more tools. There, you'll find more resources and a web-based, multi-rater leadership effectiveness assessment. Because it's a multi-rater assessment, you'll be able to compare your self-ratings with how others rated you. Because the perceptions of your behavior by those around you are what matter most, you can stack your self-ratings against the way others see you. And just as you have to step on the scale before you start a weight-loss program, you'll need to see how your behaviors stack up against the behaviors in the model. This way, you can direct your "improvement energy" to the behaviors with the greatest payoff.

It is my hope that this book becomes your encyclopedia of leadership. When you're facing a problem, you'll be able to turn to the appropriate section or chapter to identify the highest-value change you can make. And to make the book even easier to use, in the index you'll find a list of common leadership challenges. In a nutshell, this book will help you deliver guaranteed team performance. In the process, you'll banish fear and uncertainty about your leadership effectiveness and replace it with confidence. And when you successfully balance people and results, your team—and you—will feel happier and more productive.

Michelangelo once said about his art, "I saw the angel in the marble and I carved until I set him free." Without a doubt, there is a Bankable Leader within you—so let's start carving.

Part I

BE HUMAN *and* DRIVE PERFORMANCE

During my first conversation with Patty Gage, I asked her to sum up her team's situation in one sentence. She did—with the perfect metaphor.

"We have too many different zoo animals in the same pen," she explained. "They're all great people, and they're not carnivorous—so they're just hiding at the edges of the pen, trying to keep to themselves as much as possible."

Patty was a whip-smart, well-respected commercial real estate banker. She had been hired by Colorado Business Bank to bring rigor and discipline to the bank's commercial real estate group. Walking into a challenging situation on the heels of the Great Recession, Patty was tasked with transforming the organization's commercial lending department to a standardized and scalable powerhouse. Given the organization's informal and flexible culture, this was a tall order. But she had a killer network and an incomparable drive for results. *How hard could it be?* she had wondered.

To get her team where it needed to be, Patty needed to bring in senior bankers with backgrounds in large banks, private equity, and private development. *This will be great*, Patty thought. But it wasn't great. Her new bankers had a markedly different way of doing things, which proved to be rather unsettling for the "old guard." Some decided that they weren't a fit for the new group and left the company. Others began to show signs of conflict, which detracted from the team's success and eventually created more turnover.

Patty felt like she was hitting a brick wall. The team was a great bunch of people who had no idea how to work together. She knew she'd have to do something—quickly—to get the team back on track. That's when she called me.

I interviewed her team members, one by one. Over and over, they complained that they didn't understand where the team was headed: How were they going to meet aggressive goals? Would they be involved in changes to how things were done? What would the changes mean for their daily work? They had lots of questions and few answers. The team also viewed Patty's disciplined approach and packed schedule as evidence that she didn't care about them as individuals, which couldn't have been further from the truth.

When I reviewed the themes from my interviews with her team, she stared at me, stunned into paralysis. Then with a small smile, Patty joked, "Wait, what? You mean that not everyone can read my mind and just automatically do things my way?" We both chuckled.

The solution was immediately clear to both of us. This was a team of relative strangers who didn't have a strong understanding of, or appreciation for, one another as people, and as their leader, Patty needed to make the first move. Most were introverts, including Patty. I would often joke that you could hear a pin drop when you walked through their work area, and it was true. There was no sign of the usual buzz of coworker chatter.

But at the retreat we conducted, the team experienced a breakthrough. "You all lived through the downturn," Patty began, "and you all know that our reputation in this bank hasn't been particularly positive. More than anything, I want us to be the best-managed portfolio in the bank—and be proud! Each of you is a critical piece of the puzzle, and I can't do it without you." Her team nodded enthusiastically, looking truly hopeful. Patty smiled.

That was just the beginning. Later in the day, Patty surprised the team again. To help her team learn more about one another, we arranged for them to take a personality assessment. Carrying the metaphor of our original conversation, Patty purchased a small stuffed animal to represent each personality type: a poodle, a bear, a giraffe. She dutifully delivered each team member their stuffed animal and explained why she chose the animals she did. For the first time, possibly ever, the team broke into a fit of genuine laughter. By being herself, Patty provided the glue that was needed for her team to connect with each other—and with Patty!

The team capped off the day with its first-ever happy hour. Almost immediately, everyone—including Patty—seemed more comfortable being themselves. As those connections continued to grow over the following weeks, the team helped each other and bravely worked through conflict when it arose.

Through a few simple but powerful behavioral changes, Patty had managed to turn her team around. In a matter of months, everything started to improve. On the people side, the "lone ranger" approach we'd seen before had been replaced by genuine collaboration. For instance, the bankers trusted their administrative staff and were more willing to let them run with things. This made the bankers more efficient and gave the administrative staff a clearer sense of purpose. The administrative staff, previously intimidated by the bankers, now felt comfortable approaching them when a problem came up. The team shared a new sense of camaraderie and met monthly to recognize its accomplishments.

On the results side, the team excelled. In the year prior, their loan-grading metric had received a "needs improvement" rating; the two ratings following its breakthroughs were "satisfactory," and the second rating received positive comments from the auditors, which is quite unusual. Patty's team now has one of the best reputations in the bank for excellent loan underwriting documentation and management. The vision Patty shared at the retreat had materialized.

As Patty learned, Bankable Leaders connect with their teams as human beings *and* drive them to top performance. It is a rare leader who can do both naturally, without careful thought and development. I often meet leaders who say things like, "I don't want to hear people's whining—I just want them to do their jobs." Less frequently, but still often, they say, "I just want them to be happy! I don't want my team to think I'm a tyrant." The spectrum might look like this:

BE HUMAN  DRIVE PERFORMANCE
The Pushover   The Tyrant

On the left is The Pushover. This leader is overly focused on the happiness of her staff, so rather than being direct and up front, she'll tell her team what she thinks they want to hear. Mediocrity is the trademark of The Pushover. Michael Scott from *The Office* is a great example. As is clear from his "World's Best Boss" coffee mug, he's so interested in being liked that he doesn't push his team to greatness.

On the right is The Tyrant, who is focused on performance at all costs. This type of leader can often create results; however, research tells us that they aren't sustainable and will come at a cost. For example, if you forced your team members to work twelve hours a day, they might get a lot done . . . at first. But after six months, they would leave the company, get sick, or at the very least start to resent you. The movie *Office Space* is a prime example of what happens when managers focus on the bottom line above all else. In that case, the protagonists start embezzling money from the company, and the downtrodden Milton burns the building down. Most of the time, the resentment is more subtle, but you get the idea.

Think about how it would feel to work for each type of leader. Both might be fine for a while, but for different reasons. The Pushover would be fun to talk to and would probably show you she cared about you as a person. But when the time came for a tough conversation, she'd start acting strangely. Instead of giving you feedback, she may beat around the bush and leave you confused about what to do differently. In times of change, you might notice that she's telling different people different things, and chaos would ensue by virtue of the sheer confusion.

The Tyrant might help you bring your "A game" for a few months, and the feeling of accomplishment might be rewarding. But over time, you'll wonder whether he values you as a person or even appreciates your work. You'll start to feel resentful that you're not being recognized, and you may be tempted to even the score by *not* going the extra mile. When another job opens up, you'll pursue it, longing for a boss who cares about you.

As I mentioned earlier, you probably lean more toward one pole than the other, but you need to do both to do either one well. For instance, to get great results, you have to connect with your team on a human level. A Development Dimensions International study found that more than two-thirds of employees report putting in more effort when their manager supports and listens to them.[1] And to connect with your team, you have to give them something to be a part of that's worth their best efforts.

Even though the behaviors of The Pushover and The Tyrant might feel opposite, they are simply different sides of the same coin. Just like Patty, you can broaden your repertoire to become a results-focused leader who also connects with her staff and helps them connect with each other. If you've ever worked for a boss like this, you probably excelled at your work and felt extremely satisfied in your job.

Bill Daniels is the epitome of such a Bankable Leader. Often called the "Father of Cable Television," Daniels created a community antenna television system in 1952, allowing television broadcasts to reach remote Wyoming communities whose reception had previously been blocked by mountain ranges. In 1958, he established Daniels & Associates, a cable television brokerage firm and investment bank. After spending nearly fifty years in the business, Daniels was inducted into Colorado's Business Hall of Fame, with Daniels & Associates having enjoyed a tremendous amount of success—in its first ten years the company brokered more than $100 million in deals.

Daniels valued his employees as people *and* relentlessly pushed them to greatness. Describing his performance/results side, a *Rocky Mountain News* article dubbed him "utterly demanding and absolutely precise."[2] One of his mottos was literally chiseled into the lobby wall of his Denver office building: "The best is good enough for me." Here's an example of how this value drove his leadership, as described in *Relentless*, a biography of Daniels:

Bill was . . . known to conduct surprise inspections of his company facilities, which could cause quite a scramble if he showed up unexpectedly. Associates at one of Bill's cable systems in California remembered the day Bill was on his way for a visit, and they realized the goldfish pond was overgrown with algae. In the last 20 minutes before Bill arrived, they removed the fish, emptied the water, took the pond apart, and placed a plant from someone's office onto the remaining concrete podium. Despite their last-ditch efforts, the employees later received a scathing letter from Bill. "You will find this company one of the easiest ones to work for, and I am tolerant of many faults, as I have many, but I will not tolerate sloppiness, untidiness, and unkempt areas." With tongue in cheek, he concluded the letter, "The good news is I write a letter like this about every five years. The bad news is you never know when I'm coming to town."[3]

Based on this story, one might conclude that Daniels was a tyrant who achieved "the best" at the expense of the people. This couldn't have been further from the truth—he was even more famous for his compassion and humanity. As Daniels told the *Rocky Mountain News*, "If people feel they're part of a company, if they feel they're part of the action, you don't think they produce more? Business is people. And the people are the company."[4]

Daniels's associates were notoriously loyal, often working with him for decades. One such associate was John Saeman, who joined Daniels & Associates in 1965. Saeman worked for Daniels for nearly twenty years. In *Relentless*, Saeman is quoted as saying, "There are few human beings that I think are any better than Bill. He's just a very warm, giving individual."[5] Daniels appreciated and understood the essential humanity in his associates, noting that:

> people want more than a paycheck for their efforts. They want to know you care about them. They want you to listen to their ideas, be open to their suggestions, and provide them with a good . . . environment. There's a common misconception in the workplace. People always feel they have to please the boss. But if a company is to be successful, it has to be the other way around.[6]

Daniels stood by his associates during tough times, no questions asked. At one point, Jerry Maglio, Daniels's chief marketing and programming executive, was in the middle of a divorce. Bill would frequently check in with Jerry, who appreciated anyone asking about his personal situation, especially his boss. One day, Bill asked Jerry how he was faring financially in the divorce. Jerry, whom Bill called "Shoes," said, "I have about forty-eight bucks. But it will be alright."

When Jerry came back from lunch that day, there was a note on his desk. It said "Shoes—I wasn't sure if you were kidding about the $48. In case you weren't, this ought to help. Just let me know what you did for my records. Go get 'em. — Bill." Enclosed was a blank check from Daniels's personal account. Jerry was so touched by this gesture that tears welled in his eyes as he clutched Bill's note. Of course, his reaction wasn't about the money—he never even cashed the check. When Jerry told me this story, he concluded it by saying, "He was always there for us. Always. And when you get right down to it, I would have run through a brick wall for that man."

Above all, Bill Daniels loved people. As one of the most generous philanthropists of his era, he donated tens of millions of dollars to worthy causes during his lifetime (often anonymously), and his estate created a $1 billion foundation with grants paid out to the "people causes" Daniels passionately supported: aging, alcoholism and substance abuse, disabilities, education, ethics, the homeless, and youth development.

Both Bill Daniels and Patty Gage learned to bridge the tension between humanity and performance. In your own team, you'll know when you start to do both, because each outcome will feed the other and the effects will be exponential. The interactions between you and your team members will start to feel easier, and you'll feel a stronger connection with them. Instead of seeing "Alex the accountant," you'll get to know Alex, the mother of two college-aged kids who wants to be a manager someday and has always wanted to travel to India. Because of these connections, your team will work harder for you. This success will feel even sweeter because of the mutual connection and respect. And this respect will make it easier to ask your team for more when an extra push is needed. Instead of rolling their eyes, they'll kick into gear.

In this section, I'll introduce four tools to help you balance humanity and performance. In chapter 1, we'll review the importance and outcomes of trust, then provide a few simple and practical ways to earn it from your team. In chapter 2, we'll discuss the importance of transparency of information and intent, and deconstruct how you can practice it. Chapter 3 will outline the importance of clear expectations and provide a step-by-step process to create them. I'll end with a discussion of compassion—why it matters and how to demonstrate it—in chapter 4.

And as we'll see, even if you can't write your employees a blank check or start a billion-dollar foundation, you can absolutely emulate the humanity and high standards that Bill Daniels bestowed on his associates.

CHAPTER 1

TRUST AND BE TRUSTED

My heart was pounding out of my chest. Had it really come to this?

In a windowless conference room, I sat across the table from Barry and Jim, two vice presidents in a small high-tech company. I waited in the uncomfortably long silence for someone to say something—anything. "So," Jim said, "is this our marriage counseling session?"

I sighed. This was going to be a tough meeting.

Six months ago, Barry's company had acquired a smaller organization where Jim worked and retained its finance department due to a proprietary technology. I was hired to conduct a strategy session with the combined teams to bring the members together, create a common vision, and drive business results.

Things had started off promisingly. Barry and Jim knew they had to work together—this had been drilled into their heads by their boss, the senior vice president of finance. It was large-scale change, and the only way it would work was if they—and their teams—cooperated. And the only way to partner effectively would be to trust one another.

Luckily, Jim and Barry seemed up to the challenge. They had known each other socially for many years and were thrilled at the prospect of working together. In the strategy session, they sat next to each other, and every time I glanced over at them, they'd be whispering like schoolchildren. I remember standing back and thinking, *This is going to be a slam dunk.*

But immediately after the session, the SVP of finance made the abrupt decision to reorganize the division and give Jim's team some of Barry's people. Jim assumed that the SVP had consulted Barry, though he hadn't. Barry felt blindsided. On top of that, the SVP's direction was lacking, without clear goals or details on exactly how the changes would be implemented.

Soon, I started hearing stories of an epic conflict between Barry and Jim. For at least a month, I figured that these were simply rumors: It couldn't have *possibly* gotten that bad.

But unfortunately, it had. Both teams had almost completely disintegrated. There was finger-pointing, gossip, and fear. Barry questioned the motive behind every little thing Jim did, and Jim did the same with Barry. Even worse, their teams were adopting the leaders' general distaste for each other.

What's more, both teams—and leaders—started to seriously question the competence of the other team. Unsurprisingly, when I spoke to the teams' internal customers, they complained of a decline in service and a general lack of effectiveness from both functions.

At that point, e-mail was the only way Barry and Jim would communicate with each other. Because of the medium's inherently ambiguous and inhuman nature, this just made things worse. Internal clients, confused about the roles of Barry's and Jim's teams, would often e-mail their questions to both men. Before considering who should respond, they'd each reply with their own thoughts on the issue, which usually differed. It perplexed clients and chipped steadily away at their remaining modicum of trust.

After a few more weeks, Barry and Jim would no longer communicate even by e-mail. *This will not be their fate*, I said to myself, undeterred. *Not on my watch.* It was my personal—if not slightly idealistic—mission to help them figure out a way to rebuild the trust they'd lost.

Each was happy to talk to me, but less so to talk to each other. "What about the strategy session?" I pleaded. "Things were good between you two, right?" Both said, almost word for word, "Things have taken a turn since then." Though both knew that the current situation was abysmal, each held back for a different reason. For Jim, it was fear that Barry wouldn't reciprocate. For Barry, it was cynicism that things would never change. It took more than one meeting to convince each of them that it was in their best interest to try to rebuild their trust.

After Jim's marriage counseling quip in that first meeting, Barry had been the first to break the ice. "My son told me he had a great time last night with your son."

Jim's face lit up. "Yes! He told me his last name—I had no idea that was your kid!" It turned out that their sons were in the same grade at the same school. All of a sudden, instead of being bitter adversaries, they were two parents talking about their kids. I noticed the shift and slowly steered us into a conversation about work.

We spent time comparing Jim's and Barry's versions of the events, identifying where they agreed, where they disagreed, and why each acted as he did. They gave each other feedback and asked questions. What had appeared to be nefarious motives and lapses in competence turned out to be true situational pressures—once we put this idea on the table, I could see each realizing, "Oh! That makes a lot of sense."

At the end of the meeting, both agreed to my challenge: to touch base by phone every workday and meet in person weekly. They vowed to be curious, to not assume negative motives, and to make decisions that would support each other's success. After that meeting, it wasn't smooth sailing every moment— they sheepishly admitted falling off the wagon for about three weeks, and it took an additional sit-down between the three of us to right the course after one particular event.

Though Barry's and Jim's trust level didn't immediately revert to where it had been before, the change was profound. They started making decisions *after* considering the other's perspective, not before. They approached each other after anxiety-provoking situations. And the two of them made it a point to walk around their teams' work areas together, laughing and talking, a development that had puzzled employees, at least at first. The tide had turned. All of a sudden, doing the work as one team seemed easier. It was Barry, Jim, and their teams against the world—not each other.

Barry recently told me that during all of this, he'd started to notice similar friction in two of his managers. He quickly set up and brokered a meeting between them. "How are you guys communicating with each other?" he asked.

"E-mail," they admitted.

"Well, let me say this based on personal experience," Barry replied, "it's nearly impossible to have critical conversations over e-mail." He proceeded to take them through the same process I had taken him through. It was confirmation that the learning had happened and the ripple effect had begun.

Think of someone in your life whom you trust completely. Take a moment to consider the reasons you trust them. What behaviors do you see that make you sure they're acting in your best interest? What do they *do* that makes you trust them? It's likely that they do things like keep confidences, tell the truth even when it's hard to hear, do what they say they'll do, and act in accordance with their principles.

Here's how I define trust: I can show you my true self and know that you won't take advantage of me. And although most of us know trust when we see it, it isn't commonplace in most organizations. Sometimes it's easiest to identify situations where trust isn't present because FEAR—the opposite of trust—prevails:

- **F**inger-pointing: Employees act territorial. The leader ends up playing referee for team squabbles.

- **E**nergy wasted: Employees burn through energy worrying or positioning themselves to look good relative to peers.

- **A**nxiety about speaking up: Employees don't share their honest opinions. People can't speak truth to power.

- **R**umors: Conspiracy theories are invented to explain the actions leaders take.

When FEAR is gone and trust is present, however, employees feel valued and are willing to go the extra mile. Team members don't waste energy worrying or being afraid, so they're happier and can devote more energy to the team's success.

Kurt Dirks, while assistant professor at Simon Fraser University, studied trust in the NCAA by looking at 355 players and coaches in thirty men's teams.[1] Dirks measured players' trust in the coach before the team's conference schedule, then measured performance as the number of games each team won. Even after he statistically eliminated factors like the coach's experience and career record and the team's talent, he found that the players' trust in their coach accounted for a 7 percent winning advantage. The two teams with highest trust levels excelled—one was ranked first in the nation before the NCAA tournament and the other played for the national championship. The team with the lowest trust in its coach only won 10 percent of its games, and the coach was fired at the end of the season! Coincidence? I think not.

COMPETENCE AND MOTIVES

So how do the best coaches—and leaders—help their teams win? They build two types of trust: trust based on competence and trust based on motive. When you earn *competence-based trust*, others see you as competent and reliable—the first step toward being bankable. Earning competence-based trust means that your team believes in what you're doing.

When you earn *motive-based trust*, people believe you have positive intentions. With this type of trust, your team will support your vision because they believe you have their best interests at heart. They will follow you to the ends of the earth and give you the benefit of the doubt when you need it. Let's say you have to cut 10 percent of your budget. If you've earned motive-based trust, employees are more likely to accept the cuts rather than calling them out as evidence of your evil nature.

Both competence-based and motive-based trust can take years to build and one moment to destroy. Earning both types of trust isn't rocket science, but it requires a series of consistent and sometimes counterintuitive behaviors. Matt Twyman, a research fellow in the Psychology Department of University College London, and his team were the first to split trust into these two types.[2] Using a sample of university students, they created an experiment to learn whom people trusted when presented with advice about risky activities like hang gliding or working in a mine. They found that students placed trust in advisors who demonstrated accuracy in past advice and with whom they shared values—like environmental responsibility, political activism, and morality—and to a lesser degree, physical characteristics. The first element, accuracy of past advice, has to do with competence. The second, shared values, has to do with the advisor's motives. (The third is less relevant to our discussion, but it might affect your dating life!)

Think of competence-based and motive-based trust as two vital organs in your body—your heart and your lungs, for example. Each is necessary, but neither will keep you alive on its own. Likewise, you need to earn both from your team. Let's learn how to do that.

BUILDING COMPETENCE-BASED TRUST

The most basic qualification for earning trust is competence. Your team members will trust you if they believe you know what you're doing. Leaders today might even supervise departments or functions in which they've never worked. For example, a chief financial officer might have a background in finance but oversee accounting, finance, real estate, and human resources. Whatever your role, your team must believe that you have the necessary skills for your position. This doesn't mean a CFO needs to complete a rotation in HR. It *does* mean that she needs to demonstrate an understanding of each function (and admit what she doesn't know—but we'll get to that in a moment).

Competence-based trust from (and among) your team encourages its members to operate at a higher level. In one study, Satyanarayana Parayitam of University of Massachusetts–Dartmouth and Robert Dooley of Oklahoma State University surveyed the top management teams of 109 US hospitals, including hospital administrators and physician executives (two groups that are not notorious for working well together). They found that when competence-based trust existed, teams *actually made better strategic decisions.*[3]

Let's review a real-world example. In 1997, Andrew Lobo was in his first month as human capital planning director at Coca-Cola when he was tasked with introducing human capital management to the company's business leaders around the world. As he opened his first few workshops, the attendees' expressions seemed to suggest they were expecting a "normal" HR presentation.

So Andrew took a rather unexpected approach at the time.[4] Instead of launching into HR, he spent forty-five minutes deconstructing the company's market capitalization. He reviewed the valuation of the company's tangible (plants, equipment, inventory, offices, etc.) and intangible assets (trademarks and goodwill) and then added them up, noting the difference between the company's market capitalization and its total assets. There was a $70 billion gap. "The remaining seventy billion dollars," he noted, "is the total of our customer contacts, our processes, and the knowledge, skills, and performance of our people. Let's say that twenty to thirty billion is the people piece. That's pretty important to our market capitalization, right? And probably worth spending some time to plan around?"

The business leaders agreed.

"Okay," Andrew said, "now let's talk about human capital planning."

Andrew had cracked the competence code. He quickly showed that he understood their goals and the things that were important to them. And that he could actually help them.

Let's look at two ways you can follow Andrew's lead and build competence-based trust among your team.

Assess and Develop Your Knowledge, Skills, and Abilities

As Andrew did, Bankable Leaders must identify the areas in which they need to be conversant. Typically, that means understanding how to speak the language of the disciplines that report to you or work with you. The goal is to demonstrate that you know what you're talking about, and therefore what *they're* talking about. I've worked with one successful senior executive for the last five years who's done this particularly well. She leads a highly technical function and is so conversant in her business that I was shocked to learn her educational background: political science!

How do you best develop your competence, both actual and perceived? First, make it a point to attend conferences and keep up to date on the latest in your profession. If you don't have a mentor, get one. You might also consider creating a dashboard of key personal indicators. This need not be a complicated exercise, and the indicators need not be numeric. Just pick four or five key measures you want to keep track of and review them monthly.

Always, Always, Always Follow Through

Competence-based trust is also an accumulation of satisfied promises. If you are not seen as someone who makes good on your word, you won't be seen as competent. Most leaders who don't follow through have good intentions; sometimes we don't even realize we've made a commitment. Once, as I was packing for a business trip, I complained to my husband that we had quite a lot of leaves in the yard. He nodded and said something like, "Oh, yes. I do need to rake them." I returned from my trip after a week and, much to my surprise, was greeted by the same pile of leaves. When I asked him about it, he looked at me quizzically and said, "I never said I'd do that! I just said I *needed* to!"

No one is right or wrong here. I had interpreted my husband's comment as a commitment and was disappointed when he didn't deliver. (Don't worry—our marriage survived the rest of this conversation quite nicely, thank you.) But just one missed commitment can be all it takes to erode trust.

Another reason leaders don't follow through is overcommitment. Take Greg Herr, a hospital radiology director who was appointed as the administrator of a newly acquired radiology practice in New Hampshire.

Shortly after the acquisition, Greg visited the practice, took a tour, and spoke to his new team. One of the sonographers showed him a broken doorstop in her ultrasound room. This was not a minor problem for her; she had to prop the door or hold it open with her backside every time she went through. Greg figured that a defective doorstop would be easy to address and said confidently, "Well, let's get that fixed!"

But other priorities took precedence. A month went by and nothing happened.

That next month, the hospital's executive team hired me to ensure that the acquisition went smoothly. Not surprisingly, I got an earful from employees about the doorstop in my interviews with them. When I delivered my report, I pulled Greg aside and said, "If you do *nothing else* in the next twenty-four hours, replace that doorstop." What Greg had viewed as a minor oversight had become a huge trust issue with his team. He'd made a promise that he hadn't kept.

Greg immediately went to the hospital and asked the maintenance staff for a doorstop. He drove to the radiology practice, took off the old doorstop, and screwed the new one in. It took him twenty minutes, and his team was positively elated. Greg continues to make bankable improvements—many of them astonishing—which we'll revisit later in the book, and his team still (lovingly) teases him about the doorstop.

I've found two approaches that work best when it comes to keeping your commitments. First, keep close track of the promises you make. In whatever manner best fits you (Outlook tasks, Post-its, good old-fashioned paper), keep a record of every commitment you make to others, as well as the time frame you promised. Don't cross any item off the list until it's complete. If you can't keep a commitment, let the person know as soon as possible, apologize, and renegotiate the deadline.

Second, commit to fewer things. Think about it: How many commitments do you make just to keep others happy? So instead, don't say you'll do something unless you believe you can *and should* accomplish the task. It's usually better to politely decline than to accept a commitment, fail to follow through, and disappoint someone. Say, "I appreciate you thinking of me for this. What I don't want to do is let you down by making a commitment I can't keep." Renegotiate the time frame, brainstorm a different way to accomplish the goal, or learn to delegate (we'll get to that in chapter 12).

One final word on competence-based trust. You should be not only demonstrating it yourself but also fostering it in your team. If your team members trust each other to be reliable and competent, the whole team's performance will improve.

BUILDING MOTIVE-BASED TRUST

Even if you trust someone's competence completely, you still might not believe that they'll act with your best interest in mind. If that's the case, that person probably hasn't earned your motive-based trust. Don't let this be you! Let's review three ways to improve your team's motive-based trust in you: self-disclosure, demonstrating fairness, and acting with integrity.

Self-Disclosure: The Most Potent Ingredient in Motive-Based Trust

In May 2011, at age fifty-nine, Pat Summit was diagnosed with early-onset dementia. She was at the top of her career—as the University of Tennessee's women's basketball coach, she had coached her team to more wins than any other collegiate basketball coach, ever. What would you have done upon receiving this career-ending diagnosis? Many would keep this information to themselves. Why? Fear of the consequences.

That's not what Summit did. She made the brave decision to go public with this information, admitting that she had a condition that could affect her performance as a coach. Yet rather than asking her to step down, the university encouraged her to coach for as long as the condition would allow. In April of 2012, Summit stepped down, but nevertheless remained a part of the team as head coach emeritus.

Imagine what would've happened if Summit hadn't told anyone. After a while, her players—and the university—would have noticed something wasn't right. And when the truth came out, they probably would have felt lied to or cheated. Her brave self-disclosure was in large part what allowed her to continue to coach as long as she did: The university was her active partner in mitigating her condition's effects.

Have you ever felt misunderstood as a leader? Perhaps you've made a decision for one reason, but you hear people inventing another reason. Perhaps your boss asked you to restructure the department, but your employees believe you're doing it because you want to cut headcount. When they don't know the context, they will invent malicious intentions for you if they don't trust your motives.

Self-disclosure is the antidote to this phenomenon. I know something about self-disclosure. My "most likely" in high school was "Most likely to tell everyone her deepest darkest secrets and then swear us all to secrecy." Seriously. When I entered the workforce, I tried to change the tendency my classmates had pointed out. I followed common wisdom: "Never let them see you sweat." "Keep a stiff upper lip." "It's best to keep your mouth shut and be thought a fool than to open your mouth and prove it." In other words, I regarded self-disclosure as a weakness.

Flash forward fifteen years. My attitude became clear to me when I recently spent a few days facilitating a leadership retreat. Halfway through the workshop, one leader approached me and said, "We know how awesome you are—all the organizations you've helped and the leaders you've transformed." I proudly beamed. "That's great. But I'm not hearing anything about your weaknesses or failures. I know you have them. We all do. You have to be authentic to get through to us."

It was like someone had punched me in the gut. I was speechless. He was right. The teacher had become the student.

The more your team understands your motives, thought processes, and personal history, the more they will give you the benefit of the doubt. Here's the leadership lesson: It is not only *okay* to show your employees who you really are, warts and all—it is *desirable*. If you do this well, your team will trust you, connect with your motives, and go out of its way to create results for you.

Here are a few specific suggestions to foster self-disclosure both with yourself and among your team:

- **Find innocuous things to disclose**. Share information about your pets, hobbies, a dream vacation spot, or a few details about your family. Start with easy topics and work up to more personal ones, while understanding what is appropriate to share (that you are going through a divorce) and what isn't (what you hate about your soon-to-be ex-spouse).

- **Attend company social functions**. Eat meals with your colleagues. Stop and chat in common areas. Make rounds at least a few times a week to check in with your team and chat informally.

- **Encourage self-disclosure among your team members**. Challenge them to have one-on-one lunches or virtual coffee with every other team member.

- **Appoint one or two team members to lead a quick team-building activity every few months**. One idea is the "Three Shining Moments" activity. Each person has five minutes to describe the three moments in their life that have made them who they are today and why. I once did this activity with an IT team. "This is a waste of time," they whined. "We've been working together for ten years!" I asked them to humor me. When we were finished, I asked them to raise a hand if they'd learned at least one thing that helped them better understand someone else in the room. Every single hand went up. This stuff works.

- **Quarterly or semiannually, hold a team offsite**. Give your team breathing room and space to spend time together, whether it's over dinner or through an activity like bowling. Don't worry—you can do work too. Just make sure not to over-schedule yourselves.

A final element of self-disclosure that leaders must master is the *art of freely admitting when you don't know stuff*. Why would admitting what you don't know build trust? This might be easier to understand when we consider the opposite. When was the last time you saw someone pretending to know something they didn't? It probably bugged you. We humans are pretty good at picking up on this. When you set off other people's BS detectors, they will assume you're hiding something. Worse still, they could feel that you're insulting their intelligence.

Though it may seem counterintuitive, self-disclosure promotes competence. If you're honest about what you don't know, your team will trust your motives: They'll see that it's more important for you to get it right than to look good.

As part of my practice, I help leaders who are new to their position get their feet on the ground, integrate with their team, and build trust (I call this "New Leader Assimilation"). I was once working with a high-potential but inexperienced leader who'd just been promoted to lead her region. We decided it would be smart to hold a meeting to set goals for her team and give everyone a chance to get to know each other.

As we were planning the meeting, she said, "I'm so nervous. What if someone asks me something I don't know?"

How many times have you felt this way? It's often called "imposter syndrome." Especially when you're new to your role, it's normal to think, *It's just a matter of time before they figure out I'm a fraud and demote me.* I listened to her concerns and said something she found rather shocking: "Tell them you don't know."

TRUST IN **VIRTUAL TEAMS**

Perhaps the greatest challenge for virtual leaders is building trust within their team. It might be hard for you to trust your team members because you can't supervise their work in the same way you could if you were co-located with them. They might also have trouble trusting you, and each other. Misunderstandings can take on a life of their own. Add this all up, and you're in the danger zone!

1. **SEE EACH OTHER AS OFTEN AS POSSIBLE:** Research tells us that meeting face-to-face even one time significantly increases trust among the members of virtual teams. So by all means, get together in person if you can. If that's not possible, try videoconferencing—the more team members see each other (virtually or live), the easier it will be to build trust.

2. **MINIMIZE UNCERTAINTY:** Virtual teams are breeding grounds for uncertainty, which is like Teflon for trust. Make sure you have a set of clear goals that everyone understands, guiding principles for how you'll work together, and agreements for how you'll communicate with each other.

3. **COMMUNICATE OFTEN AND PREDICTABLY:** Communication is a touchstone of trust in virtual teams. Rapidly provide information to team members and avoid silence at all costs. Don't let them wonder, *Is my boss not responding because she's mad at me, or is she just busy?*

4. **BUILD A VIRTUAL WATERCOOLER:** Part of the way co-located teams collaborate is through informal interactions (in the lunchroom, the hall, etc.). With a little creativity, virtual teams can create similar forums. Make time for small talk at the beginning of meetings. Or try "virtual coffee," where team members spend fifteen minutes on the phone just chatting and catching up.

Sure enough, during the meeting there were a few questions she couldn't answer. Instead of making stuff up, she would say, "Wow. You guys probably know more about this than I do. What does the group think?" When I spoke to team members individually after the meeting, more than a few pointed out how powerful her actions had been in earning their trust.

Use the Terri Wanger Rule to Promote Self-Disclosure

Let's review one final trick to help you with self-disclosure. I call it the "Terri Wanger Rule" after the person who had made this phrase her personal calling card: my mother. Terri Wanger, a successful entrepreneur born in Bay City, Michigan, was raised by two humble parents who taught her the value of individual responsibility. Her mother, my grandmother, Amelia, served in the Women's Army Corps as a dental hygienist during World War II, and her father, Wendelin, my grandfather, served in the medical services. From a very young age, they taught their three kids that *when you mess up, 'fess up, stand up, and clean it up.*

Terri Wanger raised me with this adage too. Much as I mocked it in my broody teenage years, I have grown to understand that it's one of the most effective self-disclosure tools a leader can wield. Why? Mistakes are a powerful opportunity for a leader to show his team who he really is. The simple act of admitting that you messed up helps employees understand that the current situation wasn't your intention. Everyone knows you messed up anyway. You'll just appear out of touch with reality if you don't admit it.

Teams perform best when self-disclosure goes both ways—that is, not only are you willing and able to admit your mistakes, but your team also feels comfortable doing so. In my experience, the most powerful action a leader can take to make this possible is to admit his or her mistakes. The Terri Wanger Rule will be contagious—in a good way!

Use this table to help you translate the Terri Wanger Rule into real-world statements you can put to use:

PHASE	PHRASE
'Fess Up	"I was wrong." "I made a mistake." "I'm sorry. This wasn't my intention."
Stand Up	"I take responsibility for this mistake." "This one was all me."
Clean It Up	"I will take care of the situation." "I am going to make it right."

Fairness Is Next to Godliness

Fairness is the second component of motive-based trust. Patrick Müller of Utrecht University found that there is a causal relationship between them: In a laboratory experiment, students performed an economics game where they entrusted money to each other. Results showed that they entrusted more money to others when they saw the game as fair.[5] This plays out in the "real world" too: I recently had a conversation with an employee who told me that "fairness is literally the most important thing I look for in a manager."

So what happens when employees think the way you lead is unfair? According to author David Rock, unfairness threatens us and activates the anterior insular cortex, the part of our brain that's involved in emotions like disgust.[6] Because this part of our brain also blocks empathy, employees will actually feel satisfied if something bad happens to you (the Germans call this "*Schadenfreude*").

They'll also go out of their way to even the score. Maureen Ambrose, professor of Business Ethics at the University of Central Florida, and her colleagues conducted a study to learn why employees intentionally harm, disrupt, or embarrass their supervisor or organization.[7] They classified first-person accounts of 122 incidents of workplace sabotage and discovered that 80 percent happened because of employees' feelings of unfairness. The more injustice employees perceived, the more severe the sabotage.

To be seen as fair, you must practice three types of fairness, as outlined by organizational justice researchers Jerald Greenberg and Jason Colquitt.[8] I call this the "Fairness Trifecta":

1. **Outcome fairness:** Do employees perceive that rewards (promotions, bonuses, perks) are given proportionately to what recipients put in? Do you apply these rules consistently? In Bankable Leadership terms, this is a *results* aspect of fairness.

2. **Process fairness:** Was the procedure you used to arrive at your decision appropriate? Did employees have a say? Is there a way to appeal decisions? This is both a *results* and *people* element of fairness.

3. **Interpersonal fairness:** Did you treat employees with dignity and respect before, during, and after the decision? This is a *people* aspect of fairness.

In the introduction, we discussed the challenge leaders feel in balancing humanity with performance. As a Bankable Leader, sometimes you have to make decisions that make people unhappy. But if your team trusts you to be fair, they'll be more likely to accept the decision and give you the benefit of the doubt.

Let's review an example. Scott Page, Colorado market president at Colorado Business Bank, once had to close an unprofitable part of his business. It was unquestionably the right decision, but he knew it would be difficult to break the news to the leader of that division. Despite the grim situation—or perhaps because of it—Scott and his colleagues knew they needed to do it fairly.

First, they prepared a generous severance package as a reward for this leader's effort in helping the business succeed—this ensured *outcome fairness*. Second, to show *process fairness*, they were open and honest about how the decision was made. Finally, they put a premium on *interpersonal fairness*. Scott notes that he could have asked someone else to speak with the leader, but he wanted to honor him by talking to him personally. Scott said simply, "Listen, this is hard. We are closing the department and we have to let you go." He didn't hem and haw and say things like, "This is harder for me than it is for you." Scott respected his dignity by being direct but kind.

The leader took it like a gentleman. He appreciated the severance (*outcome fairness*), their honesty (*process fairness*), and the fact that Scott did everything possible to help him transition (*interpersonal fairness*). He and Scott are still in touch. Fairness builds trust, and when you trust someone, relationships can weather surprisingly strong storms.

Here are some tips to increase your fairness quotient:

- **Outcome fairness**: Look at what your employees are putting in—their level of responsibility, their effort, their work quality, and the stress they've endured. Are you rewarding them in proportion to that? List your top performers and bottom performers. Are you differentiating rewards? Don't give your top performers a 20 percent bonus and your poor performers an 18 percent bonus. That's an insult to your top performers and will not be viewed as fair. (We'll come back to the topic of entitlement-free appreciation in chapter 8.)

- **Process fairness**: Are you applying procedures consistently? Making the process crystal clear? Giving your employees a chance to ask questions and keeping them informed during the process?

- **Interpersonal fairness**: Are you treating your employees with kindness, respect, and consideration? Are you asking for their feedback and input?

Consistent Word and Deed: The Actions of Integrity

Let's now turn to our final component of motive-based trust—integrity—and learn why it matters. Bob Chapman, while director of recruiting and organizational development at Vail Resorts, once had an employee who was getting under his skin, though Bob struggled to put his finger on precisely why.

At the end of one quarter, Bob made a decision about merit raises in one of the units he oversaw; this employee—though not directly affected by this decision—came to Bob's office to question his call. He implied that Bob was simply toeing the company line. *I don't need to explain anything to him*, Bob thought. *It's the best thing for the company!* When Bob didn't have a reason, the employee declared, "Then that's not the right decision, because it isn't based on any principle."

A few months later, Bob called this employee into his office to give some feedback: Apparently he had a reputation for not doing things quickly enough. Upon hearing this news, the employee looked at Bob and said, "I don't care about my reputation. I care about my principles." Bob rolled his eyes and rushed to his next meeting.

It took a while for the lesson to sink in, but it did happen eventually. Up to that point, Bob had defined success as filling jobs quickly, managing the organization's talent, and developing its leaders. But he began to see that his decisions weren't centered around any personal principles. Bob realized that being a leader is really about making decisions based on your own beliefs about what's right, not the company line—and the only thing that creates a meaningful connection between your decisions are principles. Now the senior director of talent management at Xcel Energy, Bob views this as a pivotal moment in his development as a leader. It rocked his world and gave him new energy.

I define integrity as *having firm and well-articulated principles and acting in a manner that is consistent with them.* Integrity is a key ingredient of trust: If your team can't predict how you'll behave with relative accuracy, they will feel uneasy. Have you ever trusted someone who didn't have integrity? Never! Convince me that you have, and I'll promptly send you $50.

So how can you build your integrity? The first step is to write your leadership story. You can't help your team understand your principles until you understand them yourself. And you can't understand your principles until you recognize how they developed.

Morre Dean, CEO of Parker Adventist Hospital, believes that if you can articulate your story, people will be less likely to question your motives. Morre's own story is a powerful one. The son of a bricklayer and a mother who died of cancer when he was five, he spent his childhood summers working on a farm. No one had any expectation that he'd become the CEO of a hospital, but after he lost his mother, he'd wanted to go into healthcare. At sixteen, he got his first hospital job and soon met the hospital's CEO, Ron Sackett. "I have the best job in the world," Sackett told him. "Every day, I get to help the people who make a difference in

CHAPTER 1   Trust and Be Trusted   39

other people's lives." From that moment on, it was Morre's goal to become a hospital CEO—he just didn't think he'd end up achieving it by age thirty.

Morre was even more surprised when he didn't feel the sense of satisfaction he'd always envisioned. It didn't take him long to realize that he wasn't the type of person who found a sense of fulfillment because his business card read "CEO." More important to him were his marriage, his kids, his team, and the impact he had on people's lives. So when Morre's family decided to move to Colorado, it made perfect sense to Morre that he would leave a prominent CEO position at a 500-bed hospital in Glendale, California, to lead a smaller hospital in the Denver area.

It didn't, however, make sense to the people who were interviewing him. Morre immediately shared his story. "What drives me," he told them, "is wanting my family to be happy. And I want to make a difference in an organization, whether it's nine hundred employees or twenty-four hundred employees. I don't find self-worth in how high the numbers are."

He got the job.

This story illustrates the power of telling your leadership story. I also recommend reading Bill George's *True North*, an exceptional resource for understanding your own values and principles.[9] Here are some questions to get you thinking:

1. What were the most important or consequential things that happened in your childhood? How did those events shape your view of the world?

2. As a child, what did you want to be when you grew up? How has that changed or evolved as you've matured, and why?

3. What was your first working experience? What did it teach you about work and leadership?

4. Who was the best leader you've ever worked for? The worst? What did each teach you about what successful leaders value?

5. Think back on your best and worst moments as a leader. What did they teach you, and how have they changed how you view your leadership?

Once you've answered these questions, you should have a good start on crystallizing your leadership principles. You're now ready for the second step, building your leadership credo. Ultimately, you should aim for a list of three to five principles that drive you and are essential to who you are as a leader. For example, mine are *responsibility, compassion, service, involvement,* and *drive*. I believe that I, and others, must take responsibility for our behavior and work products, treat others with kindness and compassion, approach what we do with a service mindset, engage in open and participative leadership where those who are affected by decisions help make them, and exhibit a deep commitment to achievement and success. I'd tell you the personal stories that led me here, but we'd be here all day. And yours are more important, anyway!

Once you have your leadership credo, share it with your team. This can be particularly helpful if you're in a new role, but it will provide value for any team. Explain why you're sharing it and why it's important. Ask your employees to keep you honest by examining your behavior and ensuring that your actions and credo are consistent. For example, if participation is one of your principles and your team sees you making a closed-door decision without their input, you are in the danger zone. In your daily decisions, particularly when you're struggling to make one, match up the options with your principles. The answer might become clear faster than you think.

A final step you can take to develop your integrity is to respect the confidences of your team. Secrets always have a way of spreading. I have a mentor who told me: "Everyone in this company has two people they can trust. And those two people have two people. You get the idea."

Here's an example of the power of keeping confidences. To determine the best approach to boosting the performance of my clients' teams, I often conduct interviews with team members. My standard preface is to tell them that as a psychologist, I follow the American Psychological Association's code of ethics.[10] An important part of that code is confidentiality, I say, and their responses will be completely anonymous. I was once working with a leadership team in the financial services industry, and a few months after we finished our work, I ran into one of the team members at a party. As we were chatting, she told me that this statement earned her trust immediately.

Even if you're not a psychologist, you can use this principle. If you respect the humanity of your people, they will inevitably share sensitive or confidential information with you. Unless the information violates ethical or legal requirements or presents concerns for the safety of others, it is imperative that you keep it to yourself. It's also important to make sure you hold sensitive conversations in a private area; I worked in a hospital for a few years, and the types of conversations I would see people having at nurses' stations within earshot of everyone amazed me.

If you're not sure whether something is confidential, ask, "Am I correct in assuming that this is information you'd like to keep just between us?" If the answer is yes, then zip your lip. Don't discuss it with anyone, and that includes close confidants—even your spouse or partner. Just imagine how you would feel if your manager told a personal secret of yours to two people whom she trusted, and they told two people, and so on. Talk about a trust-defeating behavior.

Finally, as a parting piece of advice, consider the words of Anton Chekhov: "You must trust and believe in people or life becomes impossible." When you trust your employees, you're appreciating their deepest sense of humanity and their ability to perform their role. They'll usually grant you the same in return. And when they trust you and you trust them, everybody wins.

BANKABLE ACTIONS

Earn Competence-Based Trust

✔ Understand the skills and knowledge needed for your role through honest reflection and feedback.

✔ Continuously develop your competence by prioritizing continued learning and tracking your success.

✔ Create a system to ensure that you're keeping track of your commitments, and only make those you can keep.

Earn Motive-Based Trust

✔ Help your employees understand who you are—both at work and outside work—and encourage them to do the same with each other.

✔ Spend informal time as a team and experiment with team-development activities.

✔ When you don't know something, admit it! It is better to admit where your knowledge ends and ask for help than to pretend you know and annoy your team.

✔ Be like Terri Wanger: When you mess up, 'fess up, stand up, and clean it up.

✔ Ensure that your employees are getting back what they are putting in and that you're applying consistent rules for decisions and rewards. Create transparent and participative decision processes. Treat your employees with dignity and respect before, during, and after important decisions.

✔ Understand your story as a leader. What events in your life shaped your views on success and leadership? Share your leadership credo with your team—and ask for their thoughts on theirs!

✔ Ensure that your employees feel safe telling you their fears, weaknesses, and problems. Shun gossip like the plague. Really, it's tempting, but it's tacky!

CHAPTER 2

BE UNMISTAKABLY TRANSPARENT

I was once hired to coach a leader in an oil and gas company. One day, I was conducting interviews with his team, person by person, in a very nice corner office the organization had set me up in. The day went very well, and the team members seemed pleased to provide their input. I patted myself on the back and went on my way.

During my next visit, I heard that an interesting rumor had cropped up. Apparently, the employees who sat outside "my office" had decided that I was a recruiter interviewing people to see if they'd keep their jobs! My client's team knew exactly why I was there, but we hadn't been transparent with the folks down the hall.

Has something like this happened to you? Are you ever shocked by the elaborate stories people make up about the run-of-the-mill goings-on of your department or company?

On the people side, failing to share information is a serious issue: It dramatically erodes trust, motivation, and success. If your team members think you're hiding something, they will begin to resent you for not being forthright with them, and they may throw you under the proverbial bus when the opportunity arises. It's even worse when you actually *are* hiding something significant and your deception is revealed. Now those upset and frustrated employees have positive confirmation of their suspicions! And don't bet on hiding anything for long; as Charlene Li, author of *Open Leadership*, notes, "There is information leakage everywhere."[1]

On the results side, if your team doesn't have the right information about your department and organization, they can't make choices that are aligned with the organization's goals. They'll also be doing unnecessary or duplicative work, making poor decisions, and failing to innovate.

As we saw earlier, when employees don't have the information they want and need, they search for explanations for what's going on around them. And the conspiracy theories people invent are usually far more dire—and creative—than the truth. These theories travel as rumors, usually concerning organizational decisions like layoffs, promotions, or other types of change, and can seriously damage people and results.

Studies show that the average manager will encounter one damaging rumor per week.[2] These rumors tend to increase in times of stress; for example, the abundant rumors that circulated around World War II reflected anxieties and uncertainties the public was experiencing due to the war, and these rumors have been studied extensively by researchers.[3] More recently, Prashant Bordia, a professor at the Australian National University, argued that rumors go beyond conversations in the break room—they hurt people (causing mistrust and stress) and results (hurting the company's reputation and lowering stock values).[4]

In an ingeniously named study, "Managers Are Aliens! Rumors and Stress During Organizational Change," researcher Prashant Bordia and his team examined rumors at a large public hospital in Australia that was undergoing massive change: the building of a new facility, implementation of new technologies, internal restructuring, and the introduction of multidisciplinary teams. The researchers distributed surveys asking employees about the last rumor they'd heard. There were more negative rumors than positive ones, and among them were these: "There will be fewer staff required because of new technology," "[we're going to] have to do more work with less money," and my personal favorite, "The hospital is being moved to the CEO's home state to save relocating for his mates." Employees who heard negative rumors reported higher stress than those who didn't. But perhaps the most important of Bordia's findings was that rumors are less likely to crop up when employees are provided information.

Although thinking about rumors circulating at your company might cause a spike in your blood pressure, remember that the intentions behind rumors are not as wicked as they appear. I promise. At a basic level, employees need to make sense of what's happening to them at work. When they don't know something, the explanations they invent are based on their greatest fears.

Likewise, in my experience, when most leaders fail to share information, it's not intentional—they just don't appreciate how bad the ramifications will be. Here are some common reasons leaders aren't transparent:

- We're busy and we don't have time.
- We want to hedge our bets if things change.
- We're afraid of getting in trouble for sharing information.
- We don't want to upset or confuse people with bad news.
- We don't want to demotivate the team.
- We hoard information because it makes us feel powerful.

Bankable Leaders create two kinds of transparency. *Transparency of intent* builds on our discussion of self-disclosure and fairness by telling your employees why you're making decisions. *Transparency of information* means sharing your department and company's strategy, financials, and operations. There is danger in having one but not the other, and certainly even more danger if neither is present.

Let's look at both types of transparency together. In the model below, you can see that the ideal state is the top-right box, at the intersection of "Clear Intent" and "High Information." If your intent is fuzzy, you can compromise human outcomes (*People*); if you give out too little information, you can hurt performance (*Results*).

	LOW INFORMATION	HIGH INFORMATION
Clear Intent	Disorderly Devotees	Aligned Enthusiasts
Fuzzy Intent	Confused Conspiracy Theorists	Informed Skeptics

The first—and worst—possibility is that you provide neither intent nor information, creating *Confused Conspiracy Theorists*. Your employees don't know what's going on or why, so they'll direct their energy to the wrong things and rumors will become rampant. The less intent and information you share, the more employees will believe you are hiding something.

The second possibility is that you share information but not intent, creating *Informed Skeptics*. Here, your employees know what is happening strategically, operationally, and financially, but they don't know why. They might, for example, understand that all budgets are being cut by 15 percent but not understand the reason behind this decision. Or they might know that a merger with another company is on the horizon but not understand why you're holding closed-door meetings with consultants. They could easily invent conspiracy theories in these situations about plans to reduce the size of the team.

The third possibility is that you share your intent, but not information on the department or company's strategy, operations, and financials. This creates *Disorderly Devotees*, employees who see the reasoning behind company decisions but lack a complete picture of the state of the organization. This could result in high regard for you and the organization but may also cause uncoordinated activity because of uncertainty about what needs to be accomplished.

The ideal situation is to communicate clear intent and high information, creating *Aligned Enthusiasts*. A team of Aligned Enthusiasts operates like a well-oiled machine—its members trust and respect their leader, asking direct questions when things feel uncertain rather than whispering rumors behind closed doors.

FIVE ACTIONS OF UNMISTAKABLE TRANSPARENCY

Now that we've seen how transparency of intent and transparency of information fit together, we can learn about how to create both. But before we look more closely at these, let's discuss the five actions of unmistakable transparency—then, you'll learn what to be transparent about.

First, before you share information, *make sure you, your manager, and your peers are aligned*. If each of you is interpreting things differently, you could each be telling your team different things, and chaos will usually ensue. This is especially true if the information you're sharing is difficult or confusing. Take the time to agree on how you'll each explain your decisions and commitments. Patrick Lencioni calls this "commitment clarification."[5] You might want to brainstorm the questions you anticipate receiving and prepare aligned and clear responses.

Second, *be transparent about transparency*. One approach I use comes from a mentor and former manager, Jim Downey: When you know something and can say it, say it. When you know something but can't say it, tell them why. And if you don't know something, tell them when you'll know and how you'll follow up.

Third, *build structure around transparency*. Create forums to regularly share information. This can take the form of monthly town-hall or staff meetings, weekly stand-up meetings, or daily huddles. It's important to prioritize face-to-face or phone communication over e-mail whenever possible. One common complaint I hear from employees is that their leader hasn't set up these systems for frequent communication.

Fourth, make it your mission to *be a detective who ruthlessly ferrets out rumors*. A former boss of mine used to ask the following question in all-employee meetings: "What rumors are you hearing?" The responses she would receive were incredible, including one rumor that the company was going out of business—and this was shortly after we had received $30 million for a capital improvement project! When you unearth a rumor, the best approach is to address it directly without attacking employees. It takes courage for an employee to share the rumors they're hearing. Thank them for their bravery, then set the record straight.

Finally, *know when* not *to be transparent*. Sometimes sharing information can do more harm than good. For example, if things are in flux, you can do a lot of damage by announcing specifics before they're solidified. Let's say your organization is going through a restructuring. To minimize anxiety and cynicism, don't share details—like the organizational charts—until they are finalized. Imagine being an employee, seeing a new organizational chart that involves a significant change to your role, then seeing a different one a week later. This is an area where transparency can be disastrous. Instead of sharing in-progress items like this, explain the process that is being used and give a time frame for when you will be able to announce the change.

These five actions will help you be unmistakably transparent, with information and your intent. Let's now examine these two types of transparency on their own.

TRANSPARENCY OF INTENT

In chapter 1, we discussed the concept of self-disclosure, and there is a strong overlap between self-disclosure and transparency of intent. But with transparency of intent, you're not just sharing information about *who you are*, you're telling your employees *why you've made the decisions you've made*. It's also similar to *process fairness*, which we discussed earlier; along with explaining the process you used to make a decision, you're clarifying the reasoning behind it. When you do this, employees will see your humanity and repay it with performance.

To be fully transparent about your intentions, you must first understand them yourself. The work of creating your leadership credo from chapter 1 will give you a leg up in making your intentions clear, because your principles and experiences as a leader will strongly influence them.

For each action or decision that will be visible to your team, ask yourself:

- How does this decision relate to my leadership credo?
- Why did I do this (what were my intentions)? Why *didn't* I do this (what were *not* my intentions)?
- What do I want for my team as a result? What *don't* I want for my team as a result?
- What do I want for myself as a result? What *don't* I want for myself as a result?

Margaret Kelly, CEO of RE/MAX, is famous for her straight-talk commercials about the real estate market. Her strongly held value of transparency also influences the way she treats her employees. Recently, under advisement of RE/MAX's information technology group, Margaret and her executive team made the decision to move the company to a new e-mail application. The decision seemed straightforward and the benefits appeared to be numerous. But after the switch, the application wasn't as functional as they'd predicted. And employees hated it. After a few months, it became clear to Margaret that the move had been a mistake. So she sent an e-mail to the entire company, praising the IT group for its effort in implementing the system exactly as the executives had asked. But, she said, they had made the wrong decision; their intent had actually been to make things easier! Margaret got many e-mails thanking her. RE/MAX went back to the old system, and the employees knew that the intention behind this decision was pure.

You might not be a CEO. And you might be thinking about decisions your superiors have made that you've had to explain to your team—decisions you might not have understood. If you are not able to learn the reason for a decision after a good-faith effort, don't make up an answer for the sake of having one—it's OK to say, for example, "I don't fully understand the reason for this decision yet, but I do know that our company deeply cares about its employees and wouldn't do something like this unless there weren't other options." As a general rule, even if you don't know why a decision was made, you can talk about it in the context of the organization's strategy, values, and culture. How does this decision connect to those? Communicate that connection to your employees and you'll see the payoff for both people and results.

TRANSPARENCY OF INFORMATION

Every decision a leader makes should be aligned with the goals and strategies of the company. Transparency of information isn't just sharing the direction your company is headed; it means explaining how your team fits into the company's goals. If you can't do this, your team will be confused. They'll drag their feet and fail to deliver.

And the more senior your role is, the more challenging it is to communicate to your people. I work with an executive who confided in me that when she was a first-level employee, she used to think that the executives in her company were completely inept. The importance of sharing even the most basic information,

TRANSPARENCY FOR **EXECUTIVES**

Generally, as leaders ascend the organizational hierarchy, they share less and less information. This isn't always on purpose—when you have access to so much information, it's easy to forget that others aren't so fortunate. For executives, transparent communication with employees can often be the difference between success and failure.

1. **FIND OUT WHAT EMPLOYEES WANT TO KNOW:** Ask your direct reports to regularly inform you about the "word on the street." What are the rumors, challenges, or items of confusion floating around the organization? When interacting with employees, make it a point to ask what's on their mind, or even ask them directly what they think about a recent change. Use this information to tailor your communications.

2. **CREATE REGULAR FORUMS FOR EMPLOYEES TO HEAR THINGS DIRECTLY FROM YOU:** The more employees can hear from you, the more you'll be able to help them understand what's going on in the company. Whether it's a town hall, a Twitter or Yammer feed, a blog, or a video stream, create regular opportunities to speak directly to your organization.

3. **HELP EMPLOYEES WITH THE BIG PICTURE:** One of the greatest opportunities you have is to help your employees understand how decisions tie in to the big picture. Every time you're communicating information, talk about how and why it aligns with the organization's mission, vision, goals, and values. Be explicit—don't assume that your employees already know.

like how the company was doing financially, seemed to escape them. She used to sit in her office and stew about what a bunch of hapless jokers were running the company.

But then she became one of those hapless jokers and quickly understood that things weren't as simple as she had thought. Sometimes she would have access to information and want to share it, but was asked not to. Or she would have incomplete information and feel reluctant to communicate it in case things changed. Or she'd have information in fairly complete form but would be afraid it would scare or upset her employees.

Despite these fears and challenges so many leaders face, the research on transparency is clear: It builds loyalty and fosters performance. For example, Jacob Eskildsen and Kai Kristensen, marketing and statistics professors at Aarhus University's School of Business in Denmark, examined how companies scored in Sweden's national measurement of customer satisfaction.[6] They found that among banks, mobile phone operations, and supermarkets, the companies that were transparent with pricing and products had more loyal customers who were willing to spend more money on their products.

Providing information to employees has a similar effect. I once worked with a client that was implementing enormous changes in how it did business. We noticed that because of different leadership styles, some groups were being communicated with and some weren't. The groups that weren't getting information about the organization's vision, goals, and strategy reported feeling paralyzed and devalued. Those that had information weren't always happy about the changes, but they were able to manage their reactions and choose the best response. The difference was striking.

Bankable Leaders are transparent about three major types of information: their department and company's strategy, operations, and financials. Let's review each one so you can foster it in your team.

Strategy Transparency

It was two weeks before the start of the fiscal year at Disney Interactive Media Group, and Brad Davis had just taken over the sales department. The budget had been set, and the company's national sales conference was in fifteen days.

The year was 2005, and revenues were down. The unit had never quite recovered from the bursting of the dot-com bubble in 2002 and the sales department wasn't delivering on its true value to the organization.

Brad knew that to succeed, his team members would have to become experts in marketing to kids and moms. When he was hired on, Brad was given a three-year time frame to accomplish this. He knew that the death knell for his team would be for him to enter with a fully formulated plan that no one understood.

So he flew all twenty-five people in his team, from his VP of operations to his sales assistants, out to Los Angeles for a retreat. Brad brought a framework that everyone could follow and laid out the results they needed to deliver, and the team hashed out the details of their new strategy.

Throughout the process, Brad helped his employees understand their role in implementing the strategy. "I am not here to close business behind you," Brad told them. "That's your job. My job is to coach and counsel you to close business, and to help you see your role in the greater picture. You're empowered to achieve our goals, and I'm here to help." The important choice Brad made was to bring his employees into the process, help them understand their goals, and make each of their roles in achieving them clear.

So how can you help your employees understand your strategy in a similar way? Here are some questions to get you started:

1. Why does your team exist? What value does it provide to customers and the organization?

2. What is the future you want to create?

3. What does the competitive marketplace look like in your industry and how will you compete?

4. What are the top goals your company and team must achieve in the next three to five years?

5. How does each person's role fit into the bigger picture?

Leaders who answer these questions in partnership with their team will see the most powerful results. After Brad's team collectively charted its strategy, for example, it managed to take revenue from $15 million to $26 million in one year while creating a cohesive and engaged team in the process. Now that's Bankable Leadership—literally!

Operational Transparency

Christy Martello, nurse manager of the Orthopedic, Neurology, and Spine Unit at Rose Medical Center, had just stepped into her role as a first-time manager. As one of her first actions, she solicited feedback about the biggest operational challenges her employees were facing. She was able to address many of them, but others proved more difficult. For example, her team was frustrated by the company's vacation policy—they complained about not being able to take days off when they wanted to. Staffing a unit 365 days a year, twenty-four hours a day can be challenging. So Christy set out to educate her team on the process she used for vacations. By the time she posted the next schedule, she noticed that when she went to balance it across her team, she didn't have to make the usual changes. All she had done was help them understand this operational reality.

Here are a few questions to ask as you discuss operations with your team:

- What day-to-day issues are most frustrating to you?
- Why do we do things this way?
- What can we change?
- How are our day-to-day decisions tied to the strategy of the company (i.e., why we're not just doing this to annoy employees)?

Financial Transparency

As a privately held company, RE/MAX had kept its finances confidential for decades. Without an annual report, neither the public nor RE/MAX's employees knew where the company stood financially from year to year.

During the housing crash of 2008–2010, CEO Margaret Kelly had been asking her employees to grow the bottom line while clamping down on operations. Suddenly, she realized that what she was asking was virtually impossible: to grow the company without giving them a number to aim for.

In an unprecedented move, Margaret gathered her employees and said, "Here's our bottom line, and here is what we're trying to reach. I trust you with this information and want to give you the big picture." Margaret's decision to open the books helped her employees turn around the business. RE/MAX rebounded significantly, and employees played a pivotal role in getting things back on track.

Employees aren't the only ones who benefit from understanding the financial realities of your organization. According to Eric Ooi Lip Aun of PricewaterhouseCoopers, publicly held companies that are transparent about their finances boast stock prices as much as 25 percent higher than companies that aren't.[7]

Regardless of whether your company is publicly or privately held, you have the power within your sphere of influence to educate your employees about the financial realities and goals of the company. Here are the questions to answer when talking about financials with your team:

- *(If possible)* How is our company doing financially? What are our goals for revenue growth and expense management? Why did we set those goals?

- What are the key financial metrics used to evaluate our department's performance, and how does each person contribute?

- How can our team make decisions aligned with the financial goals of the company on a day-to-day basis?

■ ■ ■

As a final note, it's worth noting that Bankable Leaders are transparent about both the big stuff and the small stuff—holding back either can have disastrous consequences.

Remember Greg Herr, the radiology director who put off replacing the doorstop? Well, after the outpatient radiology practice was acquired by Greg's hospital, the leaders started to design a new, state-of-the-art facility. When I was on site interviewing employees, we were holding our meetings in a conference room the employees rarely entered, and the plans for the new facility happened to be sitting on the table. Many told me this was the first time they were seeing them.

Those who had seen them would knowingly show me the number of desks in a certain area and compare it to the current number of employees in that department, certain that downsizing was looming.

The irony was that Greg and the senior team *were* being transparent about the big things. For example, they were clear from the beginning that even though they'd guarantee everyone's jobs for the first year, there were some departments that would be eliminated or reduced in size (and they were specific about which ones). But employees still felt anxiety about the little things, including the architectural drawings for the new building.

In a recent conversation, Greg confided in me about his struggle to be transparent. "There will always be sensitive information," he said. "But if you're not transparent with everyone, you'll never have trust or a team or success. You have to find that fine line but still keep the things that are somewhat private, private. We've been very up front from day one about the big things. Some organizations might have said, 'We hope everyone can come to the new building.' But we were truthful and promised to work with the staff to make them a part of this. But not showing them the plans for the building made them feel we were hiding something." What Greg ended up doing next is pretty amazing, and we'll discuss it in chapter 5. For the time being, the lesson is that leaders must be transparent about both the big stuff *and* the small stuff.

BANKABLE ACTIONS

How to Be Transparent

- ✔ Make sure you're aligned with your manager and peers on information and intent. Anticipate questions and prepare clear and consistent answers.
- ✔ If you can't tell your team something, communicate why you can't and when you will be able to, and then follow up.
- ✔ Create forums to share information like huddles or town-hall meetings.
- ✔ Actively seek out and address rumors.
- ✔ Be careful about being transparent before decisions or changes are final.

Create Transparency of Intent

- ✔ Tell your employees why things are happening in the organization.
- ✔ If you can't learn why, tie decisions to strategy, culture, or values.

Create Transparency of Information

- ✔ At least twice per year, share and discuss company and department strategy and goals, as well as the competitive landscape.
- ✔ Ensure that employees understand how they fit into the bigger picture.
- ✔ Educate your team about operational realities and ensure that they see how these realities are connected to the company's strategy.
- ✔ Regularly communicate how your company and department are doing financially and ensure that employees understand how their daily actions are tied to company finances.

CHAPTER 3

SET CRYSTAL CLEAR EXPECTATIONS

Steve Gelman had a math professor in college who had a rule he called "My Way." The professor insisted that his students complete their math problems the way *he* wanted, even though there were multiple ways to solve them. Otherwise, they wouldn't receive credit.

Steve never liked the "My Way" rule.

Flash forward a few decades. Steve had recently been appointed president of CH2M HILL's Industrial Business Group. It was the winter of 2009 and the team had been working largely on the backlog of client work they'd won prior to the recession. They'd just experienced the shutdown of their biggest project due to the plummeting price of oil and had no way of predicting what the next year would bring. There was no room for error, and they would have to be prepared for anything.

Steve's team members shared a strong commitment to the success of their business, though they were geographically spread out and had few opportunities to meet in person. Tension had started to crop up, and they'd recently had trouble acting in a coordinated fashion. There were epic weekly conference calls, but Steve wasn't seeing the results he needed.

Steve knew he needed help when he contacted me, but like many leaders, he was perplexed about the cause of the problem. Steve didn't like pecking orders and knew that his team was full of smart, capable—and very senior—people. *I shouldn't need to break this down for them! How could they not know what they're supposed to be doing?* he wondered. How many times have you scratched your head, asking that same question about your team?

As I interviewed Steve's employees, the real issues started to emerge. The team—and Steve—felt that he was responsible for everything. He was invited to almost every conference call where decisions were made. Because the team didn't understand what Steve wanted from them, and despite their affection and respect for him, they were afraid to guess. One direct report lamented, "I just want him to tell me what to do!" And since team members didn't understand each other's roles, they would go to Steve when issues came up. This is a pattern I see often, and it usually starts with vague expectations. Going back to Steve's math professor, he hadn't wanted to tell them *how* to solve the math problem, and in doing so was less clear on *what* the problems were and *who* was responsible.

Steve and I dove into the issues headfirst, planning a three-day offsite to assess the team's functioning and turn it around. Steve's meticulous focus as an engineer was evident as we spent weeks planning the meeting.

Then, on three cold January days in Colorado, the team hashed things out. It wasn't a particularly sexy process, but it was an essential one. The team had exhaustive discussions and generated clear agreements on their mission, their critical success factors, their goals, acceptable and unacceptable ways of working together, their different roles and responsibilities, and the principles that would guide their decision making.

The watershed moment of the meeting was when Steve outlined his own expectations, which looked like this:

- We will enhance decision making by increasing trust.
- Decisions are to be made and issues resolved at the lowest level possible, with the least number of people involved; defer up through the organization only when necessary.

- Gross margin sold is a key metric for all; and gross margin generated per business development dollar is the metric of organizational effectiveness.

- Team members are accountable to each other and are interdependent.

- Early warning is better than a late surprise.

I remember actually hearing a sigh of relief when the team heard this—they finally understood what he wanted. As a Bankable Leader, Steve uses this exercise of outlining his expectations to this day. His learning and growth were absolutely remarkable—as was the team's subsequent performance. It was one of the most powerful team turnarounds I've witnessed.

The early decisions that led to these issues are surprisingly common. Steve was so confident in his team's abilities that he didn't feel he needed to set crystal clear expectations. But ironically, this behavior fostered a lack of confidence within the team. Many leaders who don't create clear expectations for their team have good intentions; like Steve, they don't want to micromanage. But as we discussed in the previous chapter, people need information to reduce uncertainty. Leaders who set clear expectations drive not only results but confidence within the team as well.

This doesn't mean you should be a dictator, but the rules and the outcomes of the work your team is doing should be clear. When you clarify your expectations, you reduce anxiety and respect the human need for predictability, while also making it easier for employees to focus on performance rather than wasting time guessing what you want from them.

One study by Richard Ronay of Columbia University and his team supports this idea. It revealed that teams get more done (and experience less conflict) when there were defined leaders and followers, rather than flat structures that didn't clarify everyone's roles. This was particularly true when collaboration was important.[1]

Why was this the case? One explanation lies in the brain. Despite the focus on leaderless organizations and some of the benefits they may offer, ambiguity of roles interferes with our brains' ability to focus. Wolfram Schultz and his colleagues used functional magnetic resonance imaging (fMRI) to observe activity in the brains of people who were placing bets on a card game. They studied the difference in brain activity between people making "risky" choices (where outcome probability is known) versus "ambiguous" choices (where probability is not known). The fMRIs showed stronger responses in the frontal cortex and amygdala for ambiguous situations—in plain English: The brain reacts to uncertainty with the same mechanisms it uses in "fight or flight" responses—as it would when you're facing a grizzly bear.[2] Uncertainty is *that* scary. It's serious business, not to be taken lightly by any leader.

FIVE TYPES OF CLARITY

Attempting to magically infer your boss's expectations is like trying to figure out why your spouse or partner is mad at you without talking to them about it. Both are pretty unlikely, unless you can read minds.

As a relatively new leader, Christy Martello, the nurse manager we met in chapter 2, knew she wanted to lead by example. She didn't want to be seen as the out-of-touch boss who sits in her office all day (the kiss of death in hospitals—and frankly, anywhere). Taking over for a manager who was rarely on the floor, Christy jumped into her new job by putting on scrubs and working with patients, even serving as a nursing assistant when needed. She hoped her staff would understand her expectations by watching how she herself acted.

But there was one problem. She never *said* anything to them about those expectations. And within a few months, her patient-satisfaction scores—a major results metric—plummeted.

In a flash, Christy realized that she needed to be clear with her team—they weren't mind readers! So she called a staff meeting. "You're a group of hardworking professionals," Christy asserted. "We can do better."

Christy explained that the team needed to focus on three things: courtesy, compassion, and pain management. Their low compassion scores were particularly disturbing to Christy, because most nurses enter the profession to help people. She asked them how they'd feel if she walked around the floor and didn't show any interest in how their day was going. "Would you feel any respect for me?" They shook their heads. "So how do you think our patients feel?" All of a sudden, something clicked. And before long, Christy's unit went from having some of the lowest scores in the hospital to a spot in the top quartile.

Both Christy and Steve fell into an easy trap: neglecting to tell their team exactly what they needed and expected. Bankable Leaders create clarity in five key areas: *picture of the future, roles, results, individual behaviors,* and *team behaviors.* Let's review each one to learn how you too can set clear expectations for your team.

Clear Picture of the Future

I was once working with a team that was implementing an internal merger of operations, and the process was causing a huge amount of strife and confusion. Initially, I was asked to create a competency model for their leaders for the newly merged organization. In an early session with one of the first departments being merged, there was a mutiny. "We can't even *think* about this leadership stuff," the leaders told me, "until we understand where this department is headed." Until the team understood the bigger picture, it would be impossible to discuss anything else. We took three huge steps back and started there. By the time the meeting was over, we'd agreed on a vision and mission for the department, a few short-term goals, and a list of issues that had to be resolved as we moved forward.

The bottom line is that you must communicate a picture of the future to your employees, whether you're in a new position, are leading your employees through a change, or whether it's business as usual. Here are some questions to help you hone your vision:

1. What are our group's strengths? What can we do better than anyone?

2. What are our group's weaknesses? What issues do we need to address?

3. What are the threats and opportunities in our industry or marketplace?

4. What will the industry look like in five to ten years?

5. What do we want to be different around here in three months? Six months? A year?

Clear Roles

Think back to Steve Gelman's team at CH2M HILL, where many issues stemmed from a lack of defined roles. Psychologists sometimes talk about "role ambiguity," which happens when team members aren't clear on what they're supposed to be doing. This uncertainty creates anxiety and wastes energy, hurting results, people, and even health. Role ambiguity has been linked to increases in blood pressure, heart rate, stress hormones, and cardiac disease, and to decreased immune system functioning. People who don't understand their roles are also more likely to be hostile and disengaged.[3] It follows that once Steve provided clarity to his employees, he saw better results and had a happier team.

In addition to the actions Steve took, there's one more tool you can use to help distinguish roles within your team: the RACI model, which comes from the project management literature. For each project, work through each of the questions below. The ideal end result is a list of names with a letter beside them (R, A, C, or I) for each task or project.

- **R**esponsible: Who is the team/individual who will work on this project and be "the doer(s)"?

- **A**ccountable: Who is the *one person* responsible for the success or failure of the project? (In some teams, this person can be part of the Responsible team).

- **C**onsulted: Who are the stakeholders who will be interested in the results of the project or have a pocket veto? Who has expertise that could be incorporated?

- **I**nformed: Who needs to know the status and results of the project? Sometimes these are higher-level leaders; sometimes they are customers. The difference between Consulted and Informed parties is that Consulted parties have input while the Informed are simply provided updates.

Below are a few questions to help your team define roles. These can be worked through individually or as a group (though I typically find the latter to be most efficient):

1. What are each person's primary contributions to the team? What are his or her most important projects?

2. How do you expect team members to allocate their time?

3. How do team members need to interface with one another, and what shared and unique responsibilities exist?

4. What does each team member need from other team members to be successful?

When clarifying roles within your team, imagine that you're the conductor of a renowned orchestra, guiding each musician to clearly understand the notes they're playing. To achieve a beautiful symphony, your employees must each have their own sheet of music and know their part to play.

Clear Results

Brad Davis, a leader at Disney Interactive Media Group whom we met in chapter 2, had his best and worst points as a leader within a span of two years. He had exceeded his sales goals by 60 percent for two years running and did so well that he was promoted to senior vice president of online advertising sales. In the midst of these wins, a new executive was appointed to lead his division. And one day, she summoned him to her office to deliver a warning to Brad about his leadership style. She explained that he wasn't exhibiting the behaviors that were expected from executives at Disney.

Brad was just as devastated as he was confused. *How could I have known this?* he wondered. *They just promoted me! Clearly I was doing a damn good job!*

Earlier in his career, he might have tendered his resignation then and there. But he loved his job and wanted to make things work. "OK," he said to the new executive. "Help me understand what you need from me. And if I could, let me take this home and determine whether it's something I can deliver." As the executive responded, Brad discovered precisely what was expected out of an executive at Disney. She told him about his fiduciary responsibility to the company, and said that he traveled too much and was expected to be available for internal meetings. And most startlingly, she told him that many felt he was advocating for his team (as he had done in his former role) rather than serving as an advocate for the entire corporation. It was a challenge to listen calmly, but he immediately understood that the rules of the game had changed.

Brad went home, considered his options, and decided to stay at the company.

He scheduled meetings with his superiors and laid out a five-point plan for what he would do differently. The meeting went well, and three years later, he went through the organization's senior executive program, the highest level of training that leaders can complete at Disney. Brad went from the brink of termination to the pinnacle of leadership success, all because he learned the results he was expected to create.

How often do you make your team have to guess about the results you expect? Most leaders who don't outline the results they expect say they want to "empower" their employees. But this isn't empowerment—it's abdication. If you want to make the results you expect completely clear to your team, effective goal setting is an absolute must.

Goals: Creating Clear and Motivating Results

Andrew Lobo and his partners were in a tough spot. It was the year 2000. They had founded eSkye Solutions in 1999 and were in the middle of their Series B round of funding. Already having raised $6 million, they were at the term-sheet stage with a funding source of $70 million. But before the signatures were inked, the market tanked and the funding fell through. They had more than fifty employees and less than six months' payroll in the bank.

Andrew admitted to his team that this was upsetting. But he urged them on: "We have to get out of bed in the morning and do something," he said. Since their funding fell through, the financing side of their balance sheet had changed, certainly, but the left side—the assets represented by their ideas and market opportunity—was the same. He knew that they had the best people and could raise money again if they got back on the horse. And in just three months, the team met its goal, closing their Series B round for $48 million, which incidentally was the largest amount raised to date for that type of business!

Andrew's story is a perfect example of the power of goals. Goals motivate us to create results, and we derive self-esteem and confidence from achieving them. One study by Robert Wood and colleagues in 1987 reported that the relationship between goals and performance is so strong that we wouldn't gain much by continuing to research the relationship.[4] Think about that for a moment. How often have you heard an academic say that we should stop researching *anything*?

Before we dive into how to create great goals, let me answer a question you might be asking: "Just how high should my expectations of my team be?" As is often the case, science has an answer. A team of researchers led by Peter van den Berg of Tilburg University in the Netherlands looked at the influence of leaders' expectations on their employees. The authors collected survey data from more than nine hundred employees and their managers from Dutch organizations. They found that leaders with high expectations developed higher-quality relationships with their employees, set more difficult goals, and provided more learning opportunities and feedback. These behaviors in turn made employees more engaged.[5]

In short, like Andrew and his partners at eSkye, Bankable Leaders drive results and take care of people by holding high expectations for their team. Let's learn how they do it.

SMART Goals Drive Performance

You've probably heard about "SMART goals" at least once in your career. First introduced by George Doran, Arthur Miller, and James Cunningham in 1981,[6] the framework defines what good goals look like:

- **Specific**: Is the goal stated specifically enough that you'll know you've reached it?
- **Measurable**: Is the goal able to be evaluated, either qualitatively or quantitatively?
- **Attainable**: Can the goal be achieved?
- **Relevant**: Does the goal align with the goals of your company or function?
- **Time-based**: What, specifically, is the target date for its completion?

I've sat through—and built—countless trainings on how to set SMART goals. I've seen them in strategic plans, performance goals, and coaching plans. I hate to be the one to tell you this, but SMART goals have not, in fact, saved the world. Here's why: They're results-oriented, but usually not people-focused. (Have you ever dated someone who looked good on paper, but it just didn't *feel* right? Same idea.) That's where SAIL goals come in.

SAIL Goals Embrace Humanity

SMART goals are helpful, but because they usually don't incorporate people elements, they're like a boat without a sail—it may be beautiful, but it isn't going anywhere. Below is a framework to make SMART goals SAIL:

- Stretch: Is the goal challenging enough to make the person raise their game?

- Ability: Does the person completing the goal have the ability (or can reasonably learn) to accomplish it?

- Importance: Does the goal *feel* personally important to the person?

- Learning: Does the goal help grow their skills in a way that *they* want to grow them?

Let's start with Stretch. Stretch goals (similar to Jim Collins's BHAGs: Big, Hairy, Audacious Goals) have received a great deal of attention from researchers and management authors.[7] The science on goals tells us that there's a strong relationship between goal difficulty and performance. Difficult goals help us to perform better because they force us to think of different ways of doing things. For example, if a wealth management professional has to double his clients, he probably won't do it by making twice as many sales calls. He'd almost certainly need to incorporate different approaches, like seeking referrals from his current clients.

The best stretch goals are ones that the person has a 25 to 50 percent chance of accomplishing. It's important to set these for your team, but do remember that by their nature, stretch goals aren't always attainable. Ensure that you're not punishing employees for setting their sights on excellence by giving them both an "official" and a "stretch" goal.

The next SAIL element is Ability. Let's say that the wealth manager above has been asked to double his clients in one year. But even though he may be great at managing money, his sales skills are abysmal. Is his goal SMART? Yes. Is it a stretch? Sure. But will he be able to do it? Likely, no. And if he tried, especially without development or support, he'd probably end up demotivated and demoralized.

Before setting a goal, take an honest look at the skills an employee currently has and stack them up with what's needed. If the employee can't reasonably learn through training, coaching, or mentoring, or doesn't have the resources needed, the goal will likely do more harm than good.

The next SAIL element is **Importance.** The science on goals shows that specific and challenging goals lead to higher performance, but *if and only if* the person has accepted and is committed to the goal.[8] If a goal feels trivial, your employees probably won't get out of bed in the morning and say, "I can't wait to go in to work today!" Important goals have the ability to give us a sense of involvement, meaning, and confidence—human needs that Bankable Leaders acknowledge. We'll come back to the idea of meaning in chapter 6.

Sometimes simply stating the goal differently can mean the difference between importance and meaninglessness. An assembly line worker in one of Henry Ford's factories might have had a goal of one hundred widgets per day, and the work might not have felt particularly important. But what if, instead, the goal was stated as it relates to the big picture: To help change the world by making cars that give Americans access to transportation by working on one hundred widgets per day? That's something almost anyone could get excited about.

The final SAIL element, **Learning,** is often neglected in goal setting: Performance goals are stated simply in terms of the inputs and results needed rather than what the employee will learn in the process. Learning goals, even when they have the same result as a performance goal, include a focus on increasing skills. Learning goals foster better performance and help employees be more resilient.

Let's say our wealth manager and his supervisor are setting his goals for the year. Consider the difference between these two:

- **Goal A:** I will earn five referrals for new business in the next six months.

- **Goal B:** To grow my influence abilities, and to help me become a successor to the general manager, I will earn five referrals for new business in the next six months.

Goal A is a performance goal, which has an inherent limitation. When we are focused only on the outcome, we tend to attribute setbacks to a lack of ability and get discouraged. Conversely, Goal B is a learning goal—it provides a greater context for what the person is learning in the process of achieving that result. When researchers have examined reactions to both types of goals, employees have more consistently positive feelings about learning goals.[9] When you think about learning goals in terms of humanity and performance, this makes sense—they encompass both.

Which goal in the example is more like the goals you set for yourself and your employees? My prediction is that about 90 percent of you, fair readers, write performance goals. And frankly, that is understandable! It's all about performance at the end of the day, right? But if you can help minimize your employees' feelings of discouragement when the going gets tough, you will almost always guarantee performance.

Clear Individual Behaviors

Pat Lawrence grew up in the hospitality industry. Early in her career as a human resources leader, she'd found a mentor who shaped her into a businessperson who just happened to work in HR. Pat's mentor taught her to always consider how to help the overall business with each of her decisions.

So when Pat started as vice president of human resources at RE/MAX, she spent about a month meeting her team and listening before she laid out her expectations for how she expected her team to approach its work. Her expectation, she clearly told her team, was that everything everyone did needed to support customers' happiness—even though they worked in HR. "Don't tell me about activities," Pat said. "Tell me about the results you achieved for the business and our customers." She went on to explain that she didn't want her team dreaming up distracting "initiatives" but wanted them to help the company serve its customers above all else.

She told them a story of her work at Keystone Resort. During the holidays, when hiring was down and her team members had less on their plates, she had them work on the mountain as lift operators, maids, and front desk staff. The ultimate aim of HR was keeping their guests happy, so sitting in their offices as the year came to an end just didn't make sense. She wanted to bring the same approach to the HR team at RE/MAX, and was very clear about what each person on the team needed to do to support it.

Bankable Leaders don't just lay out expectations for what gets done; they clearly and frequently communicate their expectations for acceptable and unacceptable behavior. Most employees want to do the right thing, and your team doesn't want to disappoint you. But if they don't clearly understand the behaviors you're expecting from them, they will be lost.

Having to guess how your boss expects you to behave harms both people and results. I once worked for a boss who was notoriously unpredictable. His expectations seemed to change hourly. Not sure which mood he'd be in, I'd usually create two reports to bring to our meetings, and this duplication of work pulled my focus from the results I was there to deliver. The sheer amount of energy I wasted trying to guess what he wanted was exhausting and demoralizing.

If you don't want to end up like this, here are a few questions to consider when communicating behavioral expectations to your team:

1. What five behaviors are most important for you to see from your employees? For each, give an example of a situation and the behavior you want to see.

2. What behaviors are deal breakers for your team—the things that make you go off the deep end? What behaviors bug you to no end?

3. If employees run into a problem or issue, what is your expectation for how they will handle it?

4. How do you want your employees to contact you and how often? If employees want to meet with you, what's the best way for them to get on your schedule?

5. When employees are creating reports or written documents, what do you typically want to see? Brevity? Thoroughness? Spell it out!

EXPECTATION SETTING IN **VIRTUAL TEAMS**

Uncertainty can be crippling for virtual teams. Whereas co-located teams can sometimes function with less-defined roles or expectations, this is a much bigger problem for virtual leaders. In co-located teams, expectation setting normally takes place in face-to-face meetings and is reinforced through casual interactions. But virtual leaders can't leave anything to chance.

1. **TELL THEM EXACTLY WHAT YOU NEED:** As early as possible, take time with your team members on a call (or, ideally, in person) to tell them exactly what you expect of them. Give them time to ask questions. Then ask what they need from you.

2. **PRACTICE CONSTANT COMMUNICATION:** I recommend getting together on the phone at least weekly—instituting a common and frequent touch point can make all the difference in the world for virtual teams. Your goal is to create a culture of reliable, effective communication.

3. **BE PREDICTABLE WITH FEEDBACK:** Make it a point to quickly provide feedback to team members after they have completed a task. Doing so will decrease uncertainty and give team members a chance to understand what you need from them.

Clear Team Behaviors

In 2008, I was asked to help with a billion-dollar engineering, procurement, and construction project in the oil sands of Alberta, Canada. The project had been set up so that some of the design work would be outsourced from the team in Calgary to a team in Buenos Aires, but issues started to emerge soon after the project launched. The teams in Calgary and Buenos Aires didn't clearly understand their respective roles and faced constant communication problems that were somewhat, but not entirely, due to the language barrier.

The teams' two project managers contacted me to help steer the ship back on course. Through a series of meetings in Buenos Aires and Calgary, we set out to define how the teams would work together. We created a set of guiding principles that outlined the expectations team members had of each other, things like total honesty, kindness, respect, accountability, patience, and no surprises. We established clear guidelines and communication structures. The project leads would meet weekly by phone, and new information would be shared via phone with e-mail follow up.

These agreements allowed the team to make substantial progress toward getting the project up and running quickly. The team thrived. Unfortunately, the project was shut down in 2009 because of the sharp drop in the price of oil (evidence that Bankable Leaders can't control everything). But there's still a good lesson here.

Here are a few questions to help your team learn the best way to work together:

1. How do you expect the team to work toward accomplishing the results you expect from them?

2. How will you communicate with team members individually and as a group? How often? How should team members communicate with each other? What will meetings look like? Which meetings have tight agendas and which are ad hoc? Which are stand-ups and which are longer meetings?

3. What is the preferred method of communication? What will you use e-mail for, and what *won't* you use it for?

4. What behaviors would you and the team like to see continue? What behaviors need to change or improve to help you work better together?

5. What are your general guidelines for decision making? Which decisions do you expect your team to make independently and which do you expect to be consulted on?

The behaviors referred to in the fourth question above are often called "team norms," "team guiding principles," or "ground rules." Frankly, I don't care what you call them as long as you have them! I recommend agreeing on no more than five, because if your team can't remember their principles, they certainty can't apply them.

One team I recently worked with in the City of Cincinnati came up with two highly focused team norms: (1) efficient and disciplined conversations, and (2) something they called "The Goober Factor," which meant that above all, team members would ask questions until they clearly understood what was being asked of them by their sometimes verbose leader, Mary. (Don't worry—Mary thought The Goober Factor was hilarious.) The power in this list was its simplicity, and not surprisingly, the team saw almost immediate improvement.

■ ■ ■

A few years ago, my husband and I were celebrating his fortieth birthday in Barcelona. Some friends had given us a list of not-to-be-missed restaurants. One evening, we decided to visit Cal Pep, one of the most popular tapas bars in the city. Unless you make a reservation months in advance, it's impossible to eat there after 9:00 or 10:00 p.m. (peak dining hours in Spain). We decided to show up a few minutes before the restaurant opened, at 7:00 p.m., for the equivalent of the early-bird special in most North American restaurants. We had heard that many tourists show up early, so we were prepared for a long line. But when we arrived, all we saw were people pacing by the restaurant.

We were afraid of being the first in line, so we decided to sit at an outdoor café across the way. Still we saw nothing—just people milling about. At about ten minutes before 7:00, I got antsy and decided that it was time to make a line. We planted our feet firmly outside the front door, and within thirty seconds, twelve people lined up behind us. Everyone had been doing the same thing we were: awkwardly pacing around, waiting for someone to form a queue.

There was a waiter inside the restaurant who chuckled as we passed by and didn't seem to be interested in helping us—it was pretty frustrating. Though this was one of the best meals I've ever had in my life, the restaurant didn't do a very good job of clarifying its expectations for how we'd get in line for a table. Don't let the same thing happen on your team! The world is full of situations without clear expectations, but the responsibility to communicate your expectations as a leader falls on you. And once you take your place in line, they'll know where to stand.

BANKABLE ACTIONS

Create Clarity of the What

✔ Make sure you set high expectations for your team. High expectations lead to better relationships, more difficult goals, more learning, and more employee engagement.

✔ Vision: Create and communicate a picture of the future to guide your team's work and thinking about their roles.

✔ Roles: Clearly define each team member's role, asking questions and defining specific contributions using the RACI model.

✔ Results: Create clear expectations with your employees regarding the results you expect from them by setting SMART SAIL goals.

Create Clarity of the How

✔ Individual Behaviors: Tell them exactly what you expect from them individually, outlining acceptable and unacceptable behaviors for how they get their work done.

✔ Team Behaviors: Give your employees clear direction on how you want them to engage with you for meetings, issue resolution, reports and written documents, etc. Help your team clarify how they will work together, including how meetings will run, preferred methods of communication, team operating principles, and decision making.

CHAPTER 4

BE A LIGHTNING ROD OF COMPASSION

The TV show *Undercover Boss* is proof positive that leaders can learn compassion. A prime example is an episode chronicling the journey of Rick Arquilla, president and COO of Roto-Rooter, who went "undercover" and worked with his employees on the front lines.

There he met three people in particular who showed him the value of compassion. The first, a sewer technician named Chris, reminded Arquilla of his father, a blue-collar factory worker who was an alcoholic at the end of his life. Chris, a recovering addict himself, was not afraid to share his struggles. During the episode, Arquilla admitted that he lost a lot of sleep thinking about Chris.

Then Arquilla trained with Candace, a dispatch operator, and learned about her struggles working nights and caring for an autistic child during the day, all while trying to keep up on her mortgage. By watching Candace operate the dispatch system he had helped design, Arquilla learned how confusing it was.

Then he rode for a day with Henry, a dedicated technician who in only three years had become the go-to expert for his coworkers. He witnessed Henry heavily discount a repair for an older customer. Arquilla was angry at first, but then he realized that because Henry works on commission, he was losing money too—the woman was on a fixed income and Henry just wanted her to be able to live in a house with working plumbing. After an exhausting fifteen-hour day, Henry proudly told Arquilla that he coaches a youth basketball team after work. Arquilla could hardly believe his employee's dedication to keeping the kids off the streets. It almost brought him to tears.

At the end of the show, Arquilla reflected on his experience. For perhaps the first time, he understood how hard his employees worked. He noted that he didn't want to be the guy who just made lots of money but didn't care about his people. In the end, he shed some tears, came clean to the people he'd worked with, and thanked his employees for helping him be a better leader.

Arquilla didn't start off as a bad leader, but he fell prey to a common mistake: forgetting to show compassion to employees. When you don't understand and support your team members, they will feel like cogs in a machine. This feeling almost always prevents employees from forging a connection to you or their jobs—they'll be likely to leave when the next position comes along.

There's scientific evidence that compassion drives business results: One Center for Creative Leadership study with more than 6,500 managers across thirty-eight countries found that leaders who demonstrated empathy (a component of compassion, as we'll see in a moment) were better performers than those who didn't. This was true for leaders in all countries, though the correlation was stronger in some cultures than others.[1]

Few would disagree that compassion is essential for leadership success. But for many reasons, it's surprisingly difficult to demonstrate on an ongoing basis. You may be too busy to notice when an employee needs support. You might not know enough about your employees as people to understand their world. Or perhaps you're so focused on driving performance that you don't notice when your team is struggling.

In this chapter, we'll uncover the importance of showing compassion—and rest assured that it is indeed a learnable skill.

TEACHING COMPASSION

Let's review an example. As a newly minted PhD without much industry experience, Ray Vigil had just met Ernie, a crusty older gentleman and the leader of a high-tech machine shop. Ray had been asked to figure out how to improve employee morale in the company, and Ernie's shop had the highest in the plant. Naturally, Ray went searching for a rational and reasonable cause.

He spent time with Ernie, watching him and getting to know him. One day, Ray asked him his secret. "Ray," Ernie said, "it's easy. The foundation of morale is the concept of love."

Ray was floored, "What?!" he replied. Then, ever the scientist, "How do you measure that?"

Ray was initially skeptical that such a fuzzy, hard-to-measure concept was the key to the high morale Ernie instilled in his team. But as Ray got to know Ernie, he realized that he was right. Ray witnessed the profound connection that Ernie had to his people—when Ernie spoke to Ray about his employees' struggles, Ray would occasionally see a tear welling up in Ernie's eye. Leadership is about love: Concern for people. Love for your team. Love for your customers. This lesson carried Ray through many decades as a successful leader, and as my mentor, it was one of the first things he taught me.

You might be reading this and thinking, *That is easy enough for Ernie, but I can't be like that.* Au contraire. Almost everyone possesses this capacity, and it's not as complicated as it seems. Compassion is about connection—arguably *the* essential element of being human. Don't worry: It isn't about hugging and crying with your employees and talking with them about how horrible their childhood was. It's much simpler—and more practical—than that. Douglas Noll, a California-based lawyer turned mediator, says it best: "Compassion is not sympathy nor it is emotional . . . Compassion is a state of consciousness."[2]

And luckily, almost everyone is hardwired for compassion.[3] Some researchers believe that it evolved as an emotion to promote something called "prosocial" behavior, or behavior that helps the survival of our species. And in fact, our brains are programmed to feel what others are feeling. Researchers have identified what they call "mirror neurons" in the brains of macaque monkeys (a primate genus that's eerily similar to humans). When monkeys, or humans, see someone else who is experiencing a strong emotion, mirror neurons trigger the limbic system—the part of our brain responsible for emotions—and we actually feel what the other person is feeling.[4] Why else would we cringe when we see people in movies slip on banana peels?

But not everyone is capable of compassion: About 4 percent of the population are born sociopaths, meaning that they aren't physiologically capable of feeling empathy for human suffering. The rest of us, however, don't have any excuse for not showing compassion every day. We may not always feel like doing it, but we can work on it. A team of researchers led by Johanna Shapiro of the University of California–Irvine took on the audacious task of helping medical students, a population often maligned for its lack of compassion, to improve their skills in this area.[5] They took a cohort of twenty-two first-year students through eight reading and discussion sessions of poems, skits, and short stories covering human aspects of medicine like doctor-patient relationships and listening. At the conclusion of the study, many showed empathy improvements of up to 54 percent, evidence that the majority of us can improve our capacity for compassion if we try.

In another study, Michael Krasner (University of Rochester Medical Center) and his colleagues tackled the even tougher task of teaching compassion to physicians.[6] Krasner and his team believed that most physicians' lack of compassion was situational. Their jobs are so stressful, the researchers reasoned, that it's easy for them to lose awareness of their surroundings, including the patients who need compassion.

The team studied seventy primary care physicians who completed a one-year course on mindfulness. The training included simple activities to increase awareness of their surroundings, such as storytelling, focusing on attention and awareness, and reinforcing positive personal experiences. The physicians reported improved well-being, less burnout, and more empathy.

The best leaders know they need to exhibit compassion, but for many, it takes a firsthand experience with an employee to show them why this is so important. Let's try to shorten the learning curve a little and delve into exactly what you can do to reap the benefits of compassion, first through *empathy*, then through *supportive action.*

THE INGREDIENTS OF EMPATHY

Christy Martello, the nurse manager we met in chapter 2, thought that being a manager was easy—until she became one. Before, dealing with poor performers seemed fairly straightforward: You simply reprimanded them. But shortly after assuming her role, she had an employee who kept showing up late to her shifts. Rather than reprimanding her, something instinctively told Christy to sit down and talk to her first.

Christy learned that this employee was having a difficult time at home. Letting the nurse talk through her situation, and even vent a little, proved to be the best approach. Christy ended the conversation with a message of support and a reminder that the nurse would need to watch her attendance issues even with the extenuating circumstances. After that conversation, the nurse stepped up and her absenteeism was no longer an issue. By showing empathy, Christy had fixed the problem without chastising her. The nurse even went on to be nominated for Nurse of the Year. Christy believes that if she had simply given her a warning (in other words, chosen not to be compassionate), the nurse would have quit. Compassion helped Christy avoid a serious loss.

If you empathize with your employees when they're struggling, you'll boost their confidence and they'll do the same thing for you when you need it. In this section, we'll review the three essential elements of empathy: taking their perspective, understanding the impact of your title, and realizing that names go a long way.

Learn to Take Their Perspective

Jill McClure was in her last semester of college when she fell and broke her arm, causing her to need emergency surgery. At the time, she worked as the afternoon-drive DJ at a local radio station. Dropping everything to get the surgery, she missed a lot of work and school. The day that she returned to the station, she was feeling especially sorry for herself, as she had to work with a broken arm while trying to catch up on her last semester of school. The station's program director saw her in the hallway just after she arrived and pulled her aside. "You should really consider sending a note to the staff thanking them for taking your shifts," he told Jill.

"What?" Jill exploded. "It's not like I broke my arm on purpose!"

"Yes, Jill," said the program director. "But even though you didn't do this on purpose, your absence has been a real burden for your team. Acknowledging that they helped would go a really long way."

This was a whole new way of thinking for Jill, but she noticed as her first day back progressed that she was getting the cold shoulder from quite a few people in the station. Later that night, she did as the program director recommended and sent out a round of sincere thank-you notes expressing her appreciation, imagining how it could have been frustrating for her colleagues to cover for her, even though it was no fault of her own. By the end of the week, she noticed a pronounced difference in her coworkers, especially the ones who had seemed annoyed before—they were now supportive, friendly, and grateful for Jill's act of empathy.

Jill, who now serves as COO at the Colorado Oil and Gas Association, thinks of this story frequently. When something happens (intentionally or unintentionally) that will be a hardship for her team—whether it's an office move or a rush deadline—she makes it a point to take their perspective and thank them.

When your team knows that you understand what they're going through, they will cut you a lot more slack and will be able to better manage difficult situations. Please note: This is not a free pass to keep piling things on your team as long as you thank them and point out that you know it's horrible. But you get the idea.

You might be reading this and thinking, *Well, that's pretty straightforward. I just need to be more empathetic. I'll start tomorrow!* But here's a dose of reality: By virtue of your position as a leader, this is easier said than done. We've all heard the saying "Absolute power corrupts absolutely," and there may be something to that. Research by Adam Galinsky of Northwestern University's Kellogg School of Management and his colleagues provides evidence that power causes us to over-rely on our own perspective, making it difficult to appreciate the perspective of others.[7]

The researchers primed participants by asking them to recall an experience when they had either high power or low power, then asked them to draw the letter "E" on their forehead. The high-power participants were three times more likely to draw an "E" that *they* could read in the mirror—even though it would look backwards to anyone but them. They were drawing it from *their* perspective rather than others'. High-power participants also showed more errors in judging other people's emotional responses. Let's make sure you draw your "E" correctly, so to speak, shall we? Here are some ideas to help you understand the perspective of your team:

- Like Jill McClure, when you're making a decision, make sure to ask yourself, "If I were someone who would be affected by this, what challenges would I face?"

- Like Christy Martello, as often as possible, ask your team members how things are going in their world. What challenges are they currently facing? How can you help?

- Like Rick Arquilla, make sure that you visibly—and frequently—walk in your employees' shoes. Tour the shop floor. Spend a day shadowing the civil engineer. Go on the road for a day with your sales team. Then share what you learned with your team and show them that you get it!

Appreciate the Impact of Your Title

Margaret Kelly understands the power of titles. When she was promoted from senior vice president to president and COO at RE/MAX, the outgoing president told her, "Today you are Margaret. Tomorrow, you will be The President, and you won't be Margaret anymore."

As soon as you have a title, things change. Even if you're the supervisor of the mailroom, your title will get in the way with mailroom clerks. This can be good and bad. It's good because people are more likely to listen to you, but it's bad because the same behaviors you showed before assuming a leadership role can intimidate them. As we learned in chapter 1, helping your team see who you are as a person means they'll respect your title *and* see you as a human being.

You can also use your title for good. At RE/MAX's annual convention, Margaret, now the company's CEO, makes it a point to shake about three thousand agents' hands. She always tries to say something authentic and kind. One year, Margaret greeted a short, heavyset woman in a blue dress and exclaimed "You look beautiful!"

The next day, the woman approached Margaret with tears in her eyes. "I want to thank you so much," she said. "You made me feel beautiful last night."

"Yes," Margaret said, "you had the blue dress on!"

"What you didn't know is that I just had a lumpectomy," the woman said. "I'm bandaged and I didn't want to wear that dress. I felt ugly until the moment I talked to you. It meant a lot that the CEO would say that to me." Four seconds of contact with Margaret had changed this agent's feelings about herself, and she'd remember it forever.

The title you hold will almost always impact how your team sees you. As a leader, your actions become magnified, good or bad. Bankable Leaders understand the power of simply noticing and appreciating others. So, the next time you pass one of your team members in the hall, for goodness' sake, say hello!

Know That Names Go a Long Way

Morre Dean was pleased with himself. A month after becoming the CEO of a 2,400-employee hospital in California, he was sitting at the dining table with his family when his son asked, "How many names have you learned so far, Dad?"

"About two hundred," Morre bragged.

His son's face fell. "Dad, that's weak! You only know one out of every twelve?"

Suddenly, Morre realized that his son was right. In his previous organization, he called all four hundred employees by name and could list most of their spouses' and kids' names too. He knew he had work to do.

COMPASSION FOR **EXECUTIVES**

In senior roles, you're asked to focus more on "the big picture." Research shows that it's easy for executives to lose sight of the individual humanity of their people. This puts you in danger of forgetting to show compassion.

1. **MIND YOUR LANGUAGE:** Think about the jargon of business—even referring to people as "human capital" or "resources" reduces their essential humanity. Use words that remind you that they are people, just like you.

2. **BE AVAILABLE:** If your employees perceive that you're inaccessible (either because you have a large, imposing office or are never around), they won't connect with you. Get out of your office and talk to people. Ask them questions. Seeing them in action instead of just as numbers in a ledger will help remind you of their humanity, which makes it easier to have compassion for them—and vice versa!

3. **ANY TIME YOU TRAVEL, VISIT YOUR EMPLOYEES:** Even if it is only for a few minutes, arrange to spend time with employees in other locations. Make it "Breakfast with Bob" or "Coffee with Carl." Be interested in these employees and answer their questions.

4. **REMEMBER THAT YOU WERE ONCE WHERE THEY ARE:** If you remember what that time was like for you, and what you went through, you'll better understand and appreciate the struggles your people might be going through today.

Anthropologists have found that names exist in every culture.[8] Names are a huge part of our identity. They differentiate us from others and make us unique. They're the first thing we share when we meet someone. Why else would we get so annoyed when someone gets our name wrong at a party?

The CEO at a former company I worked with had an unmatched talent for remembering names. I remember meeting him in my first few weeks on the job. More than four months later, I ran into him in the elevator. "Well, hello Tasha," he said without missing a beat. "How is the new job going?" I beamed, feeling like the most important person in the company.

You can create a similar effect by learning the names of your team members' spouse, partner, kids, and pets. There is something fundamentally more personal in saying, "Joe, how was your weekend? Did you and Barbara do anything fun?" rather than "How was your weekend, Joe?" From that simple question, Joe knows that you care about him enough to learn his wife's name.

I've heard many a leader say things like, "Well, I'm just not good at names." Nonsense. You just aren't making a commitment to learn them. How many times have you met someone and let their name go in one ear and out the other because you didn't really care about learning it? A large part of being good with names is having the mindfulness to really listen to them the first time. Here are some pointers:

- Repetition improves memory. When you meet someone, say their name twice: "Nancy. It's nice to meet you, Nancy."

- Write down their name or ask for their business card. Often, seeing it in writing will help you recall it later.

- Sometimes it can help to associate the name with something: an animal, object, or famous person. These mnemonic devices make the information easier for the brain to manage and recall new information.

- When learning large groups of names, think about using photos. Most companies will have badge photos on file or easily accessible. Get ahold of them, study up, and impress everyone.

- To remember your team's family, keep track of their names in your day planner or in the contacts database of your e-mail application.

SUPPORTIVE ACTION

Remember, Compassion = Empathy + Supportive Action. The supportive action part of that equation is about lending a hand to help your team. Think about a time when you knew someone was in pain but didn't reach out to help—unfortunately, empathy isn't always enough. In addition to understanding and valuing your employees' essential humanity, you have to help them. If your employees need your help and you don't provide it, you might lose them, or let them get burnt-out and bitter. And because helping your employees will encourage them to help you, they'll pay you back with an increased vigor and commitment to the work they're doing. In the following pages, you'll discover three ways to lend your support to the team: standing with them in the line of fire, giving them your full attention, and reaching out when the going gets tough.

Stand with Them in the Line of Fire

Emeka Ene knows that one of the greatest things a leader can do is to stand beside his team, literally and metaphorically. As the CEO of Oildata Wireline Services, Emeka's energy service company delivers hydrocarbon energy enhancement solutions to operators from West Africa to the Middle East to South America. Many of his employees work in oil fields, which can sometimes be dangerous. But Emeka never asks his team to do anything he wouldn't do himself. Some years ago, the company was working on a gas operation where they were opening a particularly dangerous well. So he put on his coveralls, drove to the field, and took his place beside the crew. He didn't want to put them in the line of fire without showing them he'd put his life on the line too. Thankfully, the crew opened the well safely, and Emeka earned his team's undying respect.

Emeka's actions spoke volumes to his crew—he showed that he didn't see himself as different or better just because of his title or position. King Arthur famously sat his knights at a round table so they'd each have equal standing. Or

COMPASSION FOR **GLOBAL LEADERS**

Leading with compassion can be a particularly important skill for global leaders, who must work to bridge cultural differences. One meaningful difference between cultures is "power distance," a measure of how equally or unequally power is distributed in a culture. Low–power distance cultures are more collaborative and "flat," whereas high–power distance cultures are more hierarchical or paternalistic. Here are a few examples:

- **HIGH–POWER DISTANCE COUNTRIES:** Malaysia, Guatemala, Panama, Mexico, China, Egypt, India, the United Arab Emirates, Brazil.

- **LOW–POWER DISTANCE COUNTRIES:** The United States, Australia, Costa Rica, Germany, the United Kingdom, Austria, Israel. (Fun fact: Although the United States is in the low–power distance list, it has higher power distance than others!)

Although empathy is important in all cultures, a 2010 study conducted by the Center for Creative Leadership found that the relationship between leader empathy and employee performance is stronger in high–power distance cultures than in low–power distance cultures. Why? In essence, the bigger the power differential in a country or organization, the more of an impact a leader's support and protection will have.

So, although this is not license to be less empathetic or compassionate in low–power distance cultures, global leaders must be aware of these differences and go out of their way to show empathy in cultures with higher power distance.

take the CEO of a Fortune 500 company I work with: He refuses to have his own parking space. If he comes to work late, you'll see him driving around the parking lot with everyone else. It's pretty great. He's human, just like his employees, and they're all the same. There is power in this.

The action here is simple: Stand beside your employees, especially at critical points. Put in a late night with them before a big proposal is due. Spend time in the call center when a new product launches. Visit the construction site. The important thing is for you to physically (or virtually) be there, and to be one of them.

Give Them Your Undivided Attention

I was once facilitating a strategic planning retreat for a senior team I'd worked with before. I was seriously concerned about the group's ability to focus for a whole day. Not because any of them had attention deficit disorder—because they had iPads. One person would check his e-mail, and then, like a rapidly spreading virus, everyone else would be glued to their device within moments.

We live in a hyperconnected society, and getting anyone's full attention these days feels nearly impossible. Unfortunately, this fact of life makes your job as a leader even more difficult—especially when you're the distracted one. Imagine that one of your employees has scheduled thirty minutes with you. She has been storing up items to discuss for days or weeks. When she comes in and sits down, you say, "Thanks for coming. Just let me finish up this e-mail—I'll be fast." You then begin your conversation and the phone rings. You stop listening for a moment to glance over and see who's calling you, decide not to answer it, and turn back to your employee, apologizing. A few minutes later, you see your boss pass by in the hallway and wave to her.

If you were the employee, how would you feel?

I call this "Shiny Object Syndrome." Although these are relatively innocuous behaviors, you're doing everything possible to say, "I'm not paying attention." This almost immediately is interpreted as "You are not important." Not only might you upset the employee, she may hold back from telling you something important in the future because she doesn't feel heard. Then, before you know it, the team's performance suffers.

The best boss I ever had would set aside one hour of her time every week to meet with me. She would shut her door, turn off her phone, and close her laptop. She showed me that she valued me, my time, and my contributions. I can't remember everything we talked about, but I will always remember how I felt. It is no coincidence that I put in extra effort and time on the projects she assigned me.

Undivided attention is a simple but powerful ingredient of supportive action, and, luckily, it is 100 percent under your control. *Harvard Business Review* columnist Kare Anderson agrees: "Giving undivided attention is the first and most basic ingredient in any relationship. It is impossible to communicate, much less bond, with someone who can't or won't focus on you . . . what we focus on comes to control our thoughts, our actions, and indeed, our very lives."[9]

So, go ahead. Make the choice to give your undivided attention. Here's one surprisingly simple trick: When interacting with a member of your team, picture a frame around their head, so that you're looking at them as if they're a framed photograph. Your job is to look within the frame only. (One caveat here: Avoid overdoing the eye contact! Try to look them in the eyes about 80 percent of the time. Any more and they'll think you're a serial killer.)

But often, competing demands on your time might make giving your undivided attention—with or without creepy eye contact—easier said than done. Well-intentioned leaders often ask me, "What if someone needs my full attention but I can't give it at that moment?" Fair question. Let's say one of your team members knocks on your door one day and you're working on a report with a tight deadline. To acknowledge them while allowing yourself to focus on the task at hand, you can say something like this: "Thank you for coming to see me. It's really important that I give you my full attention. Let me finish this up and I will come find you in an hour. Will that work?" It almost always does, and you can get your work done without disrespecting your team.

Help When the Going Gets Tough

Just like Bill Daniels did with Jerry Maglio at the beginning of part I, you have to be there for your people when the chips are down, whether it's a personal tragedy, overwork, stressful conditions, layoffs, or a merger. When you see that one of your employees is suffering, approach them and say, "Is everything OK? You seem [insert emotion]. Is there anything I can do for you?" Asking whether they want to talk about it is usually a good idea. It shows them you care without obligating the person to talk about it. If your employee does want to discuss what's bugging them, let them: Putting our feelings into words (scientists call this "affect labeling") physically reduces the intensity of negative emotions.[10] Of course, use your own judgment on what level of discussion is appropriate—for example, I know lots of leaders who would feel perfectly comfortable with an employee sobbing in their office for an hour, while others might be less inclined. Finally, there's always the good old standby: "I'm here if you need me."

■   ■   ■

Remember earlier when I said that for most leaders, compassion usually isn't about hugging and crying and talking about your feelings? Well, sometimes those things are necessary, especially when the leader has been decidedly *un*compassionate for long periods of time.

I remember one especially difficult moment during a meeting with such a leader and his employees. This team was led by a brand new, and exceptionally task-oriented, manager. I was helping the team plan for the year ahead, but the real issue was clear to me: The leader wasn't showing his team an iota of compassion.

In fact, a few minutes before the meeting started, a member of his team covertly pulled me into the mailroom to talk about her struggles. "He just doesn't care about us—we're like robots to him. I just can't take it anymore. I've never felt so devalued."

I knew that if we didn't directly address these issues, the team would never meet its aggressive plan that year. So I designed an exercise that I knew would surface them. The employee I had talked to before the meeting bravely volunteered to share her feelings about how the team was functioning. She could barely get through a sentence without beginning to sob, "When you come into work every single day and pass by my office, you've never once said hello to me.

When I bring you problems, you never seem to care about how stressful things are around here. You've never—not once—asked me anything about who I am or what I do here. It's like you don't care about us at all."

The manager listened intently to her words, which clearly stung him to the core. I could see tears welling up in his eyes. He turned to wipe them away, hoping no one would see. I asked him if he wanted to respond.

"I am absolutely devastated to hear this," he began. "I always knew that I was pretty task-focused, but I had no idea that you felt this way. For whatever pain or anger I've caused you, I am so deeply sorry. Please know that this was never my intent. I do care about all of you as people, even if I don't know quite how to show that to you." From there, we agreed on a plan to never let things get that bad again. After a hug, some tissues, and a quick break, the team got back to work, crafting an incredible strategy and jelling for the first time.

So occasionally, a few leaders may need to hug and cry. But whether or not this drastic step is needed for you, the message is the same. As beautifully said by the Dalai Lama, "Love and compassion are necessities, not luxuries. Without them humanity cannot survive."

BANKABLE ACTIONS

Exhibit Empathy

✔ Take their perspective when making decisions.

✔ Remember that your title multiplies the impact of your behavior.

✔ Regularly find out what is going on in your employees' lives.

✔ Commit to learning the names of your employees, their spouse or partner, their kids, and even their pets.

Show Support

✔ Make the choice to give your employees your full and complete attention when interacting with them.

✔ If you can't give them your undivided attention, tell them why and schedule the soonest opportunity to talk.

✔ Stand with your employees during important and challenging moments.

Part II

BE HELPFUL *and* DRIVE RESPONSIBILITY

Leading people wasn't always easy for Samer Al-Faqih, a Morocco-based, Jordan-born business operations director for the Africa region of MSD (as Merck is known outside the United States).

After six years at MSD, Samer fiercely competed for—and landed—the role of development and delivery leader of the company's HIV and AIDS products in the Persian Gulf. He inherited a team of field sales coordinators, and one of them simply wasn't meeting expectations. She spent most of her time in her office—a tendency that's anathema to most sales professionals—and became exceedingly frustrated when she had to change her schedule to meet her clients' needs. Even though Samer hadn't hired her, it was his responsibility to address her performance (as is often the case with leaders who inherit poor performers). He met with his boss to discuss a solution to these performance issues, but nothing came of their talk. Samer eventually elected to let the coordinator go. When he spoke to his boss about this situation, he was furious. He told Samer that he had failed at managing people, and that he would not recommend he manage additional employees in the future. He also said that Samer had neglected to hold this field coordinator accountable or help her adjust her behavior to meet the requirements of the role.

Samer had a supreme moment of clarity that day. Where most would have gotten defensive or upset, he felt a new level of focus as a leader. He would turn this into a learning experience, he decided, and be the best leader he could possibly be for his team.

Despite his former boss's objections, Samer went on to lead high-performing multi-disciplined teams across the Middle East North Africa Region. Rather than "holding people accountable" when they fail, Samer learned the importance of first supporting his employees' success by empowering them, helping them own their core duties, and coaching them to make good choices. The results speak for themselves: Samer's team had no voluntary attrition. And his employees have become wildly successful. One was placed in a highly visible product champion role; another succeeded Samer when he was promoted. Perhaps most impressively, the African region of MSD is achieving its top-line results, growing at a rate of 47 percent. Clearly, Samer learned a valuable lesson that helped him transform into a Bankable Leader.

In this section, I'll explain how Bankable Leaders help their employees succeed even as they drive responsibility for the employees' actions and decisions. Doing both can feel difficult, and as in the other areas of the Bankable Leadership model, the tension often pulls leaders to one pole at the expense of the other, either Being *Too* Helpful or Driving *Too Much* Responsibility. In Samer's case, he was so focused on ensuring that his employee was responsible for her actions that he hadn't created an environment that helped her succeed.

Leaders who fall on the left side of this spectrum are *too* helpful—they don't allow their employees to own or feel responsible for the work they do. Leaders on the right side of the spectrum are so focused on making sure their employees are responsible for their work that they micromanage them. Both types of leaders treat employees like children, but for different reasons. Left-side leaders don't give them the responsibility adults are entitled to, and right-side leaders don't allow them to make their own decisions.

BE HELPFUL   DRIVE RESPONSIBILITY

The Enabler   The Dictator

Though The Enabler, the left-side extreme, almost always means well, the results of her leadership style can be catastrophic. Enablers tend to be too helpful, doing things for employees instead of allowing them to take ownership of their work. Instead of coaching an employee to find the right course of action, for example, The Enabler might tell her the answer to save her the agony of finding the solution herself. Or if an employee experiences a failure, The Enabler may step in and fix things, showing him that he doesn't really need to own the quality of his work. The Enabler may accept mediocre performance or jump in to redo employees' subpar work—anything to avoid angering or embarrassing anyone on their team.

Equally dangerous is the right-side extreme, The Dictator. This leader is so focused on employees taking ownership of their work that he doesn't help them by creating the conditions for success. He might enact excessive policies that stand in for employees' good judgment, or he may fail to provide the flexibility employees need to make the best decisions. In general, this leader pushes employees instead of pulling them. And if employees don't do what The Dictator wants, he might wax poetic about the importance of holding people accountable.

As we uncover the nature of this dichotomy in the following chapters, it helps to understand the Theory X and Theory Y paradigms of leadership, as coined by management professor Douglas McGregor in his famous 1960 book, *The Human Side of Enterprise*.[1]

In a nutshell, Theory X is micromanagement at its finest. Theory X leaders assume that workers are lazy by nature, and they must be pushed to get their work done. Theory Y leaders, in contrast, assume that workers are naturally motivated and interested in their success as well as the company's, and that leaders should focus on helping them succeed rather than controlling them.

Theory X is a predominantly right-side leadership style that needs to be left behind where it was forged—the Industrial Revolution. At the beginning of the twentieth century, factories focused on mass production and were built around owner-managers, and they lacked the typical governance structures we have today: CEOs, presidents, boards of directors. On the factory floor, a premium was placed on output. The work employees did was largely unskilled, leading to a perception that workers were replaceable. I'd bet that the words "If you can't do it, I'll find someone who can" were first uttered sometime during this time period. The predominant management style of the day was strict control through process, ostensibly to drive maximum output.

"Holding your people accountable" is a modern-day outgrowth of Theory X so pervasive that it has become a cliché. The phrase implies that employees aren't achieving the results they are supposed to achieve (Is anyone ever "held accountable" for good performance? Never!) But here's the problem: Accountability is merely a *reaction* to someone's work product or attitude. It is external and takes place after the fact. Holding employees accountable implies that the employee didn't have good intentions or wasn't motivated to do the right thing. Responsibility, on the other hand, is internal—and if employees feel pride and ownership for what they do, responsibility will follow. I suggest removing the word "accountability" from your vocabulary and choosing "responsibility" instead.

After the Industrial Revolution and two wars, the world—and organizations—became increasingly complex, eventually requiring a Theory Y approach. Unskilled and standardized work was replaced with ambiguous environments that required collaboration, problem solving, and continuous improvement. The role of the manager evolved from holding employees accountable to creating opportunities for them to thrive. This included providing the autonomy to make their own decisions rather than barking out orders.

Theory Y falls in the middle of the spectrum between The Enabler and the The Dictator. Leaders who use a Theory Y approach help their employees succeed *and* they drive responsibility.

Let's review an example of the powerful shift that takes place when leaders replace a Theory X approach with a Theory Y one. Between 1927 and 1932, a series of landmark studies were conducted at The Hawthorne Works, a Western Electric factory in Illinois.[2] The research was originally designed to reveal how the company could improve efficiency on assembly lines by creating optimum working conditions. The researchers, Elton Mayo and T. North Whitehead, studied six women on the company's assembly line, varying conditions like lighting, supervision, rest breaks, and lunchtime.

Mayo and Whitehead unearthed an interesting but puzzling phenomenon: No matter what they did, the output of the assembly line workers increased. This was the case even when the researchers returned workers to the conditions they had worked under before the study began!

So what was happening? Mayo and Whitehead realized that in the course of the study, by virtue of varying the conditions under which they were working and giving them more breaks and cordial working conditions, the workers had suddenly been given more autonomy and freedom to complete their work. As a result, they developed increased responsibility and work ethic. Among other things, the Hawthorne studies showed what happens when leaders give their employees the freedom to accomplish their work the way they see fit. More specifically, having skilled employees doesn't guarantee that they will perform, because skill is only part of the equation of performance:

Performance = Skill + Motivation

Have you ever had a competent employee who just didn't care about working hard? Money probably didn't do the trick as you tried to make that person feel motivated. (Less common are employees who are highly motivated but cannot gain the skills needed to be successful.)

Here's the scary thing: Most managers have no idea what really motivates employees. In a study originally conducted in 1946 from the Labor Relations Institute of New York, then replicated in 1949, 1980, 1987, and 1995, researchers asked employees to rank the factors that most contribute to their motivation.[3] They then asked managers what they believed most motivated employees.

You've probably heard the results before: Employees gave top ranking to factors like appreciation, manager support, and coaching. But what did managers rate as number one? You guessed it: money. Not only did they get that wrong, they put appreciation, inclusion, and coaching at the *bottom of the list*. In 1999, Daniel Pink published findings from more than forty years of research in his landmark book, *Drive: The Surprising Truth About What Motivates Us,*[4] arguing that the three big motivators are autonomy, mastery, and purpose. Again, money didn't make the top three.

In the movie *The Break-Up*, Jennifer Aniston's character utters a profound statement that sums up how many leaders feel about unmotivated employees: "I want you to *want* to do the dishes," she tells her soon-to-be ex. Don't you want your employees to *want* to work hard?

When you create conditions that motivate your employees, they will begin to feel a profound sense of responsibility for the results they're creating.

One sunny spring day in Ohio, I was killing time in the new Cincinnati airport terminal. I happened to be there the first day it opened. I spoke to a gate agent who proudly declared, "I came in on my day off to help paint the walls so we could get the place ready!" His sense of responsibility, ownership, and pride was palpable.

"Wow—what motivated you to do that?" I asked.

"Our supervisor really got us excited about this. She's been talking it up for months!" I knew immediately that this supervisor was a Bankable Leader.

As you can probably tell, I'm a firm believer in the Theory Y approach to leadership. In this section, I'll offer you three approaches to move toward Theory Y. First, in chapter 5, we'll talk about the people and results benefits Bankable Leaders see when they treat their employees like adults, both by assuming that they are smart people who will make good decisions and by getting rid of overly controlling work practices. In chapter 6, we'll learn how you can effectively support employees without resorting to hand-holding. Finally, in chapter 7, I'll help you become a leader who brings out the best in your employees through coaching them and building on their strengths.

Let's dive in, shall we?

CHAPTER 5

TREAT ADULTS LIKE ADULTS

I couldn't believe it. I'd only been in my job for a few weeks when human resources handed me a dress code—one that was close to five pages long.

To give you some context, I am an obsessive rule-follower. This dates back to my days in middle school where, rather than being the one causing trouble, I was busy reporting the troublemakers to the principal (don't worry—I've grown up and only do that sometimes now). And to date, I had—I believed—managed to dress myself appropriately.

But, according to the dress code, I needed help. It contained detailed guidelines and rules, clarifying the type of makeup I could wear (minimal), the length of my nails (no more than half an inch from fingertips), the style of my shoes (closed-toe only), the length of my pants (nothing cropped), and even the appearance of my undergarments (seriously, I'm not exaggerating). As I stood there with the policy burning a hole in my hands, I felt a strange feeling wash over me.

I. Was. Outraged.

Do they really not trust me to dress myself appropriately when I come to work? I fumed silently.

So what did I do? I, Dr. Goody-Two-Shoes, turned into a passive-aggressive rebel, thwarting the dress code at every turn. I'd go shopping for pants that were just long enough not to qualify as "cropped." Once, I even put on a pair of press-on nails to see if I'd get sent home, which I thought would be hilarious.

After a few weeks, I found myself standing in the shoe department of Nordstrom, clutching a pair of shoes so subtly open-toed that I knew I could get away with wearing them. Suddenly I had a moment—I hovered outside my body and looked at myself. "What am I *doing*?" I gasped.

This is apparently what otherwise-reasonable human beings do when organizations create policies to substitute for good judgment. Leaders who excessively control employees are implicitly saying that they don't believe in those employees' abilities to make decisions—they're neither helping them succeed nor driving responsibility. When managers say, "We don't have accountable employees around here," that's a warning sign that they're treating hardworking adults like children, and when that happens, both people and results suffer.

Most leaders don't do this on purpose. In my experience, at least 90 percent of unnecessary policies were created because one leader was too scared to talk to one offending employee. Most policies are for the bottom 2 percent, the people who do the stupid things that led to the policies' creation in the first place.

Overzealous policies reward terrible leadership and often don't deal with poor performers directly. Think about it: If someone on your team was wearing cutoff jean shorts, how much easier is it to complain to human resources than sit down and have this uncomfortable conversation? Then, once you have a "no jean shorts" policy, you can simply point to it and say, "Well, this is just the policy," and the offending employee won't be mad at you. It's a vicious cycle. Leaders blame the policy and employees resent it.

The clear solution here is to treat your employees like adults, letting go of tightly controlled work practices and giving them true ownership of their behavior. At Nordstrom, the site of my dress code epiphany, their policy manual consists of a concise—and genius—eight sentences:

Employee Handbook

Welcome to Nordstrom. We're glad you're here!

Our number one goal is to provide outstanding customer service. Set both your personal and professional goals high. We have great confidence in your ability to achieve them, so our employee handbook is very simple.

We have only one rule . . . Use good judgment in all situations.

Please feel free to ask your department manager, store manager or Human Resources representative any question at any time.[1]

Granted, there is an element of risk involved in trusting employees to do the right thing. But it is by far the preferable choice. As Mark Leslie, founding chairman and CEO of Veritas Software, told *Inc.* magazine, "I believe if you want to be trusted, you have to trust first. . . . You will be betrayed sometimes, but the value of engendering trust is greater than the cost of being betrayed sometimes."[2]

In this chapter, I'll review two approaches to treating your employees like adults. First, we'll discuss how you can help them perform simply by *believing in their competence.* Then we'll discuss how to *engineer ownership by empowering your team.* At its core, you'll see that empowerment is about helping employees become self-sufficient. The more power you give away, the more responsibility your employees will feel.

BELIEVE IN THEIR COMPETENCE: "ACT AS IF"

Have you ever had someone who believed in you and, as a result, you accomplished something you thought was impossible?

Clarence McDavid and I were in a bind. Clarence, Rose Medical Center's vice president of human resources, and I were sitting in his office, scratching our heads. A month earlier, I had joined the team to build a leadership development program for the hospital. Among other things, I was hired to create Rose University, which would provide every employee in the organization with opportunities for professional development. A month in, we were offering a handful of fledgling leadership courses taught by Clarence's assistant director, but she had just resigned. I had other duties and our resources were tight, so having me teach these classes wasn't an option.

"I know this sounds crazy," I ventured, "but what if we trained our leaders to teach the classes?"

I saw a glint in Clarence's eyes, and he leaned in. "Tell me more," he said.

My idea was simple but risky. With one exception, none of our senior leaders had teaching experience, let alone expertise in leadership development. But I was confident there were at least ten leaders with the potential to be excellent instructors. Clarence loved the idea. "I'm in," he said.

We invited twelve senior leaders to apply to become Rose University Leadership Faculty. To be certified, each leader would work with me to build a course, complete a dry run, receive feedback, and have me shadow their first class. At least half of them openly told us we were crazy. But we persevered.

A year later we were the envy of our division. We had twenty faculty members teaching twenty-three classes, and our employee engagement scores shot to number one in our market. Even our patient-satisfaction scores were impacted—at one point, we were ranked number four across hundreds of other hospitals. It was incredible, but not surprising. We had believed that they could do it, and they proved us right.

What We Believe About Others Comes True

In 1963, Dr. Robert Rosenthal, clinical psychology professor at Harvard University, published a paper suggesting that psychological experimenters' expectations affected participants' behavior.[3] Rosenthal warned that such self-fulfilling prophecies might also occur in classroom settings, with teachers' expectations affecting students' performance. Shortly after the article was published, Dr. Rosenthal received a letter from an unusual source—a school principal in San Francisco named Lenore Jacobson, who wanted to test this theory at her elementary school.[4]

All students were given an IQ test that was disguised as an assessment of academic potential. The researchers randomly labeled 20 percent of the students as having high academic potential; these were designated as the "bloomers." Teachers were told these students had bright academic futures but weren't told anything about how the remaining 80 percent (the control group) would perform in class. Eight months later, the IQ test was administered to the students, and the IQ scores of the first-grade bloomers were 15 percent higher than those of the control group. Let me say that again: When the teachers were told these students were smart, they actually became smarter. The differences in scores were not as marked as the grade level increased, but the pattern held: Bloomers consistently showed IQ gains despite being arbitrarily labeled as gifted. The Pygmalion effect had officially been uncovered.

A few decades later, support for the Pygmalion effect in the workplace emerged. Dov Eden and Abraham Shani studied instructors and soldiers in the Israeli Defense Forces combat command course.[5] Before the course, instructors were given a list of soldiers, each with a randomly assigned "command potential" (CP) reflecting soldiers' ability and promise for the future. The instructors were told to memorize the soldiers' names and CP scores. The researchers found that the instructors expected more from those with higher CP scores, and the students with high CP scores actually performed better. The high-CP soldiers also gave the course and their instructor glowing reviews (the left-side leader's dream: "They like me, they really like me!")

The simple leadership lesson is this: *What we believe about others comes true.* Incidentally, research shows that the reverse is also true: Managers who expect poor performance get exactly that (we'll talk more about this in chapter 9).

When you "Act As If," you are treating your employees *as if* they were the most talented, motivated, and capable people around. To "Act As If,"[6] you have to delve into the fundamental assumptions you're making about your team. And remember, *you choose these assumptions.* The following table offers a few examples of different assumptions about the same behavior:

SITUATION	NEGATIVE ASSUMPTION	POSITIVE ASSUMPTION
An employee makes a mistake.	A policy is needed.	A conversation is needed.
An employee is late to work.	The employee is lazy or disorganized.	Something might be going on at home—how can I help?
You are leaving the office for a week for a conference.	Everyone is going to leave at 2:00 p.m.	This is a chance to get my best and brightest to man the ship.

I challenge you to monitor these assumptions in real time. When you make a judgment, ask:

- "Why do I believe that?"
- "Do I know that for a fact?"
- "What is an alternative explanation for this behavior?"

End the Tyranny of Policies and Procedures

When we board an airplane, we trust the pilot to be capable of getting us safely to our destination. When we go to the hospital, we trust our doctors to be competent to address our health problem. Why, then, don't we trust our employees to be capable of making sound decisions in *their* jobs? Why do we bog them down with rules and boundaries?

Jim Collins discusses this in *Good to Great.*[7] He found that when organizations hire mediocre people instead of getting rid of them, they create policies to mitigate the damage. Soon, these companies become bureaucracies and drive away their best people. They act as if employees can't be trusted to deliver a good performance, so the employees don't.

There are a few brave leaders and companies who have bucked the trend and eliminated policies in favor of clear expectations, reliance on their employees' judgment, and the employment of clear consequences when good judgment isn't used.

Many human resource professionals *love* creating policies. But Pat Lawrence isn't just any human resources professional. When she started as the senior vice president of human resources at RE/MAX, the company had a seventy-page policy manual. Pat thought that sitting new employees down to tell them all the things they *couldn't* do was neither welcoming nor helpful. Instead, Pat helps her leaders set clear expectations up front for what employees *should* do.

And slowly, over the course of seven years, Pat whittled away the RE/MAX policy manual. About five policies needed to be retained for regulatory reasons (the code of conduct, harassment and confidentiality rules, and so on), but the rest were out. As Nordstrom knows, it's all about using your best judgment. Is this a perfect solution that solves all HR difficulties? Of course not. "Sometimes employees make bad decisions," Pat wisely observes. "But [our approach] is infinitely better than saying 'We'll terminate you if any of these five hundred things happen!'"

Courtney Harrison is another example of a Bankable Leader who helped her organization treat its employees like adults. As SVP of Organization and People Development at Asurion, a start-up technology protection company, Courtney championed the goal of treating employees like adults.

The most powerful transformation took place at the manufacturing center where customer phones were repaired. When Courtney first met the center's manager, Charlie, his turnover was high and morale was low. The center also had the highest number of policies in the company, largely because of the fear that employees would steal customers' phones.

Courtney started with a philosophical conversation. "Charlie, you'll always have people stealing from you, but should you build your company around them or the 98 percent of employees who don't? If you do the latter, they'll police each other. Instead of the parent-child dynamic, they'll act responsibly. Wouldn't that be so much easier?"

Charlie was hesitant at first, but the lightbulb went on as they discussed the center's dress code. "Would you tell an adult you trust to work with your customers how to dress?" Courtney asked.

"No!" Charlie realized.

"Exactly," said Courtney. "We don't need a ten-page policy, we just need to set expectations and create consequences if people don't follow them." It was a revelation.

Charlie held a series of town halls to clarify those expectations. "I trust you," he told employees, "but I might not have been acting like I did. We're going to start fresh. One of the things I trust you to do is to get dressed in the morning. Here's what I expect. I want you to be covered from here"—he pointed to his shoulders—"to here"—he pointed to his knees. "Nothing with holes. Nothing religious or political. No flip-flops, midriff bearing, or belly shirts. If you're not sure, go to the Gap and buy five long-sleeved T-shirts and five pairs of jeans!" The employees all laughed.

"Now," Charlie went on, "if you come to work and seem confused about this, you get three chances. The first time, you'll go home and change. The second time, you'll be sent home without pay. The third time, you're fired." The team understood. Once he started trusting his employees, they started acting like adults. Clarifying your expectations, the big point of chapter 4, is a critical aspect of treating employees like adults. It would be delusional for an organization to abandon its policies but not give some idea of what is expected. When policies go away, employees have to be responsible for their behavior, and when they make bad choices, leaders must intervene immediately.

But I don't control the policies at my company, you might be thinking. *It's not in my power to throw out the rulebook!* That may be true, but you do influence how policies are used in your team. Let's look at two policy-enforcement conversations:

Conversation 1: "Mary, thanks for coming to meet with me. When I walked by your office earlier, I noticed you were shopping on Amazon instead of taking customer calls. As you know, we have a policy against this. [Leader hands policy to employee.] I need you to follow it."

Conversation 2: "Mary, thanks for coming to meet with me. When I walked by your office earlier, I noticed you were shopping on Amazon instead of taking customer calls. When you first joined our team, remember the conversation we had about the importance of answering our calls

TREATING ADULTS LIKE
ADULTS FOR **NEW LEADERS**

New leaders are often put in the potentially awkward position of leading former peers. Yesterday, you were friends with your coworkers, now you're their boss. This reality can turn new leaders into dictators: "Since I'm the boss now, I'd better act like one and tell them what to do!" Or you may "crack down" by making and enforcing rules that insult or alienate employees. Talk about treating employees like children!

1. **DON'T CHANGE OVERNIGHT, BUT STILL CHANGE:** The first day you come to the office as the boss, you will need to do things differently. Tell them what's going to be different and what you expect of them. Also remind them that the trust and respect you share is the same as before.

2. **THINK ABOUT DECISIONS:** Rather than acting unilaterally, engage your team in the decisions you make. Be sure to communicate to them how the decision will be made (for example, will the team provide input and you will decide?). It's extremely important to clarify the process.

3. **REMEMBER YOUR PAST, BUT ACCEPT YOUR NEW ROLE:** Acknowledge the challenges of your employees' work when necessary—you were recently in their place, so ignoring their challenges will only alienate your former peers. But remember that your role *has* changed. Blindly supporting and encouraging your employees may not only make them see you as their friend, but it may also result in problems in the future (e.g., issues with respect, decision making).

quickly? We also discussed my expectation that you only use the Internet for your personal use during your lunch break. I'm asking you not to do this again, and as you know, if you do, it will result in a day without pay. I trust you to make the right decision."

Neither conversation is comfortable—Conversation 2 is probably harder. But practice shifting your perspective and put yourself in Mary's shoes. Conversation 1 insults her intelligence. Conversation 2 treats her like an adult. Which one would you choose?

ENGINEER OWNERSHIP AND LEAVE THE DICTATORSHIP TO NAPOLEON

Engineering ownership is the second approach to treating your people like adults. When you do this successfully, you can give up a certain level of control to your team members, making them—and your customers—happier in the process.

Herb Kelleher, longtime Southwest Airlines CEO and Bankable Leader extraordinaire once said, "If you create an environment where people truly participate, you don't need control."[8] Let's illustrate the contrast between control and participation with two recent, but distinctly different, customer service phone calls—both of which I had within hours of each other.

The first was with an airline that had failed to get me to my destination on a business trip (they decided to land in Albany instead of New York City, which is only off by about 150 miles!). I was interested in a credit for my trouble. I spoke to a customer service representative, who told me about all the things she *wasn't* authorized to do, one of which was issuing a credit. I said, "Fine. Put me through to your supervisor." I thought her supervisor would be able to help, but we just repeated the kabuki theater performance I'd been through with her employee. She too explained all the things she wasn't able to do. "Fine," I said. "Put me through to your supervisor." After five minutes with the boss's boss, we'd had the exact same conversation. I hung up in disgust.

A few hours later, I called the customer service department of the flash bargain website Rue La La. "How can I help you?" the customer service representative chirped. I explained that an item I ordered had been sent in the wrong size, but that it was a final sale item and therefore not returnable. After I pleaded my case, she said, "Sure thing, ma'am. I would be happy to fully refund your purchase." I almost fell off my chair. "We don't normally do this," she said, "but I can appreciate that this was our error. We want you to be happy with your experience." Bingo! This was an empowered employee who'd been trusted to make the right decision. In one conversation, I went from someone who wasn't sure I'd shop on this website again to being so loyal that they probably should start garnishing my wages!

Overly controlling organizations typically underperform compared to organizations that give their employees freedom to make the right choice. According to leadership guru James O'Toole, when hierarchical barriers to decision making are in place, as was the case with the airline, product and service quality goes down.[9] High-control organizations hold on to mediocre employees while the best and brightest flee to organizations that give them more autonomy and respect. If you take high-control practices to the extreme, you have a full-on dictatorship; all power and decision making is held at the top of the organization.

However, when employees are given power, trusted, and treated like adults, amazing things happen. Here's an example. After a long day and a long flight, a man named Peter Shankman decided to jokingly tweet "Hey @Mortons - can you meet me at newark airport with a porterhouse when I land in two hours? K, thanks. :)". He landed to find a tuxedo-wearing Morton's employee waiting for him with a full steak dinner in hand.[10] How much would you bet that Peter Shankman will be a customer for life?

Empowerment Requires Smart Risks

If empowerment is so wonderful, you might ask, why do so many companies have trouble granting it? Well, I see well-intentioned leaders fail to grant autonomy because of fear. Let's go back to Todd Habliston, the oil and gas leader whom we met in the introduction. When Todd started his journey, he made a conscious decision to assume the risk of empowerment. He wanted to take more vacations, delegate more work, and allow his team to take on more responsibility. He realized and accepted that mistakes would be made.

His first experiment was to have the team create the budget for the next year. He asked his employees if they'd present the budget to the board, noting his confidence in their ability and his willingness to help them. Most enthusiastically accepted, telling him how excited they were about the opportunity. But as anticipated, there were a few staff members who were uncomfortable with the gravity of the assignment. Todd worked with them to understand their fear. When he learned it was lack of knowledge of some elements of the budgeting process that frightened them, he offered weekly lunch-and-learns. At the end of the process, the team had done a great job. More importantly, Todd had taken a risk that paid off. He managed risk along the way, and his team was more engaged than ever. Todd's boss and the board were absolutely thrilled with the team's work.

Here are a few questions to start to help you get the empowerment process started in your own team. I recommend starting simply, as Todd did, because if you start throwing projects at your employees willy-nilly, you'll just create chaos.

- Make a list of all the things you're doing. What do you *have* to do and what do you *want* to do? Are the things you want to do really things you *should* be doing? Are you hoarding the interesting projects or the projects that you owned before you got promoted?

- Meet with your employees to figure out what makes them tick—what areas they'd like to do more work in, learn about, etc. Find one additional responsibility for each employee and give them latitude to make decisions related to it.

- Make a list of the decisions that require your approval or work product that requires your review. Can you delegate any approvals or reviews to your team?

Be Clear About the "What" But Give Them a Choice About the "How"

Another important consideration in empowering your employees is being clear about the result you expect but less prescriptive on how it should be done. Banish the "my way or the highway" mentality forever. Amazon CEO Jeff Bezos, whom *Harvard Business Review* recently named the number two best-performing CEO in the world,[11] once explained the company's success by saying, "We are stubborn on vision. We are flexible on details."[12]

In 1982, my mother—Terri Wanger, of "Terri Wanger Rule" fame—took a job working in cable marketing for Bill Daniels under Jerry Maglio. The cable TV industry was just a few years old and cable providers were struggling to keep up with customer demand.

One day, Jerry called her to his office. "Terri," he said, "Bill would like you to build a customer loyalty program. You know his standards. It has to be the best and it has to get us to number one in our industry. Stay within the bounds of ethics and laws. The rest is up to you."

"But, but no one in our industry has ever focused on customer service," Terri stammered. "He wants us to set the standard?"

"Exactly," Jerry replied. "So you just tell us what you need to get us there and it's yours." Terri had been empowered. Jerry and Bill had given her a clear, measurable goal without telling her precisely how to get there.

With that, Terri started the first customer service training and improvement program in the cable TV industry. She knew that Bill's obsessively high standards would mean nothing if they weren't trickling down to the front line. So she began by spending time with the customer service representatives who took care of billing, customer appointments, and basic troubleshooting. On her first day in one of the operations offices, she saw one representative take her phone off the hook so she could eat lunch. Another was on the phone with a customer who had called to cancel his service. "OK, how soon would you like that to happen?" she said to the customer. And yet a third put all the telephone lines on hold so she could catch up on her paperwork.

Terri's jaw dropped. "Do you think you're giving the best customer service you're capable of?" she asked the reps bluntly.

"No!" they replied.

"OK, then," said Terri. "What's preventing you from doing that?"

They quickly gave her a laundry list of challenges, from being pulled in too many directions to old phone equipment to a lack of training to coverage of the phones during lunchtime. She took that feedback up the chain of command and made the case for the investment this program would require. She got it. Then Terri helped rewrite job descriptions, bought new equipment, and created a customer service training program to help the associates internalize and buy in to the goal of being a number one customer loyalty team.

When they were finished, things were a lot different. For instance, when customers called to cancel their cable, the representatives would work with them to solve the problem: "I am so sorry to hear that. How can we keep your business?" And within just a few months, both their customer base and their customer retention shot up.

Perhaps the most incredible part of this story was what Bill did to reward Terri for her contributions to the success of the company. He knew that she had always wanted to start her own business. After she had given notice that she was going to leave his employment to do just that, Bill asked how he could support her entrepreneurial efforts. They discussed a few ideas, and shortly thereafter he agreed to move her to a contractor position *and* provided her with favorable leasing terms ($100/month) in one of his nearby office buildings. For eighteen more months, Terri was able to call on some of the resources of Bill's company while providing consulting and customer service guidance to Bill's marketing team.

Once again, Bill had modeled what a true, trust-based professional relationship looked like. By giving Terri a *what* to achieve without telling her *how* to do it, he gave her the freedom to succeed in the way she saw best. Thanks to Bill's leadership wisdom and Terri's ability, everybody won.

Give Employees Control

I have a good friend who recently had surgery to stop bleeding in his brain after he took a nasty fall. Being the highly independent person that he is, the week he spent in the hospital was absolutely miserable for him. No one likes being in the hospital, and the lack of control he felt over what was happening to him was unbearable. He couldn't eat the foods he wanted. He wasn't able to decide when he'd leave. He wasn't able to get up and walk around.

With his discharge approaching, he was told he'd need regular appointments with a speech therapist. Still fairly groggy, he looked at me and said, "I don't think I'm going to go to speech therapy." Being far too smart not to know how important this was, I think he was exerting the last bit of control he felt he had left.

Luckily, my friend recovered quickly and completely, but there is a lesson here for managers. Regardless of their age, job type, gender, or culture, human beings want to have a feeling of control over their lives. This is especially true at work, where most employees feel that very little is under their direct control.

Researcher Muammer Ozer has found that workers who feel control over how they approach their work have better relationships with their colleagues and are more likely to help others when needed[13]—solid evidence that giving your team more control helps on the people side of the Bankable Leadership spectrum.

And on the results side, when employees have autonomy, they perform better. Nancy Dodd of Montana State University and Dan Ganster of Colorado State University studied the effect of autonomy on performance.[14] The researchers asked undergraduates to complete clerical tests measuring grammar, spelling, and punctuation—to measure their baseline ability—and then gave them text and asked them to correct the errors. Told they'd be competing against others, participants were given different sets of instructions with varying levels of autonomy. The high-autonomy group could control the program, while the low-autonomy group had to ask a supervisor's assistance at each stage. When the authors looked at the corrected text, they found that participants with high autonomy were not only more committed to the task but also performed better, providing they received feedback on how they were doing.

A friend of mine once told me that "stress is responsibility without control." There is scientific support for this statement: One recent study found that senior leaders (who have more control) report feeling less stress at work. Gary Sherman and his colleagues studied military and government leaders at a Harvard executive leadership development program.[15] They collected samples of the stress hormone cortisol and asked participants to self-report their anxiety. Researchers found that leadership positions were associated with less stress, with stress decreasing the more senior a leader was! Sherman attributed this to the fact that senior leaders have more autonomy.

There are a variety of approaches Bankable Leaders can use to give their teams a greater sense of control. For example, HCL Technologies, an India-based IT company, has created a sort of help desk dedicated to improving employees' work experience.[16] At any time, anyone can create an electronic ticket if something isn't quite right in their world. Maybe they don't like the food served at company functions, or they aren't happy with their manager. Tickets are routed to the person who can resolve them. Perhaps the smartest part of this approach is the fact that *only the employee who submitted the ticket can close it.* In other words, the employee has complete control and doesn't have to close the ticket until he or she is satisfied.

Here are some other ideas for how to give your employees a sense of control:

- Ask for their input on projects and work assignments.
- Ask them what changes you could implement to make their lives easier.
- Don't constrain their ability to take time off when they want or need to.
- Have them create agendas and/or run staff meetings.
- If your company does engagement surveys, consider building a task team to own the survey.
- Allow employees to influence the strategy of your department based on their unique knowledge.

Give Your Employees Control Over Their Work Time and Nonwork Time

If I had a dollar for every time I've heard a leader whine that their employees are asking to work from home, I could donate all of the revenue from this book to charity. I'm often unsure about why they're whining—giving employees flexibility and control is actually a business imperative. This includes options like nontraditional workweeks (for example, working four ten-hour days and taking Friday off), telecommuting, flexible hours, or modified vacation and sick-day policies. For example, event production company Red Frog gives employees unlimited vacation days. Though this seems like a potential disaster, it is almost never abused.[17]

The people and results benefits of flexible work arrangements are clear. On the people side, for example, employees who telecommute are more satisfied with their jobs and less likely to leave voluntarily. Moreover, giving employees more free time through compressed workweeks drives engagement even more than things like company picnics or social activities. On the results side, researchers have found that, on average, flexible work schedules result in a 10 percent improvement in productivity.[18]

Obviously, depending on the needs of your clients and customers, some types of flexibility will work and some won't. For example, some jobs require employees to be physically present (like a car mechanic) or work certain hours (like a nurse). I recommend making a list of the "non-negotiables" in terms of flexibility, then working with your team to think about the most meaningful options you can give them. I have a client whose front desk person wanted to work from home so she could focus on a series of reports she had to complete every month. My client was able to help her work from home one day every two weeks while other employees took turns covering the front desk. It worked like a charm.

■ ■ ■

Years ago, I'd just earned my master's degree and started as a junior consultant at Somerville Partners, a boutique consulting company. The CEO, Kevin Somerville, quickly became a mentor and always believed in my ability much more than I did. One week, Kevin landed a new client, flew home, came to my office and said, "I want you to be on point for this." A shiver came over me, along with a general fear about what would happen if I messed up. A few days later, I mustered the courage to talk to Kevin.

As an avid storyteller, Kevin provided his advice through a story about a stuffed buffalo on display at Grand Central Station. Those that passed through would do everything in the book to it: throw trash on it, stub out cigarette butts on it, kick it. Kevin once asked a caretaker how he dealt with this terrible buffalo abuse. The caretaker replied simply, "There ain't no damage to that old buffalo that I can't fix in five minutes."

Wow. The new client was the buffalo, Kevin was saying, and he was the caretaker. Any mistake I made could be fixed, and he was there to back me up. Amazing things happen when leaders empower and believe in their employees. Naturally, the project went well.

I hope this chapter has helped you think about your leadership choices in a new way—many leaders I've worked with tell me the concept of treating employees like adults has been groundbreaking. I encourage you to honestly look in the mirror before every choice you make and ask, "Am I treating my employees like adults or like children?" If you have a particularly challenging workforce and try to argue that you *have* to use excessive rules or policies, remember to ask, "Am I Acting As If?" If you're acting as if your team is made up of anything other than responsible, capable adults, it's time to change your approach.

BANKABLE ACTIONS

Act As If

✔ Examine the assumptions you're making about your employees on a daily basis.

✔ Make the decision to view your employees as competent, well-meaning professionals with good judgment.

✔ Instead of writing policies, have direct and honest conversations with employees and set clear expectations for what you expect.

✔ Create clear and swift consequences for the 2 percent who use bad judgment.

✔ If you influence policy in your organization, practice the "Adult Test." Would I need to tell a high-performing employee this? If not, consider eliminating it and instead setting clear expectations and consequences for bad judgment.

✔ If you must follow policies, take them out of your conversations with your employees, emphasizing instead your expectations and the reasoning behind them.

Engineer Ownership

✔ Ensure that you're pushing decisions down so that employees closest to customers can exercise their judgment.

✔ Take smart risks, empowering your employees to own projects that will challenge them.

✔ When empowering your employees, set crystal clear expectations for what you want accomplished, but give them leeway with the how.

✔ Regularly give your employees a voice in the decisions that affect them, and listen to their input.

✔ Give your employees control over their lives at work, giving them a choice whenever possible.

✔ Give employees flexibility in how they schedule their work and nonwork time.

CHAPTER 6

SUPPORT, DON'T HAND-HOLD

Retired Major General Joseph "Bud" Ahearn's first military assignment was at the 84,000-acre Cooke Air Force Base on the central coast of California in 1958.[1] According to one of Bud's jokes, the former army mobilization base in the Korean War consisted of two posts and a rusty chain when he first arrived.

As a pimply-faced lieutenant, he'd been sent there with many others to build a space base. In 1961 the Soviets got to space first, so the mission for the US, under the visionary leadership of the Kennedy administration, was to get there with more functions like communication, navigation, and intelligence. *This is kind of cool*, Bud thought.

Back in those days, military leadership was distinctly command and control, with figures like General George Patton and General Curtis LeMay serving as role models. Camp Cooke's leaders were no different, setting up rigid controls and organizational hierarchies. Though this was a familiar model for the uniformed personnel, those from private industry—the "space guys" who dealt with evolving technology, R&D, operational testing, and launching—began to rebel. In their minds, this was no way to run the mission. They didn't want to be ordered around; they needed to be supported and encouraged, not oppressed. The mission carried an exceptionally high national priority and was technologically very risky. Such programs are often burdened with system breakdowns or setbacks before breakthroughs occur. Just think of all those movies that depict scientists fighting with military personnel over control of a project. That's precisely what Bud saw.

The leaders at the base were certainly right-side leaders, focusing primarily on results—they built inflexible procedures that were intended to instill responsibility but too often diminished it. Bud believes that the high failure rate of some of the systems was due to this rather unbalanced style of leadership.

Luckily, the leaders began to understand that they needed to find someone to bridge the gap—a Bankable Leader. Enter General Horace M. Wade. Wade was a West Point graduate who understood that while setting high standards of responsibility and results, he had to help his people realize their promise and potential. He created policies, marshaled resources, and built education systems around that philosophy. "He wasn't any less results oriented," Bud notes, "but he was a heck of a lot *more* people oriented."

Bud first met General Wade in 1963 when the general was visiting Goose Air Base, Labrador. The junior officers had protocol duty for his arrival, a highly choreographed welcome that included carrying Wade's bags to his quarters. Bud remembers Wade smiling at them and saying, "Don't be ridiculous. I'll carry my own damn bags." Bud was floored.

He was even more impressed when he spent time with General Wade. "You could really talk to him," Bud remembers. He asked Bud questions, wondering where he came from, how he was doing, what his desired career path was. Sometimes he'd ask Bud questions that were so probing that Bud wondered whether he understood Bud better than Bud himself. General Wade taught him that great leaders build great organizations one person at a time.

Horace Wade would later serve as a four-star general and vice chief of staff of the US Air Force, and Bud went on to achieve the rank of major general, serve as senior civil engineer for the air force, and become vice chairman at CH2M HILL. Would Bud's success and dedication to growing leaders and taking care of people have come about without General Wade? Perhaps. But this experience shows the impact a single great leader can have in helping people achieve great things.

What if you could support your people without creating a bunch of whiners? Bankable Leaders do just that. They breed responsibility by helping employees find meaning in their work, give them attention without solving their problems for them, and breed a supportive environment so team members understand their responsibilities to each other. Going any further turns support into hand-holding, which results in an entitled and mediocre bunch. Who wants that?

I was recently meeting with a senior vice president who had just signed on to be one of my coaching clients. He seemed hesitant to begin the process, so I asked him what was bugging him. He looked me dead in the eyes and quipped, "Well, I *will not* change my employees' diapers."

My confused expression said it all, so he continued, "I absolutely refuse to let you turn me into one of those leaders who coddles their people. They are adults, not babies. And they need to act like it." You can probably tell that he was a strong right-side leader, but I truly understood his point. He didn't want to swing too far to the left. Not only would that be inauthentic for him and confusing for his team, it would lead to rotten results.

In this chapter, I'll give you two tactics for supporting and encouraging your employees even as you give them increased responsibility. The first is *giving them meaningful work*; the second is *making sure they feel supported and included*.

MEANINGFUL WORK: IT'S BUSINESS, AND IT'S PERSONAL

It is my belief that the statement "It's not personal, it's just business" is nonsense. Bankable Leaders give their employees a sense of powerful meaning behind their work, no matter what job they're doing. So if it *isn't* personal, you're missing something. Bud Ahearn's mission at Camp Cooke is a perfect example. Though their mission started in 1958 as "to seize and maintain control of space," three years later, President Kennedy articulated the meaning behind the mission in a new way: "Now it is time to take longer strides . . . I believe we possess all the resources and talents necessary . . . of landing a man on the moon and returning him safely to earth."[2] Talk about a meaningful way to align the government and industry in the space race! This and other early experiences in the military taught Bud a crucial lesson: "You have to give your employees a reason to get up every day with their hair on fire, loving what they do and who they do it for. Then you're not going to work at all."

Meaningful work satisfies a basic human need: We want the actions that make up our day to matter. According to Kim Cameron—Distinguished Professor of Management and Organizations at the University of Michigan's Ross School of Business, cofounder of the Center for Positive Organizational Scholarship, and one of my heroes—"When people feel they are pursuing a profound purpose or engaging in work that is personally important, significant positive effects are produced, including reductions in stress, depression, turnover, absenteeism, dissatisfaction, and cynicism, as well as increases in commitment, effort, engagement, empowerment, happiness, satisfaction, and a sense of fulfillment."[3]

If you don't believe me, think about anyone you know who works for a nonprofit. Often, this type of job means putting up with low pay and meager resources. But as one nonprofit leader recently told me, "I would put up with just about anything to be able to contribute to this hugely important mission."

Leadership science has quite a bit to say about the importance of the meaning of our jobs. As far back as 1971, Richard Hackman and Edward Lawler conducted a study of 208 telephone company employees and found a positive relationship between meaning and job performance: When employees were doing work that was "intrinsically meaningful or otherwise experienced as worthwhile," their performance improved.[4] So, as a leader, how can you create meaning for your team? Let's look at a real-world example of a Bankable Leader who did so—not just for his team but for the entire organization.

Mark Gasta, SVP and chief human resources officer at Vail Resorts, was tasked with assembling a team to define and strengthen the organization's culture. At that time, many employees loved what they did (not very hard if you work at a ski resort!), but might not have found a sense of purpose in the organization overall. The senior leadership team wanted to show all employees that there was, in fact, a common purpose behind what every employee did, every day.

So Gasta brought together a cross-divisional group that reflected the different roles in the organization, from concierges to ski patrollers to van drivers. The team was asked to define what it really meant to work at Vail Resorts. In a flash of genius, they came up with the phrase "The experience of a lifetime." To them, this was the purpose and meaning that ran through every role, in every location across the world. It didn't matter whether employees were in Saint Lucia or Grand Teton National Park; everyone immediately understood what this meant and could share their own stories, whether it was epic powder, the first time their daughter skied, or creating an unforgettable experience for a guest. Employees across the company got it immediately. They were having—and creating—the experience of a lifetime.

The statement became so popular that Vail Resorts adopted it as its mission—if the company created the experience of a lifetime every day for every employee, employees could create the experience of a lifetime for every guest.

Again, no matter what industry you're in or what your team does, there is always an opportunity to find meaning. This might be easier for clinicians, diplomats, scientists, firefighters, and the military; however, even a janitor for a pharmaceutical company is doing his part to help cure cancer.[5] Let's review three specific ways you can create meaning for your team.

Show Them That Their Work Matters to You Personally

I once knew a leader—let's call him Tim—who was completely underwater. He'd just been promoted to an executive general manager position in his IT organization and was now overseeing functions outside of his experience. Facing an aggressive plan and pressure from above, Tim muscled his way through things, doling out work assignments to his sales team. But strangely, he wasn't getting any traction.

He was particularly frustrated with a senior sales executive who reported to him, who was managing to the status quo and not doing much to address their waning performance. How often has this been the case for you: You have a million things to get done, but someone on your team seems to be making things worse rather than better? It's maddening, isn't it?

To help the sales leader get the results that he needed, Tim decided he'd need to be more directive. During weekly meetings with the sales leader, he'd literally hand over a list of things he needed to be taken care of. To the sales leader, Tim's actions seemed to say, "Just get this done." Imagine how you'd feel having a piece of paper shoved in your face without a modicum of support or encouragement. In reality, the sales leader was just as overwhelmed as Tim, and Tim failed to realize the extent of it.

As time went on, Tim's team continued to miss its targets and the resentment was building. His team finally spoke their minds one day. "You're not supporting us," they bravely stated. In a flash, Tim realized they were right. He was so focused on improving their performance that he hadn't been showing them how much their work mattered to him. And he very much wanted to get things back on track.

Tim called his team together for a "come to Jesus" meeting, kicked off by a brave and honest apology. The team then had a productive discussion about the state of the department. And even though he had thought he'd been encouraging them in the past, from that point, Tim devoted more energy to showing his people that they mattered to him, both personally and professionally.

Many managers forget to do this. But just think of what your employees make possible for you, the team, and the organization. Regularly thank them for their contribution and tell them how much it means to you—as their leader, and as a person—that they are working so hard and producing so much. This small act will create more motivation than you can imagine!

Show Them the Impact of Their Work

Bankable Leaders create a line of sight from what employees do every day to their contribution to the department, organization, the community, and even society as a whole.

First, don't assume they already understand the impact of their work. Have a discussion with your team and ask current and new members the same question: "How do you think your job contributes to our department? Our company? The community? Society?" Help them talk this through, and contribute your perspective.

Another powerful way to help your employees find meaning in what they do is to connect their contribution to something they care about personally.[6] For example, if you have a customer service representative who considers herself a "people person," discuss the positive impact her contribution has on her customers' lives.

As a Bankable Leader, you should also be helping your employees connect with the broader goals and mission of the company. In every industry in which I've worked, I encounter people who are so passionate about what their company does—and so confident in their own role in that mission—that it's motivating and gratifying just to talk to them about it.

You can also help employees see the financial impact their job has on the company; this will help them feel a stronger responsibility for creating those results. If an employee just feels like a cog in the corporate machine, he might not think twice about milking the clock. But when he learns that wasting time means that his department won't have the budget for merit increases, he might feel differently.

Let's review an easy tool to help your team members understand the impact of their role. When talking with your team about what they do, add the words "so that . . ." and state the impact this role has on the employee, the team, the organization, the community, or the world. Here are some examples:

- A civil engineer builds water treatment plants *so that* the community has clean water to drink.

- An accountant keeps financial records *so that* the company can minimize its risk if audited and ensure that the company is financially solvent.

- A landman in an oil and gas company researches ownership of land *so that* the company can drill oil wells and supply energy to the community.

- An information technology professional implements systems *so that* company employees can communicate and collaborate with one another.

- A construction worker uses his trade skills *so that* buildings will last for generations.

- A sales professional sells products and services *so that* the company can stay in business and pay its employees.

SUPPORTING EMPLOYEES
DURING A MERGER OR ACQUISITION

During mergers and acquisitions, employees need an extraordinary amount of support. Morale often suffers because employees may have loyalty to a brand or organization that doesn't exist anymore (or at least doesn't exist in the same way), and they may be leery about what the future holds. Research tells us that the most common consequence of a merger or acquisition is employee departures.

1. **CLEARLY AND REPEATEDLY COMMUNICATE THE STRATEGY OF THE NEW ORGANIZATION:** This may not feel like a way to provide support, but employees will be lost unless they can see the big picture. There's a reason you bought or merged with that company; explain how it fits into the larger whole and the value that it brings. Is it products? Expertise? New geographies? Explaining what caused the change will help people understand how they can contribute to the new organization.

2. **RECOGNIZE THEIR CONTRIBUTIONS:** Employees from both organizations want and need to feel respected by their leaders. Be as open as you can with information about changes and call out instances where you see every employee contributing to the change. If roles are unclear, it's time to hash things out.

3. **SHAPE THEIR EXPECTATIONS:** Learn what motivates employees. Figure out how the new organization can cater to these needs. Warning: Don't make promises you can't keep. Breaking promises is always worse than not making them in the first place.

Give Them a Voice

Another way to impart meaning to your team is to show them that their ideas and opinions are important. Time and time again, research in this area shows that when employees perceive that they have a say in the decisions that affect them, they are more productive and engaged. For example, Yochi Cohen-Charash of the University of California–Berkeley and Paul Spector of the University of South Florida conducted a meta-analysis (a study of studies) looking at the impact of employee voice on organizational outcomes.[7]

I promise not to bore you, but to understand their results, you'll need to understand the correlation coefficient. Correlation coefficients measure the strength of relationship between two things. They can range from –1 to 1, and a positive number means that as one goes up, the other does too, while a negative number means that as one goes up, the other goes down. Zero means the relationship is nonexistent. Got it? OK, statistics lesson over. Here's what Cohen-Charash and Spector found:

	CORRELATION WITH VOICE
Performance	.45
Job Satisfaction	.43
Supervisor Satisfaction	.58
Emotional Commitment	.47
Trust in Supervisor	.55

Amazing, right? And all because leaders asked for, and listened to, their employees' opinions. And if you don't think correlations of .4 and .5 are impressive, consider that we behavioral scientists are usually beside ourselves with joy when correlations are above .3.

Greg Herr, the radiology leader whom we first introduced in chapter 2, is a great example of what happens when a leader gives employees voice. After learning that his employees felt left out of the plans to move to their new building,

Greg decided to bring them in on the decisions. During a staff meeting, he tentatively asked, "You said you wanted to be more involved in the move, right?" They nodded. Greg left the room for a moment—everyone wondered what was about to happen. He reappeared with a color board that showed all the design options for the new building: tile, carpet, and countertops. "Right now," he said to the assembled employees, "we are going to pick the colors for the new suite. Since there are thirty of us, I'm not sure how this will go. It might be a disaster, but I want us to do it together." They chuckled but soon started throwing out ideas.

To Greg's surprise, in just a few minutes, they'd agreed on the color scheme. And the colors looked good! Employees started saying things like, "Wow—I can just picture it. Those cream-colored walls will really look great when we get over there."

There are many upsides to Greg's small but powerful decision to give his employees a voice in the construction process. First, it was a clear signal that he wanted them to be a part of the process. Second, when they moved in, the employees would feel a sense of ownership and responsibility for the new building. Instead of being "the building the hospital administrators designed," it was now "the building *we* helped design." It was a far cry from the first time I visited, when employees had been surprised and disconcerted by just seeing the blueprints!

Here are a few more pointers to get started on giving your employees voice:

- Ask what's bugging them. Potential sources of data include informal conversations, employee surveys, convening a team of employees to provide input, and anonymous comment boxes.

- Create a task team to tackle one of the challenges identified above. Ask your employees to provide you with a recommendation for how to fix it. Provide support and help them make it happen. If you can't, say why and redirect them.

As a cautionary note, it's helpful to know that giving your team voice is helpful only up to the point where the final decision is made. In one study, Kristin Laurin of the University of Waterloo and her colleagues asked students to complete online surveys asking for the students' feelings about a law that would reduce speed limits in their area.[8] Participants were told one of three things: The passing of the law was very likely, somewhat likely, or definite. When passing the law seemed uncertain and further input was going to be solicited, study participants reacted more negatively to the limits. But those who were told the law would definitely be passed had more positive attitudes about the restrictions, and were even less annoyed.

This shows that when people perceive that a decision is final, they're more likely to accept the outcome and work with it—even those who would oppose the decision if they felt the point were open to debate. The take-home message for leaders is that, prior to making a change, get lots of input. But once the decision is made, the time for influence in the process should end, and very clearly.

Now that you know how to help your employees see the meaning behind their work, let's move on to how you can help them succeed without being so supportive that, as my coaching client feared, you have to change their diapers.

MANAGER INCLUSION AND SUPPORT

Penni Key thought she understood leadership perfectly. In high school, she was usually tapped to be the captain of her sports teams. But when she landed her first significant management role, as associate athletic director at the University of Miami, she suddenly had more than twenty people reporting to her. She was quite overwhelmed, especially because she had no experience with one of the departments that reported to her. Sports medicine, the department in question, was composed mostly of trainers and physical therapists, most of whom didn't seem particularly thrilled about their new boss. They told her that she couldn't possibly understand their world. But rather than viewing her lack of experience as an obstacle, Penni decided to view it as a challenge.

Several times per week, she would come down to the training room to support the sports medicine team as they prepped the athletes to go onto the field. She'd be surrounded by eighty-five pairs of ankles being taped for football and quite a few pairs of knees being iced. She would offer assistance to anyone who needed it, and she would be "transparently ignorant" while she talked to the team, asking how things worked and noting that she didn't know everything about their world. But she did make her expectations clear (a concept we discussed in chapter 3): She wanted the athletes to feel comfortable and welcomed when they walked into the training room.

Several years later, Penni was leaving the organization to start her own business. One of the trainers who had been hardest on her at the beginning pulled her aside and said, "Penni, I didn't know about you at the beginning. We had some tense moments. But you're the best supervisor I've ever had, and I can't believe I'm saying that. Nobody has ever cared about us more, showed up and fought for us so much." Penni was deeply moved, and she understood how much going to bat for her team had really meant to them.

In a study published in 2011, Guylaine Landry of Université de Sherbrooke Canada and Christian Vandenberghe of HEC Montréal surveyed three hundred employees and their managers.[9] They found that when employees believed their supervisor supported them, they felt more committed to the supervisor (people outcome) and their job (results outcome). If employees don't feel supported, they are unlikely to be happy, productive, or responsible for the work they're creating. Remember, people don't leave companies; they leave bosses. How would you feel if the person you worked for didn't understand, or care about, what you did? To help you prevent this, let's discuss two straightforward ways to regularly provide your employees with support and inclusion.

Carve Out One-on-One Time with Each Employee and Talk About More Than Just Projects

We first met real estate banker Patty Gage at the beginning of part I and learned how she turned around her team by helping them get to know each other as human beings. Patty also makes it a point to learn about the personal lives of her employees. A few times per week, she'll roam the work area and have a sixty-second conversation with her team to see how they're doing and learn more about them. Now Jenna isn't just a loan closer; she's also a mother of three. Matt is not just an admin; he's also an avid vinyl collector. Patty has noticed that having these informal interactions with her employees makes it easier for them to get their work done.

In my Bankable Leadership workshops, I often ask leaders whether they spend one-on-one time with their direct reports on a regular basis. They usually respond with a resounding yes, scoffing at me for not giving them enough credit. When I ask what they talk about during these meetings, I hear "their projects" or "the work they're doing that week." Though operational conversations with your employees are critical, Bankable Leaders must also create time for supporting their success more holistically.

I call these sessions "Development Meetings." Similar to what Kim Cameron describes as "Personal Management Interviews" in his must-read book, *Positive Leadership*, Development Meetings help your employees succeed and surface issues before they become significant. The Development Meeting must be markedly different from a performance review or an operations conversation, because the objective is ongoing support development of the employee as opposed to a clinical look at their effectiveness on the job.

Here is the simple challenge: Spend at least thirty minutes with each employee once or twice a month discussing their overall progress and development. I've worked with many organizations that have implemented this approach, and the results have been startlingly good. Employees report that for the first time, they feel important in their leader's eyes. The leaders also report more self-sufficient and productive employees.

And we have more than anecdotal evidence; the science on Development Meetings is compelling, too. In one study, W. L. Boss looked at 208 participants across twenty-three real-world teams.[10] Teams that implemented such meetings showed improvements in things like performance and accountability (results outcomes) and communication quality and conflict resolution (people outcomes). Leaders even reported *spending less time with their employees overall*, and the time they spent was of much higher quality.

I hope this is fairly convincing evidence that Development Meetings are worth the effort, so let's talk about how you can implement them. First, draw from chapter 2 and make your intentions clear. I had one client who had implemented a similar program with the best of aims but neglected to communicate its purpose. Employees began to complain about the meetings and dream up conspiracy theories for their true purpose. My favorite one was that the leaders were secretly trying to amass documentation that would help justify a round of firings. This couldn't have been further from the truth, but once the rumor got out, the damage had been done.

If you decide to implement a similar program, here is an example of what you could say: "In our busy day-to-day work, I want to make sure that I am able to support your engagement, development, and success. I'd like to start meeting with each of you once per month for about an hour [or however long or often you can manage]. We'll have an initial meeting where we'll agree on the expectations we'll have for each other—what you need from me and what I expect from you. In the monthly meetings that follow, we'll talk about the things you're most proud of in your work, how you're progressing in your goals, and what roadblocks or support from me you need. [Now talk about how you'll set up the meetings.] I look forward to supporting each of you in your success."

When you're setting up the meetings, don't forget outcome fairness—that means meeting with *all* of your employees. You might come across one or two employees with poor attitudes who won't want to participate. My advice is to do everything possible to help them see the value, but don't force the meetings upon these poor souls if they really don't want them. For the rest, you should make a commitment to the meeting times and do not reschedule or cancel unless it's absolutely necessary. I once worked with a leader who was bankable in almost every way, except he would cancel most of his regular one-on-one meetings with his team. It was demoralizing and frustrating for them and counteracted many of his best qualities.

As described in the boilerplate introduction above, the process of Development Meetings is twofold. First, you meet to agree on goals and how you'll work together. Here are some suggested questions for this initial task:

- What is my role and how does it contribute to the organization?
- What are my goals for the year?
- What skills and capabilities do I want to better develop?
- What do we need from each other to be successful?
- What are the terms for how work will be accomplished?

HOW **GLOBAL LEADERS** CAN DEVELOP GLOBAL EMPLOYEES

If your team works across multiple cultures, they'll need a more diverse set of skills. Developing your team to work cross-culturally can be complex. Smart leaders don't just expect that this will happen on its own—they create deliberate development plans.

1. **UNDERSTAND THE IMPACT OF YOUR BEHAVIOR:** If you work in a global company and you appear insensitive or ignorant of the norms or practices of other cultures, it will be difficult for your team to develop these skills themselves. Make sure that you're conversant in the norms and practices of the countries in which your company does business.

2. **PREPARE THEM FOR CROSS-CULTURAL WORK:** The best way to learn to work across cultures is to simply do it, and have the support and coaching to make it successful. Help your employees—especially the top performers—find opportunities to complete assignments in other countries. Connect them with internal resources to help them learn more about the culture they'll be working within.

3. **SHARE CROSS-CULTURAL KNOWLEDGE:** If your team is global, create opportunities for knowledge exchange. If one of your team members takes an assignment in Asia, for example, ask her to conduct a brown bag when she returns to talk about what she learned.

Second, you hold regular meetings where you can touch on these questions:

- What are you proud of right now?
- Where are your biggest struggles and what support do you need?
- What progress are you making in your performance goals?
- What progress are you making in your professional development?
- What feedback do we have for one another?

Begin your Development Meetings as soon as you can. It's a great way to carve out time to spend with your employees, and a great practice ground for many Bankable Leadership skills. Go ahead—what's stopping you?

Create a Sense of Team Support and Inclusion

Once you've started forging individual relationships with your team, it's time to work on engaging the team as a whole. The point here is to create a "work family," a place where employees feel part of a team that cares about and supports all its members.

Patty Gage's team holds quarterly meetings where members review their progress and set goals for the next quarter. These meetings are always held somewhere outside of the office. In addition to measuring results, another purpose of this meeting is to create a sense of team togetherness. To formalize this, the team has a set of plastic teeth that they pass around to each other. When you have the teeth, you're responsible for a fun activity, after which you pass the teeth along to someone else. Patty and her team would be the first to tell you that they are not "crazy fun people," so having the teeth reminds everyone to let loose and be original.

Think of a "dream team" that *you've* been a part of. Team members probably supported each other, challenged each other, and didn't want to let each other down—the essence of helpfulness *and* responsibility. Set up regular opportunities for team members to spend time together. Being part of a dream team will help your employees do as Bud Ahearn advises: "To get up every day with their hair on fire, loving what they do and who they do it for." And even if you're not part of the space race, that's pretty exciting.

BANKABLE ACTIONS

Give Them Meaning

✔ Show them that their work matters to you personally.

✔ Help them see the impact of their work on the department, the organization, the community, and society, and don't ever assume they already know!

✔ Provide your employees a voice in the decisions that affect them at work, and listen—and respond—to them when they provide it.

Give Them Your Support

✔ Carve out one-on-one time with each employee to talk about their successes, challenges, and goals, and to show them your support.

✔ Create a sense of camaraderie within the team by spending time together and creating opportunities to be supportive of one another.

CHAPTER 7

BRING OUT THEIR BEST

Tracee Hendershott was at the end of her rope with one of her brightest, most talented employees. She would constantly stir up drama and complain about how her colleagues weren't doing their jobs correctly, or bring Tracee problems and expect her to fix them. Despite the trouble, Tracee knew she had the seeds of greatness within her.

The call for nominations to the company's yearlong high-potential program—which I had just finished building—couldn't have come at a better time. Formal development opportunities had been lacking at the organization, and there was lots of buzz about the program. Tracee nominated her struggling star and committed to coaching and developing her as she completed the required coursework and projects.

Her employee was touched and honored, and after a few short months, her potential began to materialize—she was proactively solving problems, coaching her peers, and even managing conflict within the department. The program was a turning point. Instead of spiraling downward and becoming a true problem employee, she was able to uncover her potential. She is now thriving as the assistant manager of the department and has a bright future ahead of her.

Bankable Leaders help their employees take responsibility for their own growth, find their strengths, and create a vision for their learning and development. And when issues arise, they coach them rather than solve problems for them.

Our hunger for learning is powerful—in fact, it's one of our core impulses as humans. In the fascinating book *Driven: How Human Nature Shapes Our Choices*, Paul Lawrence and Nitin Nohria delve into the hardwiring of the human brain, naming the four drives that all humans share: to acquire, bond, learn, and defend. They point out that "Humans have an innate drive to satisfy their curiosity, to know, to comprehend, to believe, to appreciate, to develop understanding."[1] In other words, we are all driven to be better!

Development is a major motivator for employees, as all Bankable Leaders understand. Anders Dysvik and Bård Kuvaas researched the relationship between employee development and performance, assessing participants from a large Norwegian training institution.[2] They found that when employees perceived that they had opportunities for development, they were more motivated and helpful to others (*People*) and were better performers who were willing to go above and beyond the call of duty (*Results*).

So what happens when employees aren't learning? According to Lawrence and Nohria, nothing good: "The inability to satisfy [employees'] drive to learn at work will frustrate [them]. If they find no outlet to exercise this drive . . . they are apt to turn their energies to finding inventive ways to frustrate management intentions."[3] It's so true: As we saw at the beginning of the chapter, if you don't develop your employees, they will become troublemakers!

This chapter will show you, very practically, how to develop your employees. First, we'll talk about the importance of identifying their strengths and potential rather than trying to fix their weaknesses. Next, we'll look at coaching as a tool to help employees solve their own problems and increase their feelings of responsibility for what they do. Finally, I'll show you how to supervise your superstars—a talented but notoriously difficult group to manage.

FOCUS ON THEIR STRENGTHS AND POTENTIAL

"I'll take him," said Cathy.

As a manager at a hospitality company, she'd just volunteered to supervise an employee who had been written off by the rest of the organization. People told Cathy she was crazy for investing her time in someone who seemed to be a lost cause.

But she was sure he had a skill set no one had tapped into. Cathy spent the first few months learning about him as a person. She'd ask, "What's the best thing you've done in your career?" "What's something you once did well that you don't get to do anymore?" and "What would you like to do?" It turned out that he loved numbers, so Cathy started finding small numeric tasks for him—analyzing data, creating reports, and so on. These assignments helped him shine, and he did a wonderful job from that day forward. When he received a promotion based on his great work, Cathy had proof that people can change.

Bankable Leaders commit to finding something good within every employee. Cathy was able to help her employee go from problem child to high performer by giving him a role he was genuinely excited about—this led to better results with less energy *and* helped the employee feel a sense of competence and accomplishment.

The philosophy of focusing on employee strengths is nothing new—witness popular books like *StrengthsFinder 2.0* by Tom Rath[4] and *Positive Leadership* by Kim Cameron—and the science on developing strengths is also well developed. One prolific researcher on this topic was Donald Clifton, who dedicated his entire career to this niche. In one study, Clifton and his colleague James Harter examined over two thousand managers, labeling each as either "strengths-focused" or "weakness-focused."[5] Then, based on a combined score of measures like productivity, profitability, and employee retention, Clifton and Harter placed each manager into one of two categories: "high-performing manager" or "low-performing manager."

Their findings were compelling. Managers who focused on developing employee strengths performed better, contributing 86 percent greater profitability to their company than managers who focused on fixing weaknesses. Are you listening now?

Mark Gasta, SVP and chief human resources officer at Vail Resorts, whom we met in chapter 6, knows firsthand how powerful it is when leaders look for the good rather than the bad. At more than a few points in his life, he found himself in a situation where someone else believed in him more than he believed in himself. In eighth grade, he was an average kid with average grades. Hardly anyone noticed him. That spring, he remembers being tapped on the shoulder by his English teacher. "Mark," she said, "we want you to speak at eighth-grade graduation." Mark was shocked. She clearly saw something in him that he didn't.

Years later, when Mark was in the ROTC, his battalion commander called him at home on a Sunday to summon him to a Monday morning meeting. *Oh boy*, Mark thought, *I must really be in trouble.* Mark braced himself for bad news as he walked into the commander's office the next day, but instead he heard, "We want you to be the cadet battalion commander"—the highest ROTC position. Again, Mark was shocked. *Why would they pick me when there are so many other people who deserve this?* he wondered.

It turns out that both of Mark's mentors had been right about his potential: He was a natural leader. He now holds a top position at Vail Resorts and went on to obtain a doctorate in organizational development. Mark's stories illustrate that leaders have the power to develop the strengths and potential of their people—a concept that might remind you of the "Act As If" principle from chapter 5.

Employees who are given feedback on their strengths are more likely to feel engaged and productive than when they get feedback on their weaknesses.[6] But too many leaders I work with assume that their employees already know what they do well and think their time is better spent helping bolster a seemingly deficient area. And often, employees I speak with have a much easier time listing their weaknesses than their strengths (usually the collateral damage of a past right-side leader).

Elisa Speranza, president of CH2M HILL's Operations and Maintenance business group, grew up attending parochial school, and she is proud to have had such an experience. She learned the values of discipline, focus, work ethic, and service. But she remembers one bad day that forever shaped her leadership style. One morning, when she was four years old, she mistakenly left her pencil in the classroom next door. One of the sisters yelled at her, and to this day, she can remember thinking, *Jeez, I already feel terrible enough! Does she have to scream at me?*

Decades later, this experience sticks with Elisa: "I'm not a big fan of the approach of 'the beatings will continue until morale improves,'" she says. "Yelling at people about their weaknesses or failures does no good." Elisa has used the opposite approach, and her results speak for themselves. She's led a $380 million business through some very challenging circumstances, and her employees are outstanding. Though she was the first person to tell me that she can't take credit for her team's accomplishments, they are truly extraordinary. Here's just one example: Her group runs a wastewater plant in Hoboken, New Jersey, that was literally underwater after Hurricane Sandy blew through. They got the plant back up and running in *less than two days*. Elisa doesn't get those kind of results by pointing out people's flaws.

Many leadership thinkers also subscribe to Elisa's approach. "One should waste as little effort as possible on improving areas of low competence," writes management guru Peter Drucker. "It takes far more energy to improve from incompetence to mediocrity than it takes to improve from first-rate performance to excellence."[7] Let's think of this like a financial investment. What if I told you that you had your choice between a $100 investment with a return of $1,000, and $100 with a return of $10. The former is a great investment. The latter barely pays you back for your time. The same is true for the choice between developing strengths and trying to fix weaknesses: For the same investment, you can have a great return or a paltry one. It's your choice.

Understanding your employees' potential is going to take some energy and thought on your part, especially if, like many of us, you're used to focusing on what people *are* rather than what they *could be*. Here are a few questions to ask yourself:

- Can they do something well that isn't in their formal training or experience?

- Compare them to others with the same experience—are they doing anything faster or better?

- Do they appear to enjoy certain projects more than others?

- What kind of work do they show the most ownership for?

- What kind of work do they need the least guidance from you to do?

- What have they produced that has genuinely surprised you?

Once you've identified employees' strengths, take a few minutes in your next one-on-one meeting to tell them what they're doing especially well, or to describe the potential you see in them in a particular area. Get their perspective. Do they know what they're good at? How can you help them leverage those strengths? Do what you can, but then get out of the way! Now, here are a few practical suggestions to help you bring out hidden strengths in your team members:

- Ask them what they like about their job and what they are less enthusiastic about. Make a list. Add the strengths in them that you see that they have not listed. Discuss how—or whether—these strengths map onto their current job or role.

- Even when giving corrective feedback, talk about the strengths you see in them.

- Instead of viewing them as a problem employee, take the approach that there has to be something they do well and it's your job to help them find it.

- Do what Cathy did and see whether you can structure the job around their strengths.

- If you can't offer them a job or project that plays to their strengths, consider whether the employee might thrive in another part of the company.

The lesson is simple: Spend your time and energy developing your employees' strengths and limit your effort to address their shortcomings; in these weak areas, they need only be passable. Please note that I'm not telling you to flat-out ignore weaknesses. In fact, one of the most important aspects of Bankable Leadership is acting swiftly and decisively in the face of poor performance. We'll cover that in chapter 9, but for now, suffice it to say that you must focus more time and energy on developing your team's strengths.

Once you discover the individual strengths of your employees, you'll set them on the course to develop their true potential. But getting work done is rarely that simple, and people are bound to hit a roadblock or two on their journey. That's where coaching comes in.

COACHING DEMYSTIFIED

Jandel Allen Davis, vice president of government affairs at Kaiser Permanente, was a leader with a problem. She'd recently had a series of interactions with a team member that went terribly, and she was confident that many in her position would have terminated him immediately, or at least put him on a performance-improvement plan. Jandel knew he couldn't continue on his current trajectory, so she decided to take action. She holds quarterly half-day coaching sessions with each of her direct reports, and coincidentally, this event had happened just a few days before their scheduled meeting.

Jandel was a labor and delivery physician prior to becoming a VP at Kaiser, so she decided to take a clinical angle in solving the problem. "I'm worried about you," she began. "I don't understand what's going on and I know I am missing something. I want to help you succeed." But in the same breath, she made her expectations clear: He *couldn't* do this again, and they would need to figure out how to prevent it in the future. She asked dozens of questions to help peel back the layers of the onion, taking careful notes throughout the conversation.

She soon learned that he was a truly entrepreneurial soul who had little experience dealing with big, complex organizations. He was used to working in a fast-moving and decidedly *un*-bureaucratic newsroom. Understandably, he became frustrated and upset when things were moving too slowly for his liking. (I am sure many of you in large organizations can sympathize!) He was also holding on to too much work (rather than delegating it to his team), causing even more anxiety and heartache when he couldn't get it all done.

The next phase of the conversation was about helping him answer the question "What will we do in the future to make sure you're successful?" He had a few ideas, like walking away and taking twenty-four hours to cool down. Jandel promised him that she would help too, and that the minute she saw him boiling up, she would check in with him. And he finally took Jandel up on her offer to work with an executive coach.

This conversation, it turned out, was transformative. It led him to take a step back and evaluate his entire life: How was he managing stress in a way that he could have a long, fulfilling and healthy life? As a leader, Jandel's day-to-day world is now rarely about directly saving lives, but she remarks, "As leader, this was one instance where I think I *did* save a life." A year later, he's more confident. He and his team are happier and more productive. Jandel had successfully coached her employee to solve his own problems, while not letting him off the hook, and everyone was better off for it.

Coaching is a required skill for Bankable Leaders. Here are a few examples of situations that are perfect for coaching:

- An employee has just received a new assignment.
- An employee has moved to a new role.
- An employee is new to the organization.
- An employee is struggling with a project or hitting a roadblock on the team.
- An employee is thinking about career development.

I work with leaders all the time who say things like, "Oh, I'm not a coach. I don't know how to do it, and frankly I don't have the time. I just need to tell my employees what they need to do and be done with it." If you're feeling skeptical about the necessity of investing time in your people's performance and development, let me make this simple: In the long run, it improves results. When you coach successfully . . .

- Employees will remove barriers without your help.

- Every challenge will become a learning opportunity.

- They will be better equipped to solve their own problems.

- They will be more confident.

- They will trust you more.

- They will do their jobs better.

Now hear this: Coaching is not an opportunity to show just how good you are at solving other people's problems. From the ages of six to twenty-one, I was an actor—I even majored in theater in college, much to my parents' chagrin. They were quite relieved when I added my psychology major, and even though I am no longer an actor, it's hard to take the theater out of a theater person. And for theater people, the concept of a line reading (instruction on how to say a particular line) stirs up almost as much uneasiness as the thought of saying "Macbeth" in a theater.[8] When working with an actor on a line, the best directors refuse to read the line the way they want it said. Why? The actor can't deliver an exceptional performance by mimicking the director. He must find his own way to play the line—one that's authentic to him. Giving employees direct advice is like giving them a line reading. Even if it's what *you* think should be done, the employee has unique context and perspective. And again, if you're just telling them what to do, they won't own their behavior.

If by discouraging you from giving advice I have wiped out your whole coaching repertoire, let's discuss what you can do instead. There are many, many nuances to coaching; however, I believe it boils down to three basic behaviors: *listening, asking questions,* and *ensuring that the employee follows through on the coaching.* If you get good at these, you'll be 80 to 90 percent of the way there.

Listen: It's Not About You—It's About Them

We all know the classic break-up line: "It's not you, it's me." Though this may be a handy phrase for commitment-phobes (don't look at me!), it's a foolish coaching philosophy. Because it's really *not* about you. It's about your employee.

Though this seems rather obvious, it's actually counter to our natural tendencies. A study by Harvard researchers Diana Tamir and Jason Mitchell revealed that humans spend 30 to 40 percent of our speaking time talking about ourselves.[9] This means that when you're coaching your employees, you'll have to prevent the urge to say things like, "Oh man, that same thing happened to me back in 1987. Let me tell you how I handled it."

To overcome this tendency, use the LISTEN framework:

- **L**ook them in the eye.
- **I**ntently focus on them.
- **S**peak less than 10 percent of the time.
- **T**est your understanding by paraphrasing.
- **E**xamine the person's ideas with an open mind.
- **N**ever, ever, ever interrupt.

Let's start with Looking them in the eye. Don't spend the conversation taking notes. No matter what you're discussing, it's important to connect by looking the person in the eye. But, as I mentioned before, don't engage in *too much* eye contact; aim to look them in the eyes about 80 percent of the time.

Next, Intently focus on the employee. Remember the picture frame trick from chapter 4, where you imagine the person's head in a frame? This is a great time to use it. If you don't, it will give the impression that the conversation—and your employee—aren't important.

Throughout the conversation, you should Speak less than 10 percent of the time. Remember, the purpose of coaching is to help your employees figure out their own challenges, opportunities, and path to greater success—and they can't do that with you blabbing the whole time. When you do speak, try to ask open-ended questions (more on this in a moment) or paraphrase a point they've made.

When you paraphrase, you should be Testing your understanding. Being understood is a fundamental human need, so show your employee that you're following them by saying things like, "What I hear you saying is . . ." or "It sounds like . . ." If you get it wrong, ask for clarification.

Sometimes, your employees might share a viewpoint or idea that you don't agree with. Nevertheless, **Examine** their ideas with an open mind. The easiest way to do this is to make a choice to change your inner monologue from judgment to interest. Instead of thinking, *What a stupid idea!* try, *That's interesting—I wonder why he thinks that.*

And finally, **Never interrupt.** I hope this should go without saying, but I constantly come across successful people who have this annoying behavioral tick. I once was chairing a board committee tasked with hiring a new executive director. About two minutes into one interview, the candidate said, "I like to interrupt from time to time to make sure I am understanding what you're saying." Not only did we *not* offer him the job, he has become a bit of a legend.

Asking Questions: The Answer Lies Within

The second component of effective coaching is to encourage employees to figure things out themselves and be responsible for their own performance. When you take this tactic, the employee might say, "Hmm. I tried this approach and it didn't work. I wonder what else I should try next" instead of "My manger told me to do this and it didn't work. It's not *my* fault!"

Carolyn De Rubertis, CEO of a large specialty medical practice, once coached an employee to do something she thought was impossible. Carolyn had a long-time employee whom she decided to promote to manage their front desk, then overseeing physician credentialing and marketing. One year the doctors sponsored an all-day training session for occupational and hand therapists. Carolyn decided to delegate this event to her. She was floored, asking Carolyn, "How am I supposed to get a hundred people at a hundred dollars per head? I don't know where to start!"

"Well, neither do I," Carolyn replied. "But just because you don't know right now doesn't mean you can't do this. Let's start by figuring out what resources we have."

They also had meetings every few weeks to touch base. At the beginning, Carolyn was asking key questions to help her get her arms around the project, but after a while, she started coming to Carolyn with great ideas—the tables turned.

The training was a success. Though the employee had no previous experience securing sponsorships for such an event, she raised more than $15,000 (the goal was $6,000). Over one hundred therapists attended the event. And perhaps most importantly, Carolyn had coached her to do this entirely on her own.

A Bankable Leader's job is to ask compelling, open-ended questions to help employees find their own answers. If you ask: "So you think that's a good idea?" your employee might simply say yes. But if you say, "Tell me about why you think this might be a good approach," you'll continue the conversation and her learning process. Asking a closed-ended coaching question is like slamming the brakes on a bus while it's going sixty miles an hour. And just like Keanu Reeves did in *Speed*, you have to keep the bus moving.

To get you started, I present to you the Magic Coaching Questions.[10] I've been using these questions for many years and often joke when I share them that I'm giving out the keys to my kingdom—I charge organizations a pretty penny to ask these to their executives! I was once visiting a client who had attended one of my coaching workshops, and I noticed that she had the questions laminated and tacked on her bulletin board. "This is my cheat sheet," she boasted. "I use it every day."

The Magic Coaching Questions are intended to be a starting point. Some of them might speak to you and some might not. You may want to change the wording to suit your style. And though they're structured to help a coaching conversation progress, you don't have to ask them in order, or use them all.

1. "How can I best help you address this?"

2. "What have you tried in the past?"

3. "Imagine that overnight you've achieved your goal. What would be different?"

4. "What is in your control and what's out of your control?"

5. "What are the alternatives for achieving this?" Think of as many as you can—even silly ones—and write them down. Then ask the next question: "What are the criteria that will help you choose the best option?"

6. "What might be the best option to try first?"

COACHING TIPS FOR **NEW LEADERS**

If you're a new leader, coaching might feel especially uncomfortable at first. In your last position, you were probably rewarded for solving problems, not enabling others to solve their own. Coaching requires a totally different set of skills than problem-solving, so acknowledging that discomfort is an important first step.

1. **GET PERMISSION:** In your first meeting as manager with your new team, talk to them about how they want to be coached, how you might approach it, and set the boundaries. That will make everyone more comfortable with this new process.

2. **TAKE THE PRESSURE OFF YOURSELF:** It's common when you're coaching for the first time to put pressure on yourself to say something brilliant. Remember that the most important thing you can do is *really* listen. So when your employee is talking, don't be thinking about what you'll say when they're finished talking. Remember, as a coach you don't have to know the answer!

3. **GET A COACHING COACH:** Find someone in your organization who is an excellent coach and offer to take them to lunch. Discover their lessons learned and approaches and ask if you can consult with them on an ongoing basis as you test-drive your new skills.

7. "How do you think your behavior is impacting your ability to achieve your goal?"

8. "What are you going to do in the next week?" or "What will you do first?"

9. "What will be the early signals that you're on the path to success?"

10. "What is the biggest lesson you've learned from this experience?" followed by "How will you implement this lesson moving forward?"

Now that you have a plan to better coach your employees, let's cover one last point to prevent you from overcorrecting—that is, giving your employees too much rope.

Don't Let Them Wander off the Ranch

In the spirit of supporting your people *and* driving results, leaders must ensure that employees are actually acting on what comes out of coaching conversations. In other words, this question-based coaching model is not an excuse to abdicate your responsibility to make sure things get done.

I have one client in a manufacturing company who been closely coaching one of the managers she oversaw on two visible projects. When she met with the manager, the manager would say things like, "Oh yes, I'll make sure I take care of that." But when the manager unexpectedly resigned, my client found out that, much to her surprise, things weren't getting done. The manager hadn't taken care of, well, anything.

Even though 98 percent of your employees won't do this, you'll occasionally have a bad apple. My client learned firsthand that leaders must always follow up and ask specific questions. Instead of saying, "Did you communicate our new decision to your team?" try "So tell me what the process of communicating the decision has been like. What challenges are you seeing?" Because people can rarely fake it when questions get this specific, you can make sure that things are getting done. I once worked with a leader who was frustrated by his team's lack of follow-through. I encouraged him to start every meeting by asking each person a question like, "How are things going with this project?" "What rumors are you hearing about it from your team?" or "What early concerns are emerging?" When they looked at him blankly, we knew there was a problem. Over the course of a few months, it worked like a charm.

In a nutshell, even when you trust your employees and allow them to solve problems on their own, you have to mind the shop. Of course, there's a fine line between following up and micromanaging, so here are some guidelines:

- Be clear about timelines that emerge from coaching. Say, "So tell me when you think you might be able to accomplish this. When should you and I revisit it?"

- Ask specific questions to follow up on coaching conversations.

- Informally touch base with the people affected by what your employees do (some call these "skip level" meetings). Don't be nosy, but do innocently ask how things are going.

SUPERVISING SUPERSTARS

Many companies use rather complicated processes to identify high-potential employees. I don't mean to disparage the science behind these processes, but I've found that most leaders know who their superstars are without a fancy diagnostic. These are the people who are capable, motivated, and positive. Open to learning and willing to embrace change. Well-liked and well-respected.

Bankable Leaders understand the value of their best employees and help them thrive. But supervising superstars also has a dark side. As vice president of an academic association, Lynn Gangone spent two years working for a president who was her polar opposite. Lynn's boss was quiet and deeply detail-oriented, while she herself was a sociable person and big-picture thinker. The boss had an MBA; Lynn had a doctorate. After a while, Lynn started to believe that her new boss was intimidated by her strengths—primarily because they were so different from hers. They could have been a dynamite team, enhancing each others' gifts and supplementing each others' weaknesses. But instead of being excited about the partnership, it appeared that the president felt threatened.

The untapped potential of this partnership haunted Lynn for a long time, and she vowed to never miss out on such an opportunity when she was in charge. Lynn knows that great leaders assemble teams that are radically different from themselves, and in her current role as dean of the University of Denver Colorado Women's College, she jokes that she wants to hire people who want her job.

She pays constant attention to her reactions to her top employees, giving credit where it's due and not making everything all about her. Most leaders can learn from Lynn's honest and brave mindset.

But why are some leaders threatened by their best people? Nathanael Fast of USC's Marshall School of Business and Serena Chen of UC Berkeley discovered that when leaders don't feel confident about their own performance, they're more likely to feel threatened and exhibit aggressive behaviors toward their team. (In the study, they defined aggression as how willing leaders were to harm their partner's chances of winning money.)[11] This makes a tremendous amount of sense—many leaders were once top performers—it's why they got promoted! But as the Peter Principle cynically (but sometimes correctly) states, many people are promoted one level past their ability.[12] Being a leader is notoriously challenging, so it's no wonder that leaders feel insecure from time to time.

Here's the good news: Fast and Chen found that when participants with low feelings of competence were given positive feedback, they showed less aggression. In a nutshell, increasing your perception of your own competence and self-worth as a leader will go a long way.

Here are some suggestions to bring out the best in your superstars and simultaneously be happy for their success:

- Pay attention to your own reactions to the superstars on your team. Do you feel jealous or threatened? If so, ask, "What inadequacy am I feeling that's causing me to react this way?"

- If you're not feeling competent, get to the heart of why. Talk to a trusted advisor and find out what you're doing well and what you can improve.

- Sometimes you might just need a shot of confidence. Find out what helps you do that—maybe it's losing that fifteen pounds, maybe it's giving yourself a pep talk in the mirror in the mornings. Whatever it takes, value yourself.

- Choose to see your superstars as people who will help you be more successful: The more they win, they more you win.

- Place your superstars in important and visible projects, and get out of the way! Make sure you use your goal-setting and coaching skills. When superstars succeed, be generous and give them credit. This will make them feel valued (and it will make you look good too).

- Disproportionately invest in your superstars' development. Make a commitment to give them the time they deserve. Touch base with them often. Set up a weekly or monthly meeting. Aim for a reputation as a talent factory.

Let's review a real-world example of a leader who wasn't threatened by a top performer. Stephen Ladek founded International Solutions Group, a social and economic consulting company focused on developing and transitioning countries, in December 2005. He saw the company grow and thrive, peaking at twenty-eight employees and offices in three countries. But when Stephen had to relocate from Amman, Jordan, in 2009, where the company's main operations office was, to Budapest, Hungary, the business began to struggle. The economic crisis dried up multiple revenue sources, internal squabbles were rampant, and revenue declined 66 percent over a two-year period. International Solutions Group soon closed its physical offices and let all but two employees go.

Luckily, in a few years, Stephen and his team were able to turn the company around. At that point, Stephen knew he needed help, noting, "I wanted to find someone who could turn the fantastic yacht we built into an ocean liner." So he hired a talented, experienced superstar. Stephen's goal was clear: He wanted him to take over the company's operations, vowing not to be threatened. After all, the reward would be huge.

Stephen's actions were commendably bankable. He understood his limitations and knew that bringing on a director with different strengths was the right thing for the company. This could have been tough and sensitive if Stephen had felt threatened. But he fully supported his new director. Now that Stephen has handed over the company's operations to his new director and associates, he is able to focus on developing new products and services—his entrepreneurial sweet spot. More personally, it's helped him separate his identity from the company, enhancing his prospects for a future divestment or sale, and it has provided Stephen space for other unrelated ventures. Most importantly, this move has reinvigorated International Solutions Group and has generated a level of satisfaction for Stephen that he has created something that has grown bigger than just him.

■   ■   ■

As we conclude this discussion, here's a final piece of advice. No matter how much your employees want to develop, you cannot inflict it upon them, as Jacob Wiesmann learned the hard way. In his first year as controller at Rose Medical Center, his heart was broken—a bunch of his employees recently left. The one that hurt the most was his assistant controller, whom he'd taken under his wing. He'd put so much of his energy into coaching her; how could she want to quit?

What am I doing wrong? Jacob asked himself. *Am I not providing an environment that people want to be a part of?*

One day, as I was coaching Jacob on this matter, a lightbulb blinked on in his head: He was inflicting the development *he* wanted for his people—whether they wanted it or not. Even though he had great intentions, he was making his employees miserable! Jacob realized that his assistant controller hadn't wanted to be a leader at all—she just wanted to focus on running a great accounting department. What felt like positive coaching to him was a nuisance to her.

Luckily, this story has a happy ending. This lesson was a turning point for Jacob, and as the CFO of Parkland Medical Center in Manchester, New Hampshire, he has since developed into one of the most Bankable Leaders I know.

If Jacob can do it, so can you!

BANKABLE ACTIONS

Boost Their Strengths

- ✔ Identify what employees are good at or what they have the potential to do well in the future.

- ✔ Engage in an honest discussion with employees to mutually understand their strengths.

- ✔ Realize that you have a choice regarding how you spend your time with your team. Don't waste too much energy trying to fix weaknesses.

- ✔ Instead, reallocate your time to help develop your employees' strengths.

- ✔ Structure their job and projects around their strengths as much as possible.

Coach Them

- ✔ Remember that coaching is about helping employees solve their own problems. It's not an opportunity to solve their problems for them. Resist the temptation.

- ✔ Center the conversation around the employee, intently listening with an open mind. Make eye contact, speak less than 10 percent of the time, paraphrase what you're hearing, and never, ever interrupt.

- ✔ Assume that employees have the right answer and that it's your job to ask the right questions to surface it.

- ✔ Don't forget checks and balances: Establish clear timelines, follow up with specific questions, and touch base with those involved.

Help Your Superstars Thrive

- ✔ Great leaders assemble teams of talented people with different skill sets. These superstars enhance their leader's strengths and supplement their weaknesses.

- ✔ Pay close attention to your own reactions to your most talented employees. Assess whether you feel jealous or threatened by them in any way. Make a choice to fight that reaction and build your self-confidence.

- ✔ Give your superstars visibility and challenging projects, and make a commitment to give them the time and focus that they deserve.

BONUS: 18 (BASICALLY) FREE DEVELOPMENT IDEAS

- ✔ Help them choose a mentor (assigning them isn't usually the best approach).

- ✔ Arrange a lunch between them and a senior executive.

- ✔ Encourage them to attend a networking meeting.

- ✔ Ask them to make a presentation.

- ✔ Encourage them to join Toastmasters.

- ✔ Appoint them to lead a staff meeting.

- ✔ Have them mentor someone.

- ✔ Assign them a project that requires a stretch.

- ✔ Put them in charge while you are away.

- ✔ Have them complete a financial analysis.

- ✔ Have them prepare a budget.

- ✔ Have them shadow someone in a different department.

- ✔ Help them arrange a meeting between them and a counterpart at another organization.

- ✔ Have them read a book and create a report for the team on an important topic.

- ✔ Assign them to a task force.

✔ Ask them to represent the organization externally (conference, public event, etc.).

✔ Ask them to serve as an instructor for an internal training session.

✔ Encourage them to join a nonprofit board or other community group.

Part III

BE THANKFUL *and* DRIVE IMPROVEMENT

Think of the teacher, coach, or boss who had the biggest impact on you. What did you respect most about that person?

Let me see if I can guess. They probably refused to let you off the hook if you weren't performing at your best. Their expectations weren't unrealistic, but they knew what you were capable of and expected you to deliver it. And when you did, they probably recognized you for your hard work. That made you feel valued, and it motivated you to deliver even more in the future.

For me, this person was Anne Strobridge, my high school English teacher at Colorado Academy. Ms. Strobridge is not the kind of teacher who gives her students an A for effort. She is smart, her class is difficult, and her expectations are high. I didn't always "like" her, but I always respected her. No one has ever held my writing, whether it was an essay, poem, or story, to a higher standard.

And though her standards were high, Ms. Strobridge was tremendously encouraging, freely giving praise when I produced something strong. She would give us as many chances as we wanted to rewrite assignments and get regraded. I don't think I've ever been giddier in an academic setting than when I managed to get an A+ from her for an AP English essay on William Wordsworth entitled "The World *Really* Is Too Much with Us." (If you chuckled at that, you're a nerd.) I had spoken to her and redone the paper twice. When I eagerly turned to the last page, I saw a note: *You certainly learned a lot from our conversation.* Wow. I can say without equivocation that to this day, I am the writer I am because of her.

Many of us have had early role models like Ms. Strobridge, but it's still easy to feel like there's a trade-off between showing appreciation for what employees are doing and driving them to improve. This is a tough balancing act for any leader, and choosing one at the expense of the other can have disastrous consequences: Leaders will never have happy, engaged employees without showing gratitude, and they'll never drive sustainable results without constantly asking employees to improve.

Let's learn about the leaders at each end of this spectrum. On the left side are those who lavish too much praise or appreciation, possibly causing employees to be complacent, entitled, or satisfied with the status quo. On the right side are leaders who do nothing but tell their employees they must be better; these

BE THANKFUL
The "Everything is
Great" Leader

DRIVE IMPROVEMENT
The "Nothing's Good
Enough" Leader

leaders are usually hated, feared, or both. "I am not going to thank employees for doing their jobs!" is something you might hear from them.

The "Everything Is Great" leader is so focused on being supportive that he doesn't understand when to cheer on and when to push his team. As a delusional cheerleader, this leader might tell the crew of the Titanic that they're just doing a wonderful job of arranging those deck chairs. He might also become defensive or uncomfortable if people criticize his staff or bring him concerns. This leader is a people-pleaser to the core—he desperately wants contented employees who like him personally.

Michael Scott from the TV show *The Office* is an example of this left-side leader. In the first episode of the series, he explains that he's a friend to his employees first and a boss second. He's so afraid of upsetting them that he decides not to announce an impending layoff, a move he justifies by saying that as a doctor, you wouldn't tell a patient they had cancer. Definitely funny, but talk about delusional!

Giving feedback is uncomfortable for the "Everything Is Great" leader. Michael Scott uses the humorous phrase "constructive compliments," which is the perfect illustration of how deeply uncomfortable he is with tough feedback. When the "Everything Is Great" leader does have to give feedback, he might deliver it vaguely or indirectly, which is very frustrating when you're on the receiving end. Employees working for this type of leader may feel appreciated at first, but after some time, they will start to crave honesty. And if they keep hearing what a great job they're doing, their performance will flatline. They may even start to feel entitled to rewards or praise just for showing up!

On the right side is the "Nothing's Good Enough" leader. This leader is so focused on results that she is never satisfied, even by the team's best performance. A perfect portrait of this leader is Miranda Priestly from the movie *The Devil Wears Prada*. Truly nothing is ever good enough for this editor of the invented New York fashion magazine *Runway*. When we first meet her character, played impeccably by Meryl Streep, she's briskly walking to her office with her assistant, rattling off everything that's currently disappointing her, including the staff's failure to find attractive, slim female paratroopers for the magazine's paratrooper layout and the fact that Gwyneth Paltrow hasn't lost enough baby weight to appear on their cover.

In one scene, Priestly's staff has been preparing for a run-through to choose the styles that will appear in the next issue. She moves up the time of the meeting, then chastises the team for not being ready, wondering why it's impossible to put together a good run-through. "Nothing's Good Enough" leaders like Miranda Priestly are usually feared, and we know from part I that fear is not exactly a productive feeling to go stirring up.

Working for the "Nothing's Good Enough" leader can be incredibly demoralizing. At first, employees might value being pushed to improve, but after hearing no messages of thanks or appreciation, these feelings will quickly be replaced by resentment. Employees who work for this kind of leader might lose confidence or start to believe that they really *aren't* good enough.

As we'll see in the following chapters, when employees don't receive thanks and appreciation, their performance starts to suffer. They might wonder, *If I put in all of those extra hours and this wasn't good enough for her, what's the point of trying this hard in the future?* In *The Devil Wears Prada*, Anne Hathaway's character spends the movie wrestling with whether she wants to work for someone like Miranda. At the end of the movie, she quits, throwing her work cell phone into a fountain. That's one way to do it!

Now that we've looked at both sides of the spectrum, let's talk about how to move to the middle. As was the case with Ms. Strobridge, you can balance the tension successfully. Bankable Leaders ceaselessly push their teams to be better, knowing that in the business world, the motto is often "Improve or disappear." At the same time, leaders who live in the middle understand the importance of recognizing and appreciating what their employees are producing. They don't blindly dole out praise—it must be earned through effort and performance. This means that employees are challenged to improve *and* appreciated when they achieve it. That, in turn, inspires them to work harder next time, raising the bar with every project.

Whether you lean toward the left or the right, this section will teach you to give thanks *and* drive continuous improvement—without feeling like you're being schizophrenic! In chapter 8, we'll talk about the science of entitlement-free appreciation so you can acknowledge what your employees are contributing *without* turning them into entitled, lazy whiners. In chapter 9, we'll review the principles of giving no-fear feedback. You'll see why many leaders provide feedback ineffectively, learn how to avoid common traps, and how to provide criticism in a nonthreatening way. Finally, in chapter 10, we'll discuss the notion of change. Even though humans have a tough time doing things differently, Bankable Leaders can successfully drive change by walking the tightrope between thankfulness and improvement.

The overarching theme of this section is smartly summed up in this Anthony Robbins quote: "Affirmation without discipline is the beginning of delusion."[1] Let's learn how you can create both.

CHAPTER 8

THE SCIENCE OF ENTITLEMENT-FREE APPRECIATION

I have this flashbulb memory: I'm driving home, my temper flaring. I'm barely able to concentrate on the road. I'd just delivered a leadership workshop that my team and I had worked on for more than nine months. We happily put in more late nights than I can count because we wanted it to be a success. I remember sitting on the floor next to our industrial printer one evening the week before the workshop. Too exhausted to stand, I looked at my watch. It was 1:00 a.m.

We were delighted when the workshop was well-received, with many partic-ipants enthusiastically approaching me and offering staccato superlatives: "This was the Best. Workshop. Ever!" My team and I gathered after participants left on the last day to debrief. We heard the door swing open. It was my boss. We instinctively fell silent.

But we didn't get the long-awaited recognition I'd hoped for. He slowly approached us, pounded his fist on the table, and said, "It's time to think about next year—and that one needs to be even *better*."

It was one of the most truly depressing moments of my career. All the late nights suddenly seemed pointless. If he was going to say that all along, why did we even bother?

I'll say this in my boss's defense: I do think he had positive intentions. But he made one of the most common leadership mistakes in the book: neglecting gratitude and overemphasizing continuous improvement. According to the Society for Human Resource Management, 79 percent of employees cite lack of recognition and praise as their top reason for leaving an organization.[1] Have you ever had a job where no one appreciated your contributions? Wouldn't a "Thank you" have made all the difference? Did you start to feel resentful or depressed? You were probably working for a right-side leader. But when a leader balances right- and left-side tendencies—giving sincere appreciation that doesn't encourage complacency—employees come away with a sense of accomplishment and pride and will be inspired to do better in the future.

So what is the right way to thank your team members and acknowledge their efforts? As I alluded in this chapter's title, appreciation is a science, and the first concept we must understand is self-efficacy. Coined in 1977 by Albert Bandura, it refers to your own belief that you can perform effectively.[2]

This is especially true at work. In a meta-analysis, Timothy Judge and Joyce Bono found a strong relationship between self-efficacy and work performance.[3] In other words, when employees believe they can do something, they usually prove themselves right. This might remind you of the schoolchildren categorized as "bloomers" in chapter 1: When their teachers believed they were gifted, they became gifted.

What's more, leaders really can improve employees' self-efficacy.[4] A research team led by Josh Arnold, a California State University professor, interviewed employees in three companies: a clothing retailer, a building-products supplier, and a telecommunications corporation.[5] The researchers asked employees about their manager's behavior during a time when he or she had "contributed greatly to the successful performance of the group." One of the behaviors frequently cited by employees was encouragement. When leaders provide encouragement and appreciation, they perform better.

The opposite is also true, as I experienced with my boss after the leadership workshop. Researchers have shown that when leaders are stingy with appreciation—or worse, criticize them in the spirit of improvement—their team actually performs worse![6] And it makes sense: If you give your employees the impression that they can't succeed, their confidence will wear away. Then, because they don't believe they can perform, they won't. It's pretty simple stuff.

Yet most leaders I meet find showing appreciation difficult, or they simply forget to do it. In this chapter, I'll provide tools to make appreciation easy. First, you'll learn the benefits of hardwiring gratitude in your day-to-day life and learn three specific strategies for doing so. Then, we'll look at how you can banish entitlement by showing appreciation without making employees feel like they can just stop trying.

DO YOU HAVE A GRATITUDE STRATEGY?

Lieutenant Colonel Mark Hughes had just accepted a challenging new assignment. As an officer in the US Air Force, he'd agreed to lead a team to update the technology for a military satellite communications program. The task was daunting: He had to build his team, craft a vision, and make a case to the Defense Acquisition Board, the body responsible for approving major acquisition programs for the US military. It was a heck of a journey, and when Mark and his team were approved by the board, it was a major milestone for the multibillion-dollar program.

One Saturday, as the project was coming to a close, Mark's home phone rang. It was his program director, General Kwiatkowski. Mark braced himself for trouble, but instead heard, "Mark, based on your hard work, you've been selected as the Space and Missile Systems Center's senior program manager of the year." Mark was shocked. "We thought you did a great job," the general went on, "and we want to recognize you for your hard work." Mark was truly touched. He felt appreciated. Inspired. Proud of himself and his contributions. Full of energy to tackle his next challenge.

Mark didn't know how important unexpected and tailored recognition really was until that moment. And through his subsequent successes in the private sector (including time as executive vice president of operations for multibillion-dollar disaster-planning company SunGard and CFO for the national data center entity Inflow), he's never forgotten it.

"The two things you can't give yourself," RE/MAX CEO Margaret Kelly notes, "are recognition and appreciation." And, equally wisely, Bill Daniels once said, "You have the ability to make people happy with just a few thoughtful words. Why not start using them?"

Most leaders have a business strategy. Why not also create a gratitude strategy? It need not be based on money. According to motivation guru Bob Nelson, nonmonetary recognition improves performance 84 percent of the time.[7] In fact, as we saw in chapter 6, nonmonetary recognition may be *more* effective than incentivizing with money. Let's review three specific tools you can use to realize the benefits of appreciation.

Make Gratitude a Habit

Even well-intentioned leaders often fail to recognize and appreciate their team. This typically isn't because they don't want to; it's because they don't create habits that help them do it on a regular basis. Good "gratitude habits" are *memorable actions you commit to doing regularly.* The last word—*regularly*—is key. Let's say that a leader set a goal to write his team thank-you cards every week. Maybe she does it for a month, then falls off the wagon. It's like New Year's resolutions—we usually start out strong, but research shows that by the end of the year only 8 percent of us have kept them![8] So when the leader starts showing appreciation and then abruptly stops, employees might think, *Wait, why did she stop? Did we do something wrong?*

In 2008, Shawn Achor studied tax managers at KPMG in New Jersey and New York.[9] Every day, participants chose one of five activities designed to increase their happiness, including writing down something they were grateful for, sending a positive message to a colleague or friend, or recording their most meaningful experience of the day. After three weeks, he found that compared to a control group whose members weren't doing these activities, these tax managers were more optimistic and satisfied with their lives. (PS: Life satisfaction predicts both productivity and happiness in the workplace—results and people outcomes, respectively.) Four months later, the experimental group was still experiencing these benefits. They had successfully made positivity a habit.

Because many behaviors from Achor's study were "gratitude habits," we can extend the point to our discussion. Bankable Leaders make recognizing their employees a habit, and it's not just employees who benefit! You, the leader, will also show long-term gains in happiness and productivity.

So what are some examples of gratitude habits? When he's on airplanes, Mark Hughes makes the most of the time during takeoff and landing. He carries a set of note cards with his name on the front. He folds them in half and writes his staff messages: "Congratulations," "Thanks for a great job," or "Welcome to our team." Mark also writes down what he wants to recognize the employees for as soon as it happens, so the note-writing process is easy and fast. Above all, the most important aspect of Mark's habit is that it's a predictable and regular part of his life.

Tracee Hendershott is another Bankable Leader who's built a strong gratitude habit. As the manager of a hospital labor and delivery unit, she'd end meetings by reading thank-you notes patients had written to staff members. It was uplifting and became a deeply ingrained practice. A side benefit of this activity is that it helps employees remember why they do what they do, reinforcing the meaning we discussed in chapter 6.

Finally, and perhaps most creatively, I once met one leader who remembers to express gratitude every time he sees a yellow car. Thankfully, he doesn't live in New York; otherwise this might be an untenable proposition.

There are as many ways to hardwire gratitude as there are leaders, so it's important to find something that works for you.

Tailor Your Expression of Gratitude

Natalie Roper had made a huge miscalculation. One of her radiology technologists had gone above and beyond the call of duty with a customer. With the best of intentions, Natalie recognized her in a sixty-person staff meeting. The employee froze like a deer in headlights. After the meeting, Natalie approached the technologist and asked what was wrong. "Choosing to recognize me in that meeting was humiliating," she whimpered. Natalie felt her heart drop to her stomach—her act of gratitude had backfired.

Natalie learned that although everyone on earth wants to be recognized, we often want it in different ways. Some want public praise, some want a pat on the back in private, some prefer notes, and some prefer small gifts.

But this mistake actually helped shape a practice that now differentiates Natalie as a leader. Now, when a new employee starts work, she learns how they like to be recognized. The following questions are inspired by her approach. They are intentionally open-ended to allow you to truly understand how your employees like to be recognized; this should be a discussion rather than a "check the box" activity.

- What drew you to this company, and what makes you want to stay?

- What was the most meaningful moment of recognition or appreciation you received from a leader in your career?

- What are the most satisfying types of recognition for you and why? (Here look for whether they talk about recognition that was private or public, verbal or written.)

Don't Forget to Fill Your Own Gratitude Wellsprings

"In the event that oxygen masks are required, do not attempt to help others until you have secured your own." If you fly often, you hear this all the time. But extended to appreciation, it holds a powerful leadership lesson: To appropriately recognize the contributions of your team, you have to be in the right state of mind yourself. The late great Stephen Covey called this "Sharpening Your Saw."[10]

To show appreciation to others, leaders must first practice gratitude in their own lives. Let's review a study that powerfully illustrates why this is the case. Robert Emmons and Michael McCullough studied gratitude in 201 undergraduates in a health psychology class.[11] Researchers assigned participants into experimental groups. The first group, the gratitude group, was asked to write down five things they were grateful for every week (interactions with friends, academic success, physical health). The second group, the frustration group, was asked to write down five hassles they'd experienced in the past week, such as road rage, a difficult exam, or fighting with loved ones.

Students in the gratitude group felt better about their lives and more optimistic about their future than the frustration group. They slept better. They spent more time exercising. They were more likely to help others. Their significant others even noticed improvements in their well-being.

HOW **EXECUTIVES** CAN SHOW APPRECIATION

Remembering to show appreciation can be especially challenging for executives, who are typically rewarded for organizational performance above all else. And even though Wall Street may not prioritize it, smart executives understand the powerful impact appreciation has on their organization.

1. **FIND SMALL OPPORTUNITIES:** As a senior leader, your actions are magnified. The standard you set also sets the tone for how other leaders will behave. Remember that though a thirty-second interaction with an employee in the elevator might not have a lot of importance to you, it can mean the world to that employee.

2. **DON'T TAKE EMPLOYEES FOR GRANTED:** Employees who have done a good job in the past may not continue to do so without positive reinforcement. Make it a practice to verbalize gratitude and provide recognition to employees. Set aside time every day to e-mail or briefly chat with someone who has done a good job, and be specific about what you appreciate about his or her actions or character.

3. **GET "APPRECIATION INTEL" FROM YOUR DIRECT REPORTS:** Get details about individuals, teams, and departments who deserve recognition and make it happen. Write notes, make phone calls, or show up at department meetings to show your appreciation. This can be *hugely* impactful and takes very little time on your part.

So to improve your leadership effectiveness—as well as your personal life and relationships—Bankable Leaders should carve out time to practice gratitude. You can't appreciate others until you appreciate things yourself.

BANISHING ENTITLEMENT

I once knew a leader who, wanting to recognize her team for its hard work, bought them all bagels one Friday morning. Her employees were grateful, cheerily devouring their free breakfast. The next Friday rolled around. The bagels had gone over so well last week—why not do it again? Her employees were once again grateful.

But on the third Friday, one of her employees came to her office and asked, "Where are our bagels?"

Clearly, this leader's show of gratitude was no longer having the intended effect. After just three weeks, the team had started to see the bagels not as a reward but as something they deserved and could expect.

When I meet managers who aren't recognizing their team, many say things like, "I don't want to create a bunch of entitled slackers." This is a common—and very fair—fear. Indeed, entitlement is the enemy of improvement.

Entitled employees have overly favorable perceptions of themselves and feel deserving of praise and rewards regardless of their performance. They tend to take credit for positive outcomes and blame others when things go wrong. Entitled employees are dangerous for both people and results. They underperform in their jobs, pick fights, abuse their coworkers, behave unethically, and possess unrealistic pay expectations.

Paul Harvey of the University of New Hampshire and Kenneth Harris of Indiana University Southeast examined how leaders' communication patterns impacted their team's mood.[12] They found that although good communication from supervisors reduced frustration for low-entitlement employees, entitled employees became *more* frustrated! As Harvey and Harris revealed, entitled employees seem to reject the good leadership behaviors most other employees appreciate.

The majority of leaders who inadvertently create entitled employees follow two predictable patterns that are, fortunately, avoidable: Some damn everyone with equal praise, giving all employees rewards regardless of their contribution, while others make rewards too predictable, so employees begin to expect them. To prevent entitlement, then, you must *differentiate recognition* and/or *make it unpredictable*. Let's learn how to do this.

Differentiate Recognition

As a Millennial, I grew up in a generation where everyone got a ribbon for everything. Being somewhat of a Baby Boomer trapped in a Millennial's body, I always felt like this robbed us of the thrill of victory. If everyone gets a ribbon for participating in field day, is it special anymore when you win, say, the long jump? Not really.

I'm not saying that you shouldn't recognize your team as a whole (see the next section for more on this). What I am saying is that if the same amount of appreciation is given for mediocre performance as exceptional performance, people will start to become not just mediocre, but entitled.

This is exactly the problem with most organizations' merit pay systems. I see leaders go through rather comical discussions to decide who will get a 5 percent raise and who will get a 7 percent raise. Really? Does anyone really think that is a meaningful difference? With a salary of $50,000, that means mediocre performers get $2,500 and top performers get $3,500. That is like organizational socialism! And if you think about it, it's totally unfair to your top performers.

I was recently talking to a client who bravely wondered, "Why don't our performance-appraisal systems take money *away* from employees? If you do a terrible job, instead of getting a small raise or no raise, why don't we dock your salary?" In practice, this would come with a slew of problems and is probably not advisable, but he did have a point.

At the heart of my client's comment was a profound truth: *Leaders receive the performance they reward.* So if you give mediocre performers essentially the same rewards you give top performers, you're just tempting your best people to be mediocre. Going back to the beginning of the chapter, they might say: "Why bother?" Alternatively, differentiation prevents complacency.

I once worked at a company that gave out a "Leader of the Year" award at its annual holiday banquet. The winner—one person, and one person only—was lavished with praise and recognition. You bet it drove the rest of us to be the best leaders we could be, just imagining ourselves standing up to accept the award the next year.

It comes down to this: Though recognizing each employee is hugely important, Bankable Leaders avoid the "peanut butter" approach, where appreciation is spread so thin that it loses meaning. The perception that praise is scarce can actually work to your advantage and help drive the behavior you're looking for.

Make Team-Level Recognition Creative and Unpredictable

You might be surprised to learn that rats can help you be a better leader. Bear with me for a moment. B. F. Skinner, a behavioral psychologist, coined the term "operant conditioning" in 1938.[13] The majority of Skinner's research was conducted in the middle of the twentieth century, and though his subjects were usually lab rats, his work has taught us a lot about what drives human behavior. The principles of operant conditioning help us understand how to encourage a particular behavior when a person has a choice about whether to do it or not.

Here's an example. Let's say we want to teach a lab rat to pull a lever. To help him learn, I might give him reinforcement, like a piece of food, each time he demonstrates that behavior. This is all well and good if I give him food every time. But he will stop the behavior if I stop giving him food when he pulls the lever. If the rat is used to pulling the lever and receiving food, he'll lose interest if food no longer follows. This is called behavior extinction.

Now let's go back to our Bagel Leader (where employees' behavior was also being reinforced with food!). This team received the same reinforcement at the same time for two weeks and became used to receiving it. Taking away the bagels led to confusion and frustration, opening up the possibility that employees would discontinue the desired behavior: hard work.

In operant conditioning, there is a strategy known as "partial reinforcement," where the rewards are less predictable and behavior extinction is less likely. A good example of this effect are slot machines. Because you don't receive money each time you play, you might find it difficult to walk away. "Just one more. Then

I'm stopping," can easily turn into ten more games; at any time, you know the reward could be just around the corner.

The simple takeaway is to vary reinforcement in your team. Employees are least likely to expect—or feel entitled to—appreciation that's creative or unpredictable. Sheryl Benjamin, executive director of the Denver-based Sensory Processing Disorder Foundation and STAR Center, believes in surprise appreciation. In a former role, she took her team to a Japanese restaurant to celebrate their hard work. She bought each person an inexpensive, goofy gift. For example, one team member, who was always telling everyone "You're a rock star," received a plastic "Rock Star" crown and trophy Sheryl had found at a nearby party-supply store. Her employee was surprised and moved by this creative and personal gesture.

Finally, it's important to remember how important it is to foster recognition between team members. Not only does this take a little pressure off you, it can sometimes be more meaningful to be recognized by one's peers. Spreading around the source of recognition and appreciation may also reduce feelings of entitlement. At a former company, we had a traveling trophy that managers would pass to each other at every leadership meeting. It was a highly motivating and powerfully self-perpetuating tradition.

■ ■ ■

When it comes to entitlement-free appreciation, one last piece of guidance is to remember the Serenity Prayer: "May God grant me the courage to change the things I can, the serenity to accept the things I cannot, and the wisdom to know the difference." The good news here is that you can usually prevent entitlement. But sometimes, no matter what you do, you'll have an entitled employee who just won't change. This type of person can be like a cancer to a team. No matter how much entitlement-free gratitude they receive, they may be doomed to act entitled forevermore. If you have an employee like this, the only solution may be to remove them from your team. But, except in these rare cases, the effects of entitlement-free appreciation can be absolutely transformative for teams.

BANKABLE ACTIONS

Adopt a Gratitude Strategy

✔ Use a regular and easy-to-remember approach to make gratitude a habit.

✔ Because no two employees will want the same kind of appreciation, learn what actions will help each employee the most.

✔ Take time to regularly remember the things you're grateful for in your work and life.

Banish Entitlement

✔ Don't damn everyone with equal praise: Make sure that you differentiate recognition between average and top performers, avoiding the "peanut butter" approach to appreciation.

✔ Consider establishing prestigious and selective rewards that only the highest performers win. The perception of scarcity will drive improvement.

✔ Make team-level recognition creative and unpredictable so your employees don't start expecting to be rewarded every time they do something.

✔ Institute team-level recognition opportunities so team members can recognize each other.

✔ Accept the reality that you may have employees who act entitled no matter what you do. Take swift action.

CHAPTER 9

NO-FEAR FEEDBACK

Margaret Kelly was devastated. Her job was challenging on a good day, but this was different. After being thrown into a role as manager of her company's finance department at only twenty-four years old, Margaret had just received her first performance appraisal, and it wasn't good.

Margaret had always prided herself on working hard, but her manager told her that she wasn't pushing her team enough (the good news, he noted, was that she always pushed herself). Later that night, Margaret's husband came home and was stunned to find his wife crying in her closet.

In subsequent months, as Margaret processed the feedback, she realized that her boss was right. She wasn't pushing her staff to achieve more. You may have already guessed how this turns out—Margaret worked on her leadership approach, became certifiably bankable, and went on to become the CEO of RE/MAX. She was always grateful for the powerful lesson she learned from that performance appraisal: People deserve honest feedback—the good, bad, and ugly.

The day Margaret's boss held that review, he was surely feeling the tension—one all leaders feel—between being thankful for the work your employees do and being honest about how they can improve their performance. In a nutshell, it's hard to tell your employees what you want them to keep doing *and* ask them to step up their game.

At this point, you might be thinking back to chapter 7, where I waxed poetic about why leaders should focus on strengths. Yes, yes—that's still true. But even though focusing on strengths is important for developing your employees, it doesn't let you off the hook when the time comes to manage performance.

When I help leaders in this area, I typically see one of two mistakes. On the left side are leaders who place people above results, only providing positive feedback and failing to give tough feedback to avoid discomfort. Have you ever had a job where you received only positive feedback, or none at all? Unfortunately, this is all too common. Most employees don't get the honest feedback they really deserve.

The second mistake I see is on the right side, where leaders drive improvement at all costs. These leaders deliver primarily negative or "constructive" feedback (and usually not kindly), striking fear in their employees at every turn. But putting their employees in this constant state of threat and fear actually does nothing to drive improvement in the long run.

Most employees are afraid of feedback, usually because of a traumatic memory of a right-side leader. In fact, a recent study by Development Dimensions International reported that employees dread a difficult conversation with their manager more than they dread paying taxes, getting a bad hangover, or even receiving a speeding ticket.[1] When you think about the so-called "constructive" feedback many leaders provide, it's no wonder! I don't know about you, but reading words like these makes my stomach drop: "Hi Tasha, when you have a moment, would you mind stopping by my office? I have some feedback I want to give you."

Because most of us dread being called out for mistakes or weaknesses, leaders who hope to give honest feedback run the risk of angering employees *and* decreasing their productivity if it isn't delivered correctly. This explains research findings revealing a negative relationship between feedback and employee engagement—it's often given ineffectively. In one study, researchers analyzed more than six hundred studies of performance evaluations.[2] Their results were astonishing. In 30 percent of cases, *performance reviews made performance worse.* I'll pause for a moment so you can read that again. The authors suggest that as feedback feels more and more personal (and less about behaviors or tasks), it becomes less and less helpful in driving improvement.

Some leaders tell me that because of this tension, they feel like they're "damned if they do and damned if they don't." If they don't give feedback, it might not upset their employees, but certainly it won't make them better. If they do give feedback, it might communicate what they need to change but upset them. In short, most leaders are just as fearful about giving feedback as employees are to receive it!

But as Margaret's boss understood, the value of appropriately delivered improvement feedback is irreplaceable. He knew that even though the feedback would be tough to hear, it was important.

Your goal is to give "no-fear" feedback: There should be no fear for employees in receiving it, and no fear for you in delivering it. If you can help employees know what they're doing well *and* have the courage to help them be more successful, they'll pay you back with performance.

In this chapter, you'll learn a simple model for giving no-fear feedback that removes the negative emotion from the process. Then, at the end of the chapter, I'll discuss the best way to honor poor performers as people while ensuring that the results you need are achieved.

2D FEEDBACK: A FOOLPROOF FEEDBACK TECHNIQUE

Imagine you're driving down the highway at sixty miles an hour. There are two possibilities: You're either pointed in the right direction and need to keep going, or you're headed in the wrong direction and need to reroute. Likewise, there are two types of feedback: behaviors employees should **D**uplicate in the future (the equivalent of staying on the same route) and behaviors employees should **D**eviate from in the future (the equivalent of getting off the road you're on and onto a new one). This is the 2D Feedback Model.

There are two important aspects of this model. The first is that it's future-focused. Because the purpose of feedback is to help a person be successful in the future, there isn't a lot of value in dwelling on the past. I've seen many leaders deliver negative feedback that points out the bad choices the employee made in excruciating detail. But beyond identifying the behavior that needs to change, what good is it to focus on mistakes? Most employees already know when they've messed up, and further emphasizing it only creates fear and self doubt.

The second important aspect of "Duplicate" or "Deviate" feedback is the fact that it's behavior-based. I often see leaders give feedback that's so general it's useless. They say things like, "You need to be a better team player" or "You need to show more commitment." For feedback to do any good, it must be specific. The standard I use is this: If you were watching a movie, would you be able to see what you're describing? If you tell someone that they're "aggressive," they won't know exactly what behaviors to change. If you say, "You pounded your fist on the table two times and interrupted me three times in the course of a thirty-minute meeting," then you're getting somewhere.[3]

How to Give "Duplicate" Feedback

I am honored to serve on the faculty at the Center for Creative Leadership, one of the top executive education organizations in the world. In the course of my training, the leader who supervises the adjunct faculty—my boss—observed me instructing a class. Afterward, I received a note from her saying that she had only positive feedback and nothing "constructive." Patting myself on the back, I thought, *I'm all set! Why do I need to look at good feedback?* But when she sent me her notes, I found that many of the positive behaviors she pointed out were things I had no idea I was doing. What a realization: Had I not looked at her notes, I never would have known what to *keep* doing in the future!

The "Duplicate" feedback you give your team is as much about improvement as it is about gratitude. Many times, employees don't realize the positive impact of their behavior. So the more you pinpoint specific actions you want to see continue, the more you'll see that behavior. This should remind you of the strengths-based approach to development we discussed in chapter 7.

Not only does "Duplicate" feedback help employees continue what they're doing well; there's also evidence that it improves creativity. Jing Zhou, a professor at Rice University's Jones Graduate School of Business, has studied this effect.[4] After being given a short task, one group of students was given feedback on what they did wrong and another was told what they did well. Those who received "Duplicate" feedback showed more creativity afterward.

Here are five tips for giving "Duplicate" feedback:

1.   **Begin with thanks:** "Rachel, I want to thank you for all your great work on this project. I've really noticed how your approach to working with our team members helped them coexist peacefully."

2.   **Describe what they did:** "When things were getting tense in our last project update meeting, you spoke up and said that even though tension was high, everyone on the team was doing their job."

3.   **Explain its effect:** "This immediately diffused the tension in the room and helped everyone gain some valuable perspective."

4.   **Ask for more in the future:** "The next time you feel the team's discussion getting harmfully heated, please make sure to take a similar approach."

5.   **Keep an eye out for the behavior, and reinforce it:** "Rachel, you did it again! Thank you for being the beacon of reason in our team. It is such a great help."

How to Give "Deviate" Feedback

Natalie Roper had waited far too long to give her radiology tech some important feedback. Though this tech was talented, employees and patients were complaining about his negative attitude. Natalie outlined a plan in her head for how she'd have the conversation. She'd give him a warning and tell him that if the behavior didn't improve, he'd be out of a job.

When the tech came to her office and sat down across from her, the disciplinary speech Natalie had prepared suddenly felt wrong. She followed her instincts and took a different approach. "You're a huge asset to this department," she began, "and I want to help you be successful."

He looked at her quizzically, as if to say, "What did I do wrong?" Natalie quickly realized that he had no idea that the way he was behaving wasn't working. They went on to have a direct conversation about the behaviors he was demonstrating that were making him seem insensitive. "I . . . I had no idea," he stuttered. "How can I make this right?"

They rolled up their sleeves and began identifying the behaviors he needed to demonstrate in the future, like wording his responses differently to avoid unintentionally offending people. Natalie started by giving him scripting and tools and making training available to him. She even assigned a mentor to help him develop these skills.

And one year after that conversation—almost to the day—Natalie's department boasted the top patient, employee, and customer service scores in her organization. Her radiology tech had gone from being her most challenging employee to one of her best. Employees wanted to work with him and patients liked him. The complaints were gone. When he retired, there was genuine sadness on the part of his colleagues; a year before, it would've been more of a "Don't let the door hit you on the way out!" response. Thanks to Natalie's belief in him and her specific "Deviate" coaching, he'd made both of them proud.

Here are five pointers to help you deliver nonthreatening "Deviate" feedback:

1. **Be direct but supportive:** "I wanted to talk to you about how you might approach discussions about your clients differently in the future. I want us to talk this through because I want you to be successful."

2. **Report the weather:** Describe the *behavior* that needs to be different and why in an even, calm tone. I have a client who uses the phrase "Report the weather." Dispassionately state the issue in the same way you might say, "It's raining outside." Try, "In our one-on-one today, when I asked you for an update on our newest client, you physically closed yourself off and your tone of voice became short and tense. You told me you had it under control. I'm not sure what's going on with the client, but I need to know how things are going with our clients in case an issue gets escalated to me—that way I can back you up because I know about it."

3. **Agree on the behavior they'll try instead:** First, ask for your employee's

perspective on the situation. "Can you tell me a bit more about what was going on with this and how I can support keeping the lines of communication open?" Then, ask for their ideas with the goal of agreeing on the best approach to use in the future. "In the future, especially if something isn't going well, I want to ask you to share that information as soon as you have it." State the benefit of changing the behavior.

4. **Determine next steps:** "Why don't we take stock of how things are going next month to make sure we're both feeling positively about things?"

5. **Offer your support, and end on a positive note:** "Thanks for talking to me about this. You're a valuable member of our team and I know this will make a big difference in our ability to serve the client." When you see improvements, give "Duplicate" feedback.

When and How to Deliver Balanced Feedback

Most organizations have a yearly or biannual process where employees receive feedback from leaders. Without getting into the tedium of the endless paperwork exercise many organizations complete, I will say that this model is based on a flawed assumption that managers should "store up" feedback to deliver during these reviews.

I once worked for someone who almost never gave me feedback on how I was performing. In our first performance-appraisal conversation, my boss shared some "Deviate" feedback about a project I had completed about four months prior. I was furious. I couldn't go back in time and change anything! I left my boss's office in a huff, thinking, *Why didn't I know that earlier?* I felt like I'd been repeating the same mistakes for four months.

In one study, a team of researchers led by Ralph Pampino Jr. of University of the Pacific worked with managers in framing stores to set goals to improve store operations. They found that when employees were given daily or weekly feedback, the stores they worked in were more likely to meet their goals. Employees even reported preferring daily feedback to weekly feedback![5]

I like to think of performance appraisals as the period at the end of the sentence of the employee's performance that year. I have a good friend who adamantly points out that *nothing* a leader tells an employee in a performance review should be a surprise. If it is, shame on you as the leader!

The important lesson here is to give your employees 2D feedback as soon as the behavior happens. On the people side, your employee will feel respected. On the results side, the immediacy of the feedback will make it more productive. If your employee asks, "What exactly did you see me do?" and you say, "Oh, I can't remember exactly, but the meeting really didn't go well," you're not helping anyone.

In any feedback conversation—formal or informal—it's important to balance "Duplicate" and "Deviate" feedback as much as possible. Imagine you had a performance review conversation with an "Everything Is Great" leader where you only heard "Duplicate" feedback. You might leave the room thinking, "There must be *something* I could be doing differently. Why won't he tell me what it is?"

Or let's say you have a performance review conversation where you hear only "Deviate" feedback from a "Nothing's Good Enough" leader. Even if it was well-delivered, you might feel insecure. Find a balance that is authentic to you. For example, don't make up one kind of feedback just because you feel you should deliver it; that will make it meaningless and probably confusing. But do make sure that you're creating a balance over time, and that your pattern includes at least three to four "Duplicate" statements for every one "Deviate" statement.

While we're on the topic of performance appraisals, a note about rating scales. I have seen organizations engage in long, protracted, and highly comical arguments about whether performance ratings will fall on a three-point or five-point scale. My perspective: Who cares? I have seen no good come from assigning a number to performance—for either top or bottom performers. Employees with low ratings become demotivated or disgruntled, and the learning opportunity disappears. Employees who receive an average rating feel they should have received a higher one. And those who receive a high rating have an expectation that next year's rating will be just as high.

Even if you don't have influence over your company's performance-appraisal process, I caution you to avoid focusing on the "number" or "rating" you're assigning to employees. Instead, focus on making your feedback narrative. The more narrative feedback you can provide, the more helpful the process will be

FEEDBACK FOR **GLOBAL LEADERS**

The employee evaluation and feedback process can be tricky for global leaders given the way various cultures perceive critiques. Feedback presented in the same format could be viewed as constructive in one culture and accusatory in another. Awareness of cultural norms is critical for global leaders to know how to provide effective feedback.

1. **DO YOUR HOMEWORK:** Because even countries in the same region can have marked differences, check with your HR department for resources they might have about working with different cultures. As you evaluate employees, apply what you've learned about how people of different cultures react to feedback.

2. **BEING DIRECT ISN'T ALWAYS BEST:** In individualistic cultures (North American, European), you can be more direct with feedback. In collectivistic cultures (Asian, African, Latin), direct feedback can be embarrassing, so indirect feedback is best. Or you can practice "blurring," where you provide the feedback more generally to the group the person belongs to rather than singling them out.

3. **RESPECT THE POWER DYNAMICS AT PLAY:** North American countries have fairly low power distance, and employees at all levels are more likely to be open to giving and receiving criticism. Asian, Latin, African, and Arab countries have high power distance (meaning that they are more hierarchical), and there might be hesitancy on the part of subordinates to give their managers feedback—and hesitancy on the part of managers to be receptive to feedback from subordinates.

for your employees. Besides, how could anyone's performance in a year really be so oversimplified as to be turned into a number? Really.

Finally, and perhaps most importantly, at the end of the day it's about trust. Bob Chapman, our Bankable Leader from chapter 1, conducted his master's research on performance appraisals, and his findings ring true.[6] Collecting data from employees in a large sporting goods company, Bob found that employees who trusted their leaders were more likely to feel good about performance appraisals. Building trust with your employees, as discussed in chapter 1, can improve their attitudes about and the effectiveness of the performance-appraisal process.

WHAT TO DO ABOUT POOR PERFORMERS

I first met Andrea Gwyn when she was the administrative resident overseeing the Environmental Services and Dietary departments of a hospital. It is unusual for an administrative resident to have any departments reporting to them, so she was in uncharted territory. Based on her potential, I was asked to be her coach. At twenty-seven years old, despite her tremendous accomplishments, it was easy for people to underestimate Andrea when they first met her.

Two years into her residency, Andrea inherited a project aimed at improving the hospital's outreach to EMS crews. When Andrea was briefed on the project, she was told about one "problem" employee whom she'd need to watch closely.

Flash forward a few weeks. She, the employee, and the employee's supervisor sat in Andrea's office. Andrea and the employee's supervisor had decided to write her up. The conversation wasn't going well, and the employee was shutting down. And after that meeting, the employee's performance plummeted further.

Andrea was racking her brain to solve the problem, and suddenly remembered some advice her third-grade teacher, Mrs. Gwaltney, had given her: "Be a sponge." She had always thought it meant to learn as much as possible in every situation. But in this moment, Andrea realized that what Mrs. Gwaltney was really saying was to be open-minded. To not preconceive. To not judge. That, Andrea realized, would be the only way to turn this situation around.

From that moment on, Andrea made a commitment to learn more about her employee as a person. She had two grown kids and was getting a business degree, and Andrea helped her see the relationship between what she was learning in school and the EMS project. The metrics started to move. They were reaching more EMS professionals and involving more physicians in outreach, and the quality of her reports to the hospital leadership improved. Andrea was so successful in helping turn this situation around that she was assigned an additional department to oversee by the CEO.

Andrea learned that Bankable Leaders don't judge their employees and are genuinely invested in their success. It's important to point out that she didn't ignore her employee's poor performance. Doing so would be delusional. Instead, she thought about the problem differently. And even though you should still be focusing equal or greater attention on your best performers, many poor performers can be turned around quickly with the right focus and energy.

Remember, what we believe about others comes true. Indeed, leaders can unintentionally reinforce poor performance in their teams. Joseph Folkman and his colleagues examined a group of low-performing employees, and though they were behaving in ways that justified their moniker, Folkman found that *managers were actually treating them differently than their other employees.*[7] The problem employees reported wanting their leaders to simply believe in them. Once leaders started treating them like everyone else, their behavior improved.

To prevent the effect Folkman observed, ask yourself these questions about your poor performers:

- Do they truly understand your expectations?
- Is there something outside of their control that is preventing them from performing?
- Do they know they're not performing?

If All Else Fails . . .

My friend Andy, an excellent IT project manager, once told me, "I never regret letting someone go too soon. But I almost always regret keeping someone who isn't performing on my team for too long."

Dealing with poor performers decisively is a must for Bankable Leaders. It should go without saying that you're documenting their actions and your discussions (if you need more detail on this, your HR department can help). And if nothing is producing an improvement, it's time for a serious conversation with yourself about whether this person should be on your team. Recall from chapter 5 that part of treating employees like adults means making your expectations clear, helping them perform, and allowing them to move on if they show you they can't improve.

You have to take poor performance seriously. I have a client who recently had to fire someone who'd been stealing from the company. The employee had worked there for a decade, having been passed from manager to manager (as frequently happens among poor leaders). The company could have saved a lot of heartache and money if someone had acted sooner.

Many leaders are afraid of taking appropriate action when all other options have been exhausted. But, especially if you've been giving honest feedback, things are just as uncomfortable for the low-performing employee as they are for you. And many times, your decision to terminate the person could open up new, better-fitting options for them.

One of my first jobs was working in outplacement, helping match workers who had lost their jobs with outplacement packages. My role was to follow up at three and six months with people who had used our package. When I first spoke to them, they were often afraid. But more often than not, when I spoke to them the second time, many had started doing what they had always wanted to do. They told me that losing their job was the push they needed to pursue their true passion.

I'm not trying to dampen the seriousness of letting your employees go if that's what it comes to. But I am telling you three things: (1) Don't give up on employees until you are confident that they aren't going to improve. (2) You have to have the courage to confront the issue and quickly choose the right course of action. And (3) sometimes the best thing for a low-performing employee is giving her the opportunity (hopefully with a good severance package) to find what she's really great at.

Hopefully this last step won't be necessary, and using the tips I presented in this chapter, you'll be able to reinforce great performance and help employees deviate from their unsuccessful behaviors. And once you help turn around someone's poor performance, it's critical to give them a fresh start. Again, to create a capable, successful team, Bankable Leaders Act As If their employees are capable and successful.

Tom Horton, a former tank battalion commander in Germany, is the perfect example of what happens when leaders give their employees a fresh start. In his role, Tom oversaw tank crew maintenance activities.

Battalions have four soldiers on a tank crew: the commander, a gunner, a driver, and a loader. Tom was missing a loader. As luck would have it, Private Jackson, a loader, was assigned to Tom's crew. Tom learned that he was a rehab transfer from a battalion in Swinefurt, Germany. In the military, that's code for "this person messed up and we're sending him away"; soldiers who are court-martialed are always sent to another battalion.

But Tom was determined to give Private Jackson a clean slate. "I don't care what happened in Schnackenberg," Tom told him. "I need a good loader on my team and I have faith in you." Perhaps because of Tom's position on the matter, Private Jackson rose to the occasion and became a superb soldier. Tom promoted him as fast as he could: He arrived as a rehab transfer and left as a corporal. Tom had given him a fresh start and showed everyone that within every poor performer is a superb soldier just waiting to come out.

BANKABLE ACTIONS

No-Fear Feedback

✔ Remember that the purpose of feedback is to help your team be better in the future. Focus your feedback on the future and discuss specific behaviors to duplicate or deviate from.

✔ When providing "Duplicate" feedback, make sure to express gratitude and tell employees exactly what you want them to replicate in the future.

✔ When providing "Deviate" feedback, be direct but express support. Describe the behavior you see that needs to be different and the behavior you want them to replace it with. Establish clear next steps and then follow up to ensure that the deviation is occurring.

How and When to Give Feedback

✔ Never wait until performance appraisals to give feedback. If anything you discuss in performance appraisals is a surprise, shame on you!

✔ Make sure to balance "Duplicate" and "Deviate" feedback in an authentic way.

✔ Understand that classifying employees with performance ratings or scores does more harm than good. Instead, emphasize narrative, qualitative feedback above all else.

What to Do About Poor Performers

✔ Make sure the underperforming employee knows that they're not meeting your expectations.

✔ Act in a way that shows you're truly invested in their success, and work with them to try to find what they're good at doing.

✔ Investigate whether there is something outside their control preventing them from being successful, and do whatever is in your power to mitigate it.

✔ Be honest with yourself and take the appropriate action when you've exhausted all other options. If necessary, work with your HR department to document their performance, and have the courage to help them move on if they're not up to the challenge.

CHAPTER 10

THE CHANGE BLUEPRINT

In the 1990s, the US Army War College coined the term to describe an ever-changing world "VUCA," which stands for Volatile, Uncertain, Complex, and Ambiguous.[1] And although this term was first applied in the military, its use in organizations shortly followed. Think about what each of those four words mean for organizations: We rarely know when things will change (Volatile), have all of the information (Uncertain), or a clear understanding of the factors at play (Complex and Ambiguous).

Whether it's growth, a new business strategy, implementation of a quality program, evolving technology, mergers and acquisitions, reorganizations, shifts in organizational culture, or reductions in force, your company and team are changing all the time, and this trend is not likely to slow or reverse anytime soon. Despite the fact that change can be difficult, we shouldn't dread it: Most change by its very nature is about improvement.

You've probably heard that our DNA is strikingly similar to that of primates. Studies of primates, as it turns out, show just how hard change can be for people. In 1967, G. R. Stephenson conducted a study where he put five monkeys in a cage and hung a banana from the ceiling in the middle.[2] Leading to the banana was a ladder. The monkeys were interested in the banana, of course, but when one of the monkeys climbed the ladder to grab it, researchers sprayed him with ice-cold water. At the same time, the other four monkeys—much to their surprise—were sprayed too. Researchers continued to spray the monkeys with water every time one would climb the ladder, and the monkeys learned pretty quickly that going after the banana was not a great idea.

Next, the researchers swapped out one of the monkeys, replacing him with a new monkey who hadn't seen any of the previous events. The new monkey immediately went for the banana, but the four monkeys who'd been there earlier tackled him to the ground to avoid the water. Researchers continued swapping out the original monkeys with new monkeys. Each time, the new monkey would try to climb the ladder, and the other monkeys would stop him. At the end of the study, there were four monkeys in the cage who had never been sprayed with water, all tackling a new monkey *without knowing why they were doing it.*

We humans, too, often cling to old ways without knowing why. One oft-quoted statistic states that 70 percent of change efforts fail. Though recent research from the University of Brighton indicates that there isn't any real scientific data to back up this number,[3] the fact that it's repeated so often means that the percentage anecdotally resonates with people.

Our proclivity to become set in our ways presents a problem for leaders, whose task is often to introduce change to their department or organization. And when leaders don't successfully navigate change, people become anxious, hopeless, and angry—and that's just the beginning. On the results side, poorly managed change efforts will fail, often with negative consequences for profit, stock price, and even the company's reputation.

There are two ways leaders typically approach change, each corresponding to one side of the Thankfulness–Improvement spectrum. On the left side are leaders who resist change, showing appreciation for the way things are—even if change is needed. This type of leader may drag her feet in implementing change, or be so indirect about it that it's confusing or frustrating for her team. She might also try to minimize the impact of the change by downplaying it. This left-side leader doesn't successfully implement change even though she's trying to take care of her people. And she isn't likely to be successful in her role.

On the right side are leaders who are so focused on improving things that they implement change abruptly and often, causing shell shock among employees. This leader is likely to say, "Team, everything is awful. We're going to do this instead. Let's go!" He charges ahead before his team can catch up, and though he may initially succeed at creating rapid change, the improvement isn't likely to be sustained: People will abandon the new way in favor of older, more comfortable ways, or they simply won't continue to follow the leader in the future. I often see new leaders fail because they try to change things without taking time to understand what *shouldn't* be changed. This type of leader neglects to show appreciation for what's working and doesn't get buy-in from his team.

Several years ago, as dean of the University of Denver's Colorado Women's College, Lynn Gangone and her team were facing a six-figure deficit. In previous roles, when facing similar situations where improvement needed to happen fast, Lynn's pattern was to become gripped by fear, find someone to blame, and then drive her team hard to make the necessary changes. But she had learned that this approach didn't serve her well.

When she first felt herself drawn to drill-sergeant behavior and was tempted to bark orders at her employees, Lynn instead took a deep breath. "We're not going to panic," she told her team. "We're going to envision a different future for the college and use affirmative statements for what this place can be. We're going to do this together, and I need your help."

To give them a shared language for the change, Lynn used a clever metaphor: Change was a bridge she and the team needed to cross. "My tendency," she explained, "is to go, 'Whoo hoo—let's go!' and run across the bridge. But I don't want to run so fast that you're all freaking out and chasing me. I want you to use your energy to get yourselves across the bridge. If I get too far ahead, please communicate that to me." Lynn also made sure to recognize and appreciate her team when they were making the changes that needed to happen to get across the bridge.

This experiment paid off—big time. Lynn's team was enthusiastic, hardworking, and positive about the changes that were taking place. She, too, felt great because she was turning around the organization *and* taking care of her people. Lynn had become bankable while accomplishing something many would have thought impossible: The college turned a six-figure deficit into a surplus that next year. Could she have gotten her team there simply by running across the bridge, focusing only on driving improvement? Possibly, but it would have cost her the energy, enthusiasm, and commitment of her team in the long term, and they'd never have made it across in one piece!

The key to successful change is balancing thankfulness and improvement, which means being clear and positive about what needs to happen while honoring your team's hard work and progress on the way. Bankable Leaders also appreciate what *doesn't* need to change.

In this chapter, we'll hack the code of change. First, you'll learn how your mindset can either make or break your change efforts. Next, I'll introduce the Change Blueprint, which will help you better plan and implement change in your team.

THE CHANGE MINDSET

Anytime you're asked to drive change, you must adopt the right mindset. And unfortunately, many leaders use faulty thinking when it comes to change.

When I was working on a project in South America, I met an HR professional—let's call her Sophia—who has since started her own very successful business and become a dear friend. Many years before we met, Sophia had just been hired as a trainee at a large multinational company in Buenos Aires, Argentina. It was 2001, and the country was going through an economic crisis. She was one of thirty trainees selected from a pool of over 25,000 applicants. It was a lot of pressure, and she was determined to do the best job possible. Unfortunately, Sophia's boss didn't have much confidence in her; she told Sophia she didn't think she was up for the challenge.

Sophia's resentment for her boss grew. The more her boss told her she wasn't doing a good job, the more Sophia would defend herself against the negative feedback. And after a while, she started to feel like maybe her boss was right—maybe she couldn't do it after all. Things got so dire that after two years she decided to leave and take another position with a boss whom she adored. Sadly, the boss at her new company was dismissed just months later. Sophia was shocked and upset—the supportive, competent boss she thought she'd finally found had slipped through her fingers.

But after some time passed, Sophia realized that during those years she worked for the "bad" boss, she'd been wasting energy trying to change something that wasn't in her power to change: No matter how much she argued with the negative feedback her boss gave her, Sophia was never going to change her boss's mind. In life, no one should marry someone and then try to change them—at work, the same is true for bosses. Sophia hadn't succeeded at this pursuit, and her self-confidence was the collateral damage.

She wondered what might have happened if she'd simply accepted the situation and tried to find a few things she liked about her boss. Not only did she think she might have learned something from her boss; she also realized that she probably would have been able to do her job and keep her sanity.

Here's another suboptimal—yet common—change mindset: Many leaders become complacent when changing something *is* in their power. That is, they can implement change, but believe they can't or choose not to. When I worked at the hospital I talked about in chapter 5, I was making rounds one day, talking to patients to see how their stay was going. As I was walking down the hall toward the nurses' station, I ran into a nursing assistant who seemed so distressed that I thought she might need to be admitted to her own hospital. I asked how she was doing and got an earful: "The patient refrigerator is completely empty! Sally usually gets it restocked and she's on vacation."

"Why can't you call food services and get someone up here?" I inquired.

"Oh, I can't do that! I'm not allowed to! Only Sally can call them."

I placed one phone call and the refrigerator was filled within ten minutes. Here's the crazy part: She could have done the same thing. But just like the monkeys in the cage, something was preventing her from climbing the ladder.

So, to save you from both of these fates, allow me to present the Change Mindset Model. It will help you identify what's worth spending your time trying to improve and what's likely to lead to frustration and cynicism. When used correctly, this model helps you focus your energy so you'll get the biggest bang for your buck, even as you embrace the reality of the situation you're in.

Let's get oriented to the model. In the left-hand column are things that, in

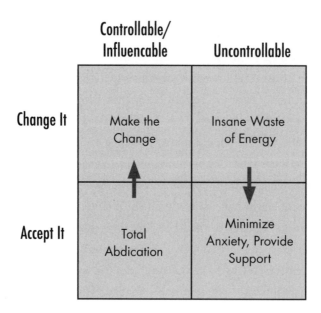

your position, you have the power to change. This could include hiring and fir-ing decisions, work distribution, and business or client decisions. In the right-hand column are things that are out of your control, either because the decisions are above your pay grade or the changes are out of anyone's control. This could include things like regulatory changes, natural disasters, or predetermined bud-gets and resources.

The rows represent the reactions you can choose. As shown in the top-left box, *Make the Change*, you can decide to change something that you believe needs to be improved. This is only advisable if this is something you can actually change. But if you're trying to change something that's out of your control, it's an *Insane Waste of Energy*, as shown in the top-right quadrant.

Most leaders can benefit from taking a step back to determine whether a desired change is within their team's control. If not, can you influence the decision makers? If not, ask yourself, *Is this a sane thing in which to continue investing our time and energy*? If the answer is no, you should cut bait. It may be hard if there are sunk costs, but you'll have more energy to focus on what you should change.

Let's move to the bottom row. The bottom-left response, *Total Abdication*, involves throwing up your hands and saying, "Oh well! Not much I can do about this." I come across many leaders who have incorrectly convinced themselves that things are out of their control when, in fact, they aren't. When something needs to change and changing it is within your power, it's foolish not to try.

Conversely, accepting the situation might be an appropriate reaction if the situation is truly unchangeable. In that case, your job as a leader is to *Minimize Anxiety and Provide Support*, as shown in the bottom-right box. Does this mean that I'm suggesting you give up? Quite the contrary. Let's look at an example of why this is sometimes the best mindset a leader can choose.

I worked with one leader whose organization was moving from one state to another, which meant that everyone, including her, would be let go. Naturally, she was devastated when she heard the news and tried to talk the board out of its decision. But once it became clear that things wouldn't change, she smartly shifted her efforts to helping her staff manage their reactions. Though many leaders in her position would have continued to try to convince the board otherwise, she knew that wasting energy trying to fight things wouldn't result in anything more than frustration.

Now that you've learned how to adopt the right mindset for change, you'll be more confident that you're spending your energy changing things that are worth your time and energy. Read on to learn how to do it.

THE CHANGE BLUEPRINT

As a leader, your approach to change can either make it a reality or doom it completely. Researcher Martin E. Smith of The Stratics Group interviewed people to learn the most common reasons change fails.[4] What topped the list? Ineffective, missing, or conflicting leadership.

That puts a lot of pressure on you, the leader.

In this section, I'll review the three elements of successful change and provide practical suggestions to make your efforts successful. Think of it like a blueprint. To build a successful change, you must have carefully drawn plans.

There are many excellent change models (including those described by John Kotter, William Bridges, Chip and Dan Heath, and Elisabeth Kübler-Ross), and underlying most are three basic elements that make up the core of my Change Blueprint:

- Does your team **understand** the change?
- Does your team **believe** in the change?
- Does your team know what to **do** to support the change?

Each of these elements corresponds (respectively) to the Head, the Heart, and the Hands. If you follow all of the elements of the Change Blueprint, you can drive improvement *and* help your employees feel supported and appreciated for their efforts. For employees to *understand* the change, you have to be transparent, arming them with information—why it's happening and what it means. For employees to *believe* in the change, you have to emotionally support them, create a participative process, and build enough momentum to sustain the change. And for employees to *do* what's needed to successfully implement the change, you have to teach them the right behaviors and recognize them when they demonstrate them.

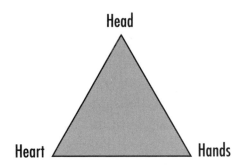

Let's look at an example. In almost every company I've worked with, asking employees for their thoughts about salary and benefits is tantamount to being trapped in a lion's cage wearing a hat made out of steak: You're going to get your head bitten off no matter what. Even if the company is providing competitive pay and benefits, employees are usually dissatisfied.

So just imagine for a moment that you are Mark Gasta. As the chief human resources officer at Vail Resorts, his organization was in a tough spot—every year, their insurance premiums were going up, and it was becoming more and more costly to provide employees the same level of coverage. Recently, the situation reached a tipping point and the company made the decision to move to a consumer-driven health plan. Typically, such plans wreak havoc when implemented, and for one simple reason: They require employees to think about cost when seeking medical care. It doesn't take a rocket scientist to see that Mark and his team were walking into the lion's cage donning fresh steak hats.

Shockingly, though, Mark and his team were able to make this significant organizational change without incurring the wrath of their employees. In fact, the rollout was a huge success. Intrigued? Let's use the Change Blueprint to understand how they did it.

We'll start with the *Head*. Mark and his team knew that they had to be honest with employees rather than giving them a stream of platitudes. So they told employees exactly what was happening: They would still get the best healthcare, but the days of seeking that care blindly and regardless of the cost were over. Vail wanted to help employees be healthy, informed consumers who are doing the best thing for the company. They did everything they could to have transparent communication, telling employees: "We'll save money, and you'll continue to get the best healthcare. We all win."

For the *Heart* element, the team involved employees in the process from the beginning. They held employee focus groups at all levels, incorporating their feedback and reactions into the plan and the communication process. And since a change like this might leave employees feeling utterly powerless, involving them early and often was an especially smart move.

To consider the *Hands* element, the HR team used two approaches. First, they trained leaders on what the change would look like and how to communicate it to their team. For employees, they provided education on how to make smart choices, including tools to help them compare costs in their area. That way, employees could bargain-shop at the same level of quality. This helped them meet their own needs while demonstrating the behavior that was necessary for a successful change.

Another way the team drove the behavior they needed was by showing appreciation. The HR team designed the program so employees could share in the rewards. When the plan outperformed cost-savings expectations for the company in the first year, employees were given a "benefits holiday"—no one had to pay for benefits for two weeks. Vail Resorts is now bucking the trend of rising healthcare costs and preventing year-over-year premium increases.

Now that we have an understanding of how the Change Blueprint works at a high level, let's look at each part more closely.

Understand It

Change efforts are most successful when you arm your team with the right information. In the fall of 1998, CNN Headline News began implementing a series of changes mandated by Time Warner during its acquisition of CNN. Time Warner had decided to replace live newsfeeds with a series of prerecorded segments to reduce operational costs. It also reduced headcount and work hours and introduced a new IT system that would allow the new format to be implemented. To better understand the impact of the leaders' actions on these change efforts, George Daniels of the University of Alabama and Ann Hollifield of the University of Georgia collected data from leaders and employees at Headline News.[5]

In interviews with the researchers, senior leaders reported taking extra effort to communicate about *why* the changes were being made, *how* they related to the company's goals, and *what* the changes meant to employees. For example, employees who would lose their positions were told more than six months beforehand. And though employees weren't happy about the change, when managers kept them informed, they reported higher job satisfaction, more company loyalty, and better attitudes about their leaders. This was especially true when leaders helped employees connect the changes to longer-term company goals. Part of the battle with this kind of change is helping employees not lose sight of the big picture.

So when leaders communicate information about change, not only is change more effective; employees also have more positive attitudes about their leaders. The takeaway for leaders is to clearly paint two pictures: "This is what we must do now and why" and "Here's what things will look like when we're successful."

I once worked with two teams that were merging under one leader during a time of vast organizational change. Though I was brought in to help the teams work better together, the sheer amount of uncertainty and anxiety I was seeing gave me pause.

I decided to sit down with their leader to share my observations and ask a few questions. I asked what the employees knew, if anything, about why the groups were being merged, or what changes to the strategy or operations they would see. "Nothing," she sheepishly admitted. She'd been so busy figuring out the details of the change that she had completely forgotten to communicate, well, anything. Once we identified the problem, it became a lot easier to solve!

Here are some essential questions you must answer if you want your employees to truly understand a change:

1.   What in our organization or environment caused us to consider this change?

2.   What was the process we used to make the decision?

3.   What alternatives did we consider and why did we not select the alternatives?

4.   What will happen if we *don't* change?

5.   What was our true intention behind the change?

6.   What will the change mean for employees' day-to-day lives? What (if anything) will be different?

7.   When will the change take effect?

8.   What are our goals for the next three months? (There should be fewer than three if you want your employees to remember them).

9.   What do we need from employees to make this change successful, whether it is an attitude or actions?

10. How will we measure and monitor our progress and know we've succeeded?

Before we leave this topic, I want to bring up one of the mistakes I see most frequently in this area. I call it the "But I Sent an E-Mail" syndrome. In their

CHANGE MANAGEMENT IN MERGERS AND ACQUISITIONS

You've acquired another company. Or perhaps your company has been acquired. Two discrete teams of people, sets of processes, and ways of working are becoming one. How exactly do you bring these two groups together? Unfortunately, there's no silver bullet. However, research shows us several actions we can take to raise our chances of success.

1. **COMMUNICATE MORE THAN YOU THINK YOU NEED TO:** Share as much information as you can with both sides, and do it often. If you're the acquiring company, remember that your new teammates are probably much more worried than you are. Share as much as possible about plans; otherwise, the best people will be the first ones out the door because they are the most marketable—the ones you most want to keep!

2. **DON'T REINFORCE "US" AND "THEM":** This is a natural mindset when two teams come together. But don't dwell on differences. The sooner you start talking about "all of us" rather than "us" and "them," the sooner your teams start thinking that way and the sooner they'll start acting like one team. What's more, take the best of both organizations— don't just let yourself default to adopting the processes of the acquiring company. Sometimes that's not the best answer!

3. **GET THE TEAM TOGETHER:** During a merger or acquisition, the CEO and senior leadership teams need to be actively engaged and drive the change process from the very top down. But it can't be just senior managers—employees at all levels must be involved in the integration process. As quickly as possible, get the combined teams—at every level—away for the day. Learn more about each other personally and professionally, and create a plan to form a team that will be better than the sum of its parts.

haste to inform employees, many leaders (or worse, communication departments) spend hours composing a single e-mail to the team, then send it and assume that employees now magically understand the change. But think about how many e-mails you get every day. How many seconds do you spend reading and processing each one? I would guess less than a minute. So, to expect that your employees have printed your e-mail, highlighted the important parts, and created flash cards to help them memorize the details is probably just a bit misguided.

A good rule of thumb is to use at least three methods of communication *besides e-mail* when you're conveying information about any important change. These methods can include staff meetings, town halls, video messages, one-on-one meetings, flyers, stand-up meetings, or brown bags. Use the rule of thumb that employees need to hear something three times before internalizing it. You have nothing to lose from erring on the side of overcommunication but everything to lose by not communicating enough.

Believe It

After decades as an emergency room physician, Andy Ziller had recently stepped into a role as medical staff president of Rose Medical Center. One of his first projects was to oversee the implementation of the World Health Organization's surgical checklist. Created to minimize human errors in the same way a pilot's checklist does, the checklist stipulated that the surgical team take a time-out before all procedures to make sure that preventable errors like confusion about the surgical site or drug allergies had been eliminated (as a patient, I just *love* having my surgeries in the right place!).

Dr. Ziller was optimistic about the change. The science was strong: Checklists consistently reduce medical errors and patient harm.[6] He assumed that explaining the science behind the checklists would be enough to convince the surgeons to start using them. But things didn't go quite as smoothly as he predicted. He was absolutely shocked to see that many were disinterested or noncompliant.

He racked his brain for an alternate approach. Having just read Chip and Dan Heath's brilliant book *Switch: How to Change Things When Change Is*

Hard, he remembered that logic makes people think and emotion makes them act. Explaining the science behind the checklists hadn't given the surgeons a reason to care.

He and his colleagues started to focus on emotion-based ways of implementing this change. One source of resistance was pride: "I don't need a stupid checklist to tell me what I've been doing for thirty years!" Dr. Ziller and his team were able to acknowledge and address these concerns directly and saw adoption increase. They also began to involve the surgeons in designing the process so that they would buy into it rather than having it "done to them." Dr. Ziller now calls this the "Transfer of Enthusiasm." Incidentally, but not coincidentally, he was later promoted to be the hospital's chief medical officer.

To help you capitalize on what Dr. Ziller learned, here are some principles to help you manage the emotional aspects of change in your team:

- When people are a part of the change, they are much more likely to buy in. Find a way to involve your team in some aspect of the change process, whether it is planning, communication, implementation, troubleshooting, or ongoing support.

- Even if it is a small change, never underestimate its emotional impact. Frequently express your support of your team during the change.

- If something is ending because of the change, give your employees an opportunity to grieve the loss, either by discussing it or marking the ending with a celebration or meeting.

- Help create momentum by finding employees who can serve as early adopters of the change. When people perceive that their colleagues are jumping on the bandwagon, they are more likely to want to do it themselves.

- Show gratitude for your employees' sacrifices. Thank them in advance, before the change happens. During the change, show your appreciation for their efforts. After the change, help them see how their efforts contributed to the success of your team or the organization and reward the right behaviors you want to see.

Do It

The final element of the Change Blueprint is ensuring that your employees actually know what they're supposed to do to adopt the change. Many change efforts fail because it isn't clear how people should behave to support the change on a day-to-day basis. For example, if the CNN Headline News employees hadn't known how to use their new equipment, the change would have failed even though the team had bought in to the change. So do your team a favor and help them understand exactly what behaviors you need from them.

And once you've made your expectations clear, you must model the behavior you want for your team. When Morre Dean assumed his role as CEO of Parker Adventist Hospital, it quickly became clear that he would need to change the hospital's culture when it came to e-mail communication. Frequently, he saw conflict escalate in e-mails: Recipients would misinterpret the tone, blind-copy others, or forward e-mails to people who shouldn't be involved. "As long as I'm CEO," Morre told his team, "we will not hash out conflict in e-mails."

In his second week on the job, a divisive issue with a physician popped up and tempers started to flare. Morre knew that this was a "make or break" moment for him, and that he'd have to act decisively. The e-mails were flowing and people started getting upset, as usual. They started asking Morre, "Aren't you going to respond to this e-mail from the doctor?"

"Yes I will," he replied, "but only to thank him for his thoughts and ask to set up a time to meet in person."

Morre successfully resolved this conflict without using e-mail, and a year and a half later, the way the staff communicates has indeed changed. Instead of assailing each other with e-mails, everyone sits down to talk in person. Morre's clear expectations for how everyone's behavior had to change paid off—they knew what needed to be done and they did it.

Here are some pointers for ensuring that your team members adopt the right behaviors during times of change:

- Help them understand how the change will affect their day-to-day decisions. Tell them exactly what you want them to do. One easy tool is "Start/

CHANGE MANAGEMENT
FOR **VIRTUAL LEADERS**

Leaders of virtual teams face a number of communication barriers that do not occur in a co-located work environment. The lack of face-to-face interaction restricts the opportunity for everyday support that may keep individuals committed to the team.

1. **CREATE A SHARED CONTEXT:** As the leader of a virtual team, you can create a shared context that is similar to that of a physical work environment. Ensure that all team members have access to the same information and share the same tools and work processes. You can foster this by standardizing certain aspects of work, such as work norms and the tools that team members use.

2. **GET ON THE SAME PAGE:** One of the biggest risks for change in virtual teams is "dramatic interpretation." That is, different team members will interpret a message differently or place emphasis on different portions of a message. This is mainly due to the lack of verbal cues that would normally help clue people in to the meaning of your message. Therefore, it is crucial that you check in to ensure that team members are on the same page if given the same message or task.

3. **SPEAK REGULARLY:** It seems easy, but in a time of rapid change, virtual teams may need a bit more hand-holding because they may not have the proverbial watercooler as a source of information. Even if it's an e-mail or a five-minute call, try to talk to everyone at least a few times per week.

Stop/Continue." After the change, what do you want your employees to *start* doing, *stop* doing, or *continue* doing?

■ Conduct a formal or informal assessment to see whether your team possesses the skills needed to implement the change. If new skills or knowledge are required, provide it early and often, through training, mentoring, or coaching. For example, the CNN Headline News employees needed to get trained on the new software.

■ When employees start to engage in the right behaviors, make a big deal out of it. Thank them for their contributions and provide reinforcement for the behavior, through praise, appreciation, or rewards.

■ ■ ■

I was recently meeting with an executive, an engineer by background, whom I'd just started coaching. I asked, "As we work to help you grow, what are your non-negotiables—the things about yourself that you never want to change?" He thought for a moment and replied, "My belief that things can always be better."

Granted, we had some work to do on the people side of the equation, but this leader had uncovered a fundamental characteristic of exceptional leaders. No matter how far they've come, they have the courage to say, "Things can always be better," even if others see it as impossible.

So in your journey as a Bankable Leader, remember this right-side refrain. And if you balance the aspiration for constant improvement with gratitude and support of your people, you will be unstoppable.

BANKABLE ACTIONS

Adopt the Change Mindset

- ✔ Distinguish between the things you can control or influence and the things that are out of your control.

- ✔ If a change needs to be made and you can control or influence it, charge ahead with your team and make it happen.

- ✔ If a change needs to be made but it is out of your control, don't waste energy. Rather, support your team and help them manage their anxiety.

Apply the Change Blueprint

- ✔ Help your team understand the change by explaining why it is taking place, how it will impact employees, what the process will be, what alternatives were considered, and what the cost will be if the change isn't adopted.

- ✔ Make sure your team believes in the change by involving them in the process, expressing your support for their sacrifices, and showing gratitude for their willingness to leave the old way behind.

- ✔ Clearly communicate what employees should do to support the change. Equip them to demonstrate the behaviors the change requires. Be generous with appreciation when they demonstrate those behaviors.

Part IV

BE HAPPY *and*
DRIVE PRODUCTIVITY

If anyone wants to annoy me as much as possible, all they have to do is say, "Tasha, you need to relax." At some point, nearly everyone I know—family, friends, clients, bosses, peers—has said this to me. Obviously, the reason I find it so annoying is because, nine times out of ten, I actually *do* need to relax.

I remember one business trip to Buenos Aires where I clocked a ninety-hour week, facilitating meetings by day and fiercely preparing for the next one each night. At the end of the week, I collapsed on the bed in my hotel room and slept for twenty straight hours. Despite being one of the most fulfilling projects of my career, this was an embarrassing Type A moment.

People with a Type A personality tend to be unusually involved in their work. They push themselves to cross things off their to-do list, lest they feel guilty for not being productive. Perhaps as a result, they tend to be disproportionately stressed out by their jobs and experience poorer health.[1]

My Type A compatriots and I may also appear anxious or wound up. Even if you haven't had a Type A boss, you can imagine how stressful it is. I often annoy my husband on Saturday mornings by interrupting his leisurely breakfast and saying things like, "OK—let's make a list of all the things we need to get done this weekend!" For me, productivity is like a drug. When I'm crossing item after item off my to-do list, I feel unstoppable. But on the days I don't, I am ridden with shame.

A recent experience helped me truly understand the value of balancing productivity and happiness. When I started working at the hospital I discussed in chapter 5, I had a huge task ahead of me: building a development program for our leaders from scratch. I'd show up to my office every day and work like crazy, often forgetting to eat lunch or informally socialize.

But all around me, things seemed to move at a different pace. I felt like I had stepped onto a different planet. Everywhere I looked, there was a celebration or a game or an event. On one hand, I was working with a group of serious clinicians who were poised to save lives at a moment's notice. But on the other hand, they were the most amicable, fun-loving bunch of people I'd ever worked with. Most meetings began with hugs, food, and merriment. And there was a genuine sense of joy. After a few months, I started to notice how great I felt when I came to work. I'd look forward to Mondays—like I was going to hang out with my friends.

About six months after I started my role, I learned about the annual employee picnic. Every spring, the employees—with the help of their leaders—would spend months planning a gathering complete with tents, games, and food.

On the day of the event, I was facing a deadline: one of our courses was about to launch. I was stressed and stuck. I'd been staring at the same PowerPoint slide for what seemed like hours when the Outlook reminder for the picnic popped up on my screen. "I do *not* have time for this today," I grumbled, sighing dramatically. But knowing it would be a career-limiting move to skip the picnic, I dragged myself to the back parking lot.

When I stepped outside, it was pure magic. There were picnic tables covered with checkered tablecloths and carnival games. Dozens of employees were smiling in the warm spring sun, waiting in line for lunch, which was being served out of large catering tins by the senior leaders of the hospital.

At that moment, it hit me like a ton of bricks. I had been so obsessed with finishing my work that I had been missing the joy of the event (thank goodness I forced myself to leave the office or I would've missed out entirely). I decided to enjoy myself and purge the guilt I felt for leaving my project. I had fun and was even more shocked when I got back to my office: The project that had been tormenting me seemed to finish itself. I learned that when you have fun, the work will get done.

Viewing happiness and productivity as mutually exclusive is one of the most common mistakes in modern organizations. As a leader, you can't take care of people without letting them enjoy themselves, and you can't drive results in the long term without helping your team produce in a smart way. Not only can these two outcomes exist at the same time; in fact, they are interdependent. You need one to optimally produce the other.

You might be familiar with Mihaly Csikszentmihalyi's concept of flow[2] or Marshall Goldsmith's term "Mojo." Think of the last time you were so absorbed in an activity that you lost all sense of time. That's flow: Where we're happiest, most confident, and most productive. Both flow and Mojo are the outcomes of leaders who live in the middle—their teams are unimaginably productive *and* loving every minute of what they're doing (or at least most minutes).

So what stops leaders from doing both? Much of the time, it's the belief that we experience happiness at the *expense* of productivity. Or we think that if we're being productive, we can't be having fun at the same time. The spectrum looks like this:

BE HAPPY

The "Only Fun Matters" Leader

DRIVE PRODUCTIVITY

The "Only Productivity Matters" Leader

On the left-hand side of the spectrum is the "Only Fun Matters" leader, who creates fun without asking for productivity. These are the leaders who let their employees leave the office at 3:00 p.m. every day, or who are so interested in creating a positive and enjoyable environment that they don't also expect hard work in return. They might be so informal or relaxed that they don't drive a sense of urgency in their team. A team led by an "Only Fun Matters" leader is fat, happy, and unsuccessful. Of course, these leaders don't stay leaders for long. They are often labeled slackers who don't apply themselves. It probably goes without saying that this is majorly limiting to a career.

On the right-hand side is the "Only Productivity Matters" leader. Many leaders are so overly focused on productivity that they exterminate fun. This could be because they are Type A, or because they want to get the work out of the way *before* they allow fun. But the work is almost never done, so this leader's team will be waiting a long time for the payoff. The result of this type of leadership is productivity in the short run but burnout and costly turnover in the long run. Being on the far right side of the spectrum also doesn't do much for the leader. In well-led organizations, they'll drive away their best employees.

Bankable Leaders are able to drive productivity while creating an enjoyable work environment. Most leaders, however, are fighting an uphill battle against the strange, joy-killing belief that pervades most modern organizations: that a team's productivity is directly proportionate to how many hours they work.

The irony is that by driving our team to work long hours, we are chipping away at the road of progress that was paved for us nearly one hundred years ago by Henry Ford. While the forty-hour workweek seems torturous enough, previous generations didn't have it so good. During the Industrial Revolution, workers in Britain and the United States were often forced to put in ten to sixteen hours a day, six days a week.

In 1926, Henry Ford, the founder of Ford Motor Company, sent shockwaves across the United States by implementing a five-day, forty-hour workweek for employees in his factories. Edsel Ford, Henry's son and Ford president from 1919 to 1943, later noted that "every man needs more than one day a week for rest and recreation . . . The Ford Company always has sought to promote [an] ideal home life for its employees. We believe that in order to live properly every man should have more time to spend with his family."[3]

But here's the interesting part. Henry Ford also made this decision *because he believed it would make his employees more productive.* He knew that when workers are less burnt out, they produce better work products than if they're overworked, sleep-deprived zombies. No matter what your team members are doing, flow simply can't be maintained if they're exhausted and worn down. In fact, neurobiology research has proven that our brains need rest to reach certain levels of activity (we'll talk more about that later).

After Ford made this bold move, other companies began to follow suit. Sometimes it was because unions were demanding shortened workweeks, but when managers begrudgingly gave in, they were shocked to see productivity dramatically increase. By the 1950s, the five-day workweek had become a way of life.

Flash forward to present day. Many of us spend far more than eight hours at work or working. But often, it doesn't result in more productivity. Think about a typical day in the office. You arrive, turn on your computer, and answer a few e-mails. Then maybe you wander down the hall to the coffee machine and leisurely pour a cup of coffee. You run into your friends in the hallway and discuss last night's football game. Then you wander back to your office, start a task but get interrupted by a member of your team. And on and on it goes. By the time you go home at 7:00 p.m., you might have had only five to six productive hours. When you're dragging yourself out of bed after too little sleep and too much work, do you ever wonder if there's a better way?

In this section, you'll discover how Bankable Leaders create a fun environment where stuff actually gets done. In chapter 11, I'll show you how ultimate productivity is achieved when you allow your team to take smart breaks. In chapter 12, you'll learn about the OLT Principle, designed to get the same amount of work done in less time. Then, in chapter 13, we'll talk about why most leaders need to loosen up—and help their team do the same. So, in the most efficient and enjoyable manner possible, let's jump in.

CHAPTER 11

WHY NO ONE CAN WORK EIGHTY HOURS A WEEK—FOR LONG

General Lester Lyles, a three-star general and vice chief of staff in the US Air Force, was hard at work one day when his assistant handed him an urgent fax. It was from his boss, General Henry Viccellio, a four-star general and commander of the Air Force Materiel Command.

Lyles glanced down at the handwritten note with General Viccellio's signature across the top. The title was "Nose to the Grindstone Nine," followed by the names of nine officers in General Viccellio's command.

"Gentlemen," the note read, "I have personally reviewed your leave balances. For the good of your family and the good of your command, I am directing you to please provide your vacation plans by close of business today. Thank you."

Lyles sighed. He put it down and called his wife immediately. His vacation plans were submitted in mere minutes.

The man who delivered that fax to General Lyles was his assistant, Mark Hughes, and Mark never forgot the lesson.

As had been the case with the "Nose to the Grindstone Nine," many of us take on the mindset that the mission is more important than our—or our team's—well-being. We live in a world where what we accomplish in a day seems to be a barometer for our value. One survey reports that 55 percent of people report that their workload has increased since the Great Recession, with 27 percent saying it has *doubled*.[1] This is shameful.

Most leaders I know are in a downward spiral of stress, and I'm guessing this may be the case for you too. You might be burning yourself out, either through a self-imposed but unrealistic work ethic or pressure from the top. Maybe you're holding on to work that you should be delegating. Or perhaps you're spending your energy in a scattered, unfocused manner. Anyone can work fifty, sixty, seventy hours a week—for a while. But trust me, it will catch up with you. It's not a matter of if, but when.

As a response to the stress you're feeling, you might be acting like a slave driver or expecting your team to do twice the work with half the people. According to The Hay Group, half of all employees report that their current workload is unsustainable.[2] And 63 percent of those putting in extra hours note that their boss doesn't appreciate the effort. This problem is pervasive. I once had a boss who was famous for calling his direct reports at 5:00 p.m. every Friday to see if they were there. It probably goes without saying that working for this person was pretty tedious.

While some leaders are overt in their slave-driver behavior, others may send subtler signals that employees aren't working hard enough. I worked with one leader who was notorious for staying late—sometimes until 10:00 p.m. He would tell his staff repeatedly, "Don't do what I do. It's bad." But what do you think his staff focused on? Not what he said, but what he did. Most felt guilty when they didn't work late themselves.

And whether you are doing this to yourself, to your team, or both, the consequences can be disastrous. You've already heard that working too much is unhealthy. But the consequences are far more sweeping. Over a period of five years, University College of London epidemiologist Marianna Virtanen and her colleagues examined the relationship between long hours and brain functioning in British civil servants.[3] The participants completed a variety of tests to evaluate intelligence, verbal recall, and vocabulary. Compared to those who worked forty hours per week, participants who worked more than fifty-five hours showed poorer vocabulary and reasoning. Let me be clear: *We actually get stupider when we work too much.*

What's more, and somewhat counterintuitively, there is strong evidence that vacations help us be productive. As referenced in a brilliant Harvard Business Network blog post entitled "More Vacation Is the Secret Sauce,"[4] Tony Schwartz cites a 2006 Ernst & Young study that showed that for each additional ten hours of vacation employees took, performance reviews were 8 percent higher the following year. So taking vacations will help your employees do a better job for you. Now are you listening?

Leaders who provide a balanced environment maximize output, employee happiness, and even employee health. The Framingham Heart Study, a massive longitudinal research program that began in 1948 (they were the first to find evidence of the link between smoking and cancer), reports that taking annual vacations reduces the risk of heart attack by 30 percent in men and 50 percent in women.[5]

Bankable Leaders understand the importance of breaks and recognize that there is an upper limit for what anyone can produce. Helping your team members break up the work they're doing will increase their well-being in the short and long term and improve the quality of their work.

I'll be the first person to tell you: This can be incredibly hard, especially for high-functioning, successful people. It's a running joke among my family and friends that I am literally addicted to work. For me, the invigorating feeling of accomplishing "just one more thing" at the end of a long day can often be too much to resist. Balancing what I know to be true (I have to pace myself or I'll have a heart attack) and what I feel compelled to achieve is a daily battle.

This affliction has a cure, but for leaders who suffer from it, resolving to work less or to give the team a break might feel vague and difficult. So in this chapter, we'll cover an approach that has made a huge difference not just for me but for many of the leaders I've worked with. First, we'll talk about the brilliance of breaks, whether it's a single day off or a month-long sabbatical. We'll then turn our focus to "power breaks," which you can incorporate into your (and your team's) daily routine to sustain focus and quality.

BREAKS MAKE US BRILLIANT—
AND PREVENT BURNOUT

About seven years after Mark Hughes delivered the "Nose to the Grindstone Nine" fax, he was working in Washington, DC, as an air force colonel. One day, he was visited by two old friends, Art Zeile and Joel Daly, who used to work for him at a military satellite communications organization. They had just founded Inflow, a start-up that managed data center operations for businesses, and they were raising their second round of funding. In need of some gray hair, they asked Mark to join them in Denver as their vice president of corporate operations and subsequently their vice president of finance.

The year was 2000. The technology industry was struggling, and Mark was working hard, often on nights and weekends. This went on for months. Then, on one blizzardy Friday in January 2002, Mark decided to leave the office early. It was his birthday and he wanted to spend it with his family. But Joel stopped him.

"Sorry, Mark, but we need to have a budget meeting. Today." Mark's stomach dropped, but he agreed to stay. Later that day, Mark entered Art's office—Art and Joel had been waiting for him. "Thanks for coming Mark," said Art. "First, you're going to need to give us your phone and your computer."

What? Mark thought to himself. *Am I getting fired?*

"Second," Art went on, "here are tickets for you and your family to go to Phoenix for a long weekend." He slid an envelope across the conference table. "They are waiting downstairs." Mark was stunned. He was rewarded with a most unexpected vacation! And how thoughtful—his leaders had planned it all for him. He proceeded to have a wonderful weekend with his family and arrived back at work on Tuesday refreshed and ready to dive into the challenges of the week.

Art and Joel had made a bankable move. Even if we love what we do, when our leisure time declines, so does our life satisfaction. Working too many hours drains and depresses us, leaving little extra energy for being productive. According to the Mayo Clinic, burnout is a special type of stress; sufferers are so exhausted—physically, mentally, and emotionally—that the value of their work, and their feelings of capability to do it well, plummet.[6] If you often feel impatient with coworkers or clients, get cynical about your job, or struggle to drag yourself out of bed in the morning, you're probably experiencing burnout. Burnt-out people have poor health and sleep habits and are more likely to engage in "passive coping" through eating, drinking, or drugs. For leaders, burnt-out employees are a huge liability: Their output is horrible and they are just about as *un*productive as anyone could be. Having even one burnt-out person on your team is dangerous.

One of the most effective antidotes to burnout is time off. Today, most countries in Europe give workers at least four weeks of vacation each year, with Germans and Swedes averaging seven weeks.[7] But according to the Center for Economic Policy and Research, 25 percent of Americans don't take any vacation at all, either because they have it but don't use it or because their employer doesn't provide it.[8] And according to the Adecco Group, only one in four workers who accrue vacation time uses all of it.[9]

Why would anyone choose *not* to take a vacation they rightfully earned? For many employees, fear is a factor—fear of missing out on that promotion, fear of topping the layoff list, fear of the work that will be waiting for them upon their return, fear of being judged by their boss or coworkers. According to Adecco, one in five employees reports feeling upset when their coworkers take time off![10] Bankable Leaders realize that employees are fighting against this current and actively help them balance time off with hard work.

More Frequent, Shorter Vacations May Be Better

Even though burnt-out employees typically need two weeks away from work to recharge their batteries, long vacations are rarely the norm in the United States: Only 14 percent of workers take a week at a time according to a Harris poll.[11] And I often hear employees lamenting that the cost of taking even a few days off outweighs the benefits. But there's good news: Even if you can't take off two or more consecutive weeks, employees who take vacations show less stress levels no matter how long the vacation is.[12] More specifically, a research team led by Jessica de Bloom of Radboud University Nijmegen in the Netherlands found that even vacations of just a few days increased health and well-being.[13] Yet, after participants returned to work, the benefits faded after only five days.

Given the benefits of any vacation and the short-lived nature of those benefits, helping your employees take even a day or two off will impact their productivity and well-being. It will pay off for them and for you!

Time Off Is Time Off

Okay, it's confession time: Do you sneak off to check your work e-mail on vacation? Or even take a few calls? This is actually okay in small quantities. De Bloom and colleagues found that even though people who worked during vacations showed smaller increases in health and well-being than those who didn't, they still showed an increase. However, when your employees feel like they *have* to work during their time off, research shows that the positive impact of their time away is shorter-lived.

So—please—give your employees space when they're out of the office! I know how hard it is to feel okay about unplugging: On our honeymoon, my husband had to literally lock my BlackBerry in our hotel safe to keep me away from it. But I did notice that after a few days, I was more relaxed than I'd been in a long time. Help your team see the benefits of unplugging while away and show them that you don't want or expect them to respond to messages. If they do need to stay plugged in for some reason, ask them to check in no more than once per day.

To help your employees believe you when you tell them to unplug while they're away, do it yourself. I once worked with a manager who would often take three weeks off to visit her family in Canada. I asked her, "How do you deal with the stress of being away?"

"It's easy," she said. "I turn my department over to my best people. They have my phone number if something goes wrong."

Before we turn to a few practical tips and suggestions, one final point: It's helpful to remember that your top performers might be the most prone to not taking enough time off to recharge.

Carolyn De Rubertis had a top-notch employee who ran her medical practice's front desk. One December, she came to Carolyn with a problem—she was struggling to cover the front desk the week of Christmas.

"Why don't we sit down and look at the moving parts?" Carolyn said. "We can try to figure out what's possible." When she looked at the rough schedule her employee had put together, Carolyn noticed that she had put herself on the schedule for the whole week of Christmas.

"I have to ask this," Carolyn ventured. "I know that you had been planning on visiting your mom in Wyoming. Why aren't you taking the time off you planned?" The employee sheepishly admitted that it had been too hard to balance the schedule, so she put herself in to solve the problem.

Carolyn smiled. "I appreciate that you're that kind of team player—but this isn't the best solution, because it isn't fair. It's important for you to go to Wyoming, and we'll find a way to make that happen."

Carolyn thought back to the reason she had made her the front desk manager in the first place: She was a problem solver. But, she realized, she had to teach this budding leader that she was not the solution to every problem. They ended up finding an eager-to-work employee who was happy to cover the front desk that week. And most importantly, Carolyn's employee got to see her mom in Wyoming.

Let's review a few takeaways to help your team enjoy the benefits of time out of the office:

- Try to explain to employees that they will gain more than they lose from taking time away from the office.

- Remember that vacations need not be long: Even a few days away can help your team recharge.

- Go out of your way to make sure you're helping your employees—especially the top performers—take vacations without feeling stigmatized.

- Realize that you set the example. Remember the "Nose to the Grindstone Nine"? Say, "It's very important to me that you take care of your health and well-being. Please, take your allotted vacation time." If they're not taking days off, find out why and help them do it.

- Before your employees leave for their vacation, make sure that you and your team have all of the information necessary to continue projects in their absence.

- When your employees are out of the office on vacation, let them unplug! Don't e-mail them. Do everything you can to resolve problems without calling them.

THE POWER OF POWER BREAKS

Now that you know the brilliance of time away from the office, we'll turn our focus to helping you make the most of your team members' energy while they're in the office.

You cannot do your best thinking in what my friend Dana calls "a deluge of minutiae." Researchers from the University of Illinois at Urbana–Champaign studied the effect of periodic breaks on tasks that require precision and attention.[14] Students were asked to memorize sets of numbers and then given a monotonous task that required attention to detail. One group was shown the numbers once and then asked to complete the monotonous task for forty minutes. Another group was shown the numbers three times during the forty-minute period devoted to the task—think of the numbers as a "power break," because the students could turn their focus away from the task for a few minutes. The results were striking: Even though students in the power-break group spent less total time on the task, they were *more vigilant* while completing the same amount of work.

Suggest that your team members take a short break every hour—even if it's just a minute—especially when they're working on projects that require focus, such as writing a proposal or preparing a budget. Encourage them to get up to stretch, look out the window, or even (Heaven forbid) check their Facebook feed. I once worked for someone who used to set up putt-putt golf outside his office. When I was working on a tedious project or report, it was nice to have something to take our minds off things for a few minutes before going back to work with a renewed focus.

In addition to taking power breaks throughout the day, consider evenings and weekends as great power-break opportunities. Many of today's workplaces are set up with the expectation that employees will be available around the clock. iPhones, BlackBerrys, laptops, web conferencing—they were all designed to help us be more efficient, but they've turned into a tether. This is especially true in global organizations. I recently spoke to a leader in such a company who told me that her day starts on the phone with the Middle East offices at 6:00 a.m. and ends at 10:00 p.m. with calls to Asia. This is no way to live, for Pete's sake. It's insanity!

My husband frequently tells me that I am in a hell of my own making: By responding to my clients' e-mails at 11:00 p.m., I'm creating the expectation that I will do the same thing in the future (remember operant conditioning from chapter 8?). But if I simply waited until the beginning of the next day, I'd have set the correct expectation—and the client would still probably perceive me as responsive.

Expecting employees to be constantly available can be dangerous. I worked with one leader who joined a fast-growing start-up. He was told he needed to get a BlackBerry and keep it with him at all times. Initially, he assumed that this was for emergencies. His naiveté became apparent when, one Saturday morning, one of the founders sent an e-mail to the senior leadership team, and by 5:00 p.m. that day, there was a string of more than thirty replies. He soon learned that at this company there was no concept of detachment from work. He grieved this loss bitterly, and his nonwork friends would mock him for stepping out of the bar to check e-mail at 10:00 p.m. while they were all out for a few pints of beer. The situation ended up interfering with his relationships with his friends and—worse—with his wife.

But here's the scariest part. In a matter of months, this leader became completely desensitized and reset his definition of "normal response time." He inadvertently started expecting his own team to meet the standard set for him—it was a terrible domino effect. He eventually—and wisely—left the company for a role that gave him back his personal life.

Think about it. If you have a brilliant idea on a Saturday and e-mail your team, how might they react? If *your* boss e-mails you over the weekend and you are a conscientious employee, you'd feel obligated to respond, right? I see leaders do this often: They simply want to write the e-mail when they have the idea but have no expectation of a response until the next business day. But the employees get the e-mail and assume that they need to respond right away. It's a vicious

TAKING BREAKS FOR **WORKAHOLICS**

Workaholics find it hard to take breaks for the simple reasons that they are workaholics: the urgency, impatience, and competitive drive that define that personality type. If you are a workaholic leader (be honest!), you must find ways to take breaks to keep your own fires stoked and set a good example for your team.

1. **CREATE A "STOP RULE:"** Stop rules tell you when you're going to say "Enough!" and stop working. They can be enjoyment-based (i.e., stop when you are no longer enjoying yourself), time-based (i.e., stop every two hours or at 5:00 p.m.), or quantity-based (i.e., an "enough rule"— stop when you believe you have done enough). If you can't trust yourself to actually stop, enlist the help of a colleague or friend.

2. **PLACE A FRIENDLY WAGER:** Find another workaholic who wants to reform and create a "Life Balance Challenge." Make things interesting: The loser donates money to the winner's favorite charity, buys the winner an extravagant lunch, etc. Track yours hours of work and see whose weekly numbers are trending in the right direction.

3. **FIND A HOBBY:** Research shows that workaholics are less likely to enjoy their at-home and leisure activities and that they show increased boredom when they're not working. Try to pick up new interests and hobbies by joining a local club or organization and you will soon find more meaning outside of work.

cycle. I'm not saying you and your team shouldn't respond to urgent issues when necessary, but it should be the exception, not the rule.

To make sure you're allowing your team enough power-break time between workdays, pay careful attention to the response culture you are creating. Tell your team directly and often, "Unless I alert you beforehand that something important might be coming through, I don't expect you to check your e-mail or respond to anything from me outside of business hours." Or you can simply save weekend and evening e-mails as drafts, or tell your e-mail program to send them later, during business hours.

■ ■ ■

If you've read this chapter and are still feeling a sense of uneasiness about your or your team's level of stress and overwork, it might be time to take a step back and look at your own beliefs. If you find that you simply can't stop yourself from working too many hours or that you're continuing to expect that from your employees, there might be something deeper going on. Below are some questions to help you discover what's really behind your singular focus on work and productivity. I'd suggest sitting down, either by yourself or with a trusted friend or confidant, to go over your responses.

Reflection Questions

- Were you raised by parents or family members who pressured you to accomplish a lot? How did they reward you for working hard or criticize you for not doing so?

- Is there a part of you that judges your team's (or your own) worth by how much time they spend working? Why? Is this fair to them? What might be the effect of this in the long term?

- Are you taking on too much work—or asking others to do too much—because you want to please people? What are you worried will happen if you say no?

- How much is your drive to achieve based on money? Is the relationship between the amount you work and your financial success a realistic or causal one? How does your drive for more affect your team?

- Are you using work to escape something else going on in your life? If that's the case, what is the effect on your team seeing you do this?

I've been wrestling with these questions for years. But as Austrian poet Rainer Maria Rilke wisely noted, there is power in the questions themselves, because if you "live the questions now . . . you will gradually, without even noticing it, live your way into the answer."[15]

BANKABLE ACTIONS

Remember That Breaks Make Us Brilliant

✔ Proactively combat burnout by encouraging your employees to take time off. Your top performers might have the hardest time doing this.

✔ If long vacations are difficult, help your team take a few short breaks during the year at a minimum. The benefits will actually be greater if they take more frequent breaks rather than one long one.

✔ Don't bother your employees while they are out of the office. Make sure everything is covered before they leave. Working during time off will diminish the benefits of the break.

✔ Use your own time out of the office as a chance to groom your high-potentials and give them more responsibility while you're gone. And if people see you unplug, they'll be more likely to do the same.

Don't Forget to Take Power Breaks

✔ When your employees are working on a long or tedious project, help them take at least one short break per hour to help them focus.

✔ Help your employees use their evenings and weekends as power breaks (and do the same yourself). Be careful about the response culture you set. As much as possible, try to avoid sending or replying to e-mails to your team outside business hours.

✔ Make your expectations clear to your team: What types of emergencies or urgent issues do you expect them to respond to, and which can wait until the next business day?

CHAPTER 12

THE OLT PRINCIPLE

I once worked with an executive team to develop a strategic plan. The process had been full of great ideas, and after a month or so of work we were almost finished.

All that was left was to take the twelve strategic initiatives they had brainstormed and choose the most important ones. I posed the question to the group. The CEO turned red. He stood up and pointed to the sea of flipcharts that surrounded us. "They're all important," he said simply. "We're done."

I looked around the room and saw confused expressions, open mouths, and a general sense of desperation. But of course, no one was going to disagree with the boss. So the team took its twelve different priorities and did the best they could. Though the company made their plan that year, it was at the expense of the well-being of many employees.

As this example illustrates, constantly having new projects or tasks added to our already packed schedules is the new normal. In modern organizations, most people have way too much on their plates. Think about it: When was the last time you received an order from your boss telling you to *stop* doing anything? And just like you, your team is bombarded with goals, initiatives, and corporate fire drills.

In this situation, most leaders choose one of two responses: They push their employees to get everything done, or they downplay the new initiatives lest they upset or overload their team. The first response often leads to questions from the team like, "When will we have time to do our day jobs?" or "Will we be getting more resources to make this happen?" These reactions are completely understandable—even the best employees can only do so much. And when your team members have too much on their plates, they'll feel helpless and hopeless.

Leaders who choose the second response and put off new initiatives might say things like, "Oh, here corporate goes again—trying to get us to do more stuff. Don't worry. I won't make you do this." Though they're often heroes to their team, these leaders are limiting their own success and probably creating a reputation for being difficult.

While these two outcomes—"get everything done" or "give your employees a break"—feel mutually exclusive, Bankable Leaders accomplish both. How? They aggressively focus their team's efforts and minimize unnecessary expenditure of energy.

When I worked at CH2M HILL, a large engineering company, my boss—Jim Downey—and I were swapping stories at the end of a very long week.

"Why do we have so many smart, *un*-lazy people in this company?" he asked. "I'd pick a smart, 'lazy' person before a smart, un-lazy person anytime."

I looked at him, somewhat perplexed.

"I don't mean lazy like they don't care or want to do a good job," he continued. "I mean lazy because they find the simplest good solution possible to problems. Lazy because they delegate. Lazy because they focus and eliminate unnecessary work."

As someone who was guilty of overcomplicating, well, everything, Jim's words caused me to reevaluate how I was accomplishing my own work.

A few years later, I met Bob Chapman (the Bankable Leader I've mentioned several times in this book), who soon became a client and good friend. In one of our first conversations, he shared his strategy for completing his master's degree while working full time. With his graduate advisor's permission, Bob outsourced the statistical analysis for his thesis—he didn't need that level of knowledge in statistics for a career as an HR leader. So he conserved the time and energy but still attained the desired result: completion of his master's degree. This is smart "laziness" in action.

It is not a crime to be more efficient. It is not a crime to focus your efforts. It is not a crime to do something in the simplest way possible. In fact, realizing when to *stop* investing time and energy in your team's projects might be just as important as knowing when to *start*.

These days, work is a marathon—if you sprint the first five miles (i.e., pile things on your team without understanding the impact it will have on their long-term performance), you might not finish the race. Focusing your team also helps them feel satisfied and productive and encourages them to enjoy what they're doing. Think about a day where you've crossed off everything on your to-do list—you leave the office triumphantly, ready to come back the next day to tackle the next challenge.

In this chapter, you'll learn a tool to focus your team's energy on the outcomes that are most important for your success. It's called the "One Less Thing" Principle—the OLT Principle for short—and it's so simple it is startling. But before we dive into the tool itself, let's review the law of diminishing returns.

THE LAW OF DIMINISHING RETURNS

As we discussed in chapter 11, most leaders feel constant pressure to work insane hours and ask the same of their team. But we saw that quantity often trumps quality, leading to suboptimal results and miserable employees.

One of the greatest evangelists for efficient, focused work is Timothy Ferriss, author of the best-selling book *The 4-Hour Workweek*.[1] Ferriss advocates the concept he calls "lifestyle design," bucking the convention that we should work hard now and rest when we retire. Ferriss wisely notes that work will always expand to fit the amount of time we've allocated to it. That explains why in school, no matter how much notice you had to complete your term paper, you always finished it the week—or night—before. And though the concept of a four-hour workweek is probably a dream for most of us, Ferriss has a point.

Building on Ferriss' ideas, most of the time, people think of the relationship between effort/time and output/results as being linear, like this:

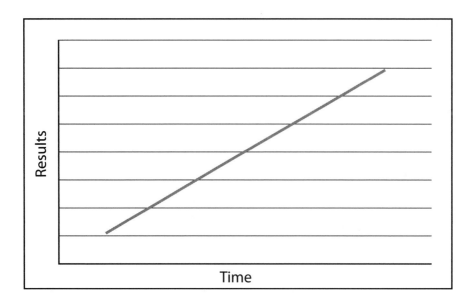

But in reality, the relationship between the two, after a certain point, is one of diminishing returns. People can only work so much before they cease to be effective. The essence of the OLT principle is to identify the point at which your team will produce less given what they put in:

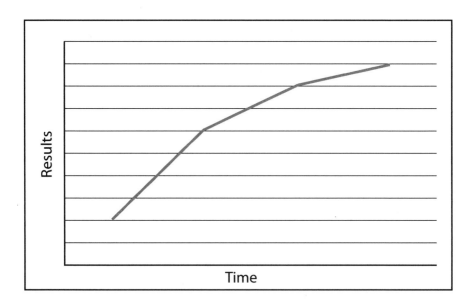

Imagine being able to help your team focus on its most important work and—*gasp!*—discontinuing activities that no longer add value. You'll earn accolades for the great work your team is doing *and* build a relaxed, energized team that is hopeful and excited about its work. Sound pretty appealing? Let's talk about how to do it.

THE OLT PRINCIPLE

The OLT principle ensures that your team is focused on the right things and spending no more time than necessary to produce the results you need. Here's how it works. For every activity your team is performing, you (and they) should ask:

- Can this activity be *focused* so less time is spent completing it?
- Can this activity be *delegated* to another person or group?
- Can this activity be *stopped*?

In this chapter, we'll review each option, I'll give you an example of a leader or team who's done this well, and we'll end with specific tips to put the tool into action. And the challenge—should you choose to accept it—is to help your team offload or reduce one task per week for a year, either by focusing it, delegating it, or stopping it entirely. At the end of the year, that'll be fifty-two OLTs, which is more than enough for you and your team to take a nice vacation (the one you now know you need after reading chapter 11).

Option #1: Focus It

There is an expression among lawyers that if you argue ten points during a trial, no matter how good the points are, the jury won't remember a single one when they get to the jury room. Similarly, if you're not focusing your efforts on the most important actions your team must take, your team is probably doing a lot of work with little payoff.

So why is it so hard to prioritize? It's simple: We're scared of failure. By having twelve priorities, the team from the beginning of this chapter was hedging its bets. But the irony here is that, much like the lawyer with ten points that the jury can't remember, having twelve goals means that all your team will do is frantically run around asking, "How are we going to get this all *done*?"

Working on more than three to five priorities reduces your team's ability to complete any of them well. Research by Paul Leinwand and Cesare Mainardi of Booz & Company shows that as an executive team's number of priorities grows, revenue declines.[2] The good news is that the reverse is also true. For example, whereas companies with more than ten priorities only grew above industry average 29 percent of the time, 44 percent of companies with just one to three priorities reported above-average industry growth. These findings might also remind you of Stephen Covey's third habit from the classic *7 Habits of Highly Effective People*: putting first things first.[3]

Leinwand and Mainardi also report that 64 percent of executives believe they have too many priorities. But bucking this trend is Lynn Gangone, whom we first met in chapter 2. When she assumed her role as dean of the University of Denver's Colorado Women's College, she and her team created three strategic priorities on which to focus their efforts: (1) expand enrollment and become an academic powerhouse, (2) continue to grow our fundraising to support student scholarships and academic programs, and (3) increase our footprint. These goals became their yardstick for how the team spent its time. Equally important, it gave them permission to *not* do things that weren't aligned with their priorities.

For instance, when a group of Lynn's students had the opportunity to travel to South Africa, they needed a staff member to accompany them. Lynn wanted to go. But when her team looked at their three priorities, the trip didn't map onto a single one. As interesting as the opportunity was, her team reported to her, it was not the way she needed to be spending her time. They were right. So, instead, Lynn traveled to Florida that week to spend time with some of their donors.

It's clear that limiting the number of priorities can help a team focus. Another strategy for prioritizing your team's efforts is to reduce the time spent on a task when perfection is not required. Imagine that an employee is working on a report that's due to you tomorrow morning. He's spent eight solid hours locked in his office to finish it. He glances at the clock. It's 6:00 p.m. He takes a step back to review the report. It looks good. He knows that it meets the criteria you're expecting. But he's a perfectionist. Should he spend that extra hour or two to give it one more pass?

In this case, my answer is no. Because the report appears to be at least 80 percent of the way there and meets your expectations, the improvement in quality would probably not justify the exhaustion he'd cause himself by staying and reviewing it one more time. This is the law of diminishing returns in practice.

This concept can be challenging for many of us, especially for leaders with backgrounds in professions like law, engineering, or medicine, to name a few. Let me be clear: I am *not* saying that you should expect your team to complete its work at 80 percent quality. That would be ludicrous and insult your intelligence.

What I *am* suggesting is something I call the 80/100 rule: Distinguish projects that need to be perfect (100 percent effort/time) from those that need to be good (80 percent effort/time). Your team should complete mission-critical work at 100 percent. Less-critical projects should get 80 percent. And always find the easiest route to your goal.

When he worked as a consultant, Andrew Lobo was assigned a cost-cutting project for one of his clients. Instead of creating a long, convoluted plan that would involve process mapping and a tremendous amount of time, he asked himself, *What do I need to deliver here?* The answer was a set of areas in the department where there was excess spending.

So instead of complicated process mapping, Andrew asked employees where there was excess. Some weren't comfortable telling him, but many did. He used their responses as a list of hypotheses; starting this way would make the budget analysis much more efficient. But Andrew is quick to note that he only reduces effort if the solution does not require that effort. This is the 80/100 rule at work. If you want to help your team members to be more like Andrew, here are some tips:

- Before tackling a project, ask your team: Have you considered all of the ways you can do this? Is there a shortcut that will get you the same outcome?

- One easy way to eliminate unnecessary work is to leverage the knowledge of others. Especially if you or your team members are being asked to do something new or challenging, have them interview a few people who have done similar projects to ask for their advice.

■ If a team member feels like they're overcomplicating a project but doesn't know how to simplify it, suggest they ask for advice from someone who knows nothing about the topic. Someone who isn't bogged down with the details may be more likely to identify unnecessary steps or find areas to streamline.

■ To discourage inefficiency, reward people who produce results, regardless of how much time they're spending. Bankable Leaders know the difference between results and activity: Just because someone put in seventy hours in a week doesn't mean they did anything productive.

Option #2: Delegate It

Delegation takes courage, trust, and thoughtfulness. It's a tough skill, but it has a huge payoff. Of course, you yourself can practice the delegation tips we'll review (i.e., making sure you're delegating to your team), but we'll focus primarily on helping *your team* offload tasks that others could do.

You may have managers or supervisors reporting to you, in which case your team members' options for delegation are considerable. But even if you supervise a group of frontline employees, delegation is still an option. Here's an example: In one previous role where I was an individual contributor, I spent my first few months on the job grumbling, "Ugh! I have to do everything myself!" But after some coaching from my boss, I learned that I had resources available to me within and outside our group. In one project requiring a great deal of communication with employees, my boss encouraged me to reach out to our marketing department. It worked like a charm—marketing was able to own a piece of the project, and frankly, they did it twice as well as I would have!

To encourage your team members to delegate, model the way by doing it yourself. After attending one of my workshops in which we covered the OLT principle, Jill McClure, whom we met in chapter 4, returned to her office and had an epiphany: She'd been spending a huge amount of time reviewing her organization's weekly newsletter before it was sent out. Every week, the task would hang over her head, and she'd put it off because she had so many other (and more important) commitments as chief operating officer. In the workshop, it dawned on Jill that this was a job her communications coordinator could learn. After she trained her to take the task over, it became clear that this was an investment with infinite returns. Jill gained back time every week and her coordinator got the chance to develop her skills, capability, and motivation.

So how can you help your employees delegate? Here are some guidelines:

- Work with them to identify the projects or tasks that someone else has the capability to do—either currently or with some coaching—especially when they're overwhelmed.

- When your team members delegate to others within or outside the department, make sure they hand over the whole project rather than pieces of it. The person or group completing the project will do a better job with the task because they feel ownership and continuity.

- Coach your team to be clear on the following when delegating: What do I need? Why do I need it? Why am I asking you to do it? What is the specific outcome and deliverable I am asking for? Be as specific as possible and give them ample time to ask questions—it will save you time down the line.

- Make sure your employees agree on a timeline and approach to follow up with the person or group completing the task. Just as with coaching, delegation isn't an excuse to let them wander off the ranch.

One final point on delegation is in order. Especially if you have managers reporting to you, be sure to help them look at delegation as something that not only takes work off their plates but that also helps develop others, as was the case with Jill's communication coordinator. I once heard someone say that the purpose of leadership is to build other leaders. Delegation is an excellent way of doing that. It's a win-win.

Option #3: Stop Doing It

The final option of the OLT Principle is to simply stop doing a task. Due to the demands placed on you and your team, this may not always be possible, but it's worth considering the option with an open mind. There are probably things

GETTING OUT OF THE WEEDS

In occupations where success means an intense focus on details, the goal of simplifying might not come easily. However, great leaders are simplifiers (who also understand the detail), and you'll need to look at the big picture to make sure your team is focusing on the *right* details, not all of them.

1. **EXPLAIN IT TO YOUR GRANDMOTHER:** If you're looking to simplify a message or assignment, especially for team members who might not have expertise in a particular area, answer the question: "If I needed to explain this to my grandmother, what would I say?" The point is to remove jargon, acronyms, and unnecessary details and instead focus on what's most important. It's not easy at first, but try it—you'll be amazed.

2. **SPELL OUT YOUR PRIORITIES:** Detail-oriented people often don't prioritize, because "all the details are important." So on a regular basis (daily, weekly, monthly) figure out what things you need your team to do and articulate those priorities. Use them to help your team focus on the right things: "If you do nothing else this week, it's important that you . . ." Don't forget to explain why they're focusing on it, too.

3. **HAVE BRAINSTORMING SESSIONS:** Have a team meeting where, instead of brainstorming about details (you already do that), you brainstorm about big-picture goals for the coming week or month. Encourage someone in your group to call "Details!" when you get into the weeds. This will help you stay focused on the big picture and will let your employees participate in direction setting and goals.

your employees are doing that they don't need to be doing. Here's an example. Betsy Hunsicker, COO of Rose Medical Center, was asked one year to create and maintain a dashboard to track progress on one of their parent company's key strategic initiatives. Every quarter, Betsy and her team would create and submit the report. After a few years, she wondered what was being done with the information. She hadn't heard anyone mention the project for a while. So just as an experiment, she had her team stop compiling the report. No one has asked about it since. As is often the case, what had started as a key business strategy had been replaced by other priorities.

Here's the lesson for Bankable Leaders like Betsy: Continuously stack your team's activities against changing priorities—and be brave about challenging previous assumptions. Here are some guidelines to determine whether you or your team can stop doing something completely—the holy grail of OLT:

- If something feels stoppable, do you think anyone would miss it if it were gone? Verify whether this is truly the case.

- If this is a deliverable being created for someone else, does it add enough value to justify the time it takes to create it?

- If it is a deliverable the team creates for itself, is this something you really need and use, or is it something that has simply become a habit?

- Even if the task had value when the team started it, have the conditions or strategy changed?

■   ■   ■

Remember, even if you feel powerless against the magnitude of your team's workload, there is almost always an opportunity to streamline or focus. Taking the time to ask the three questions of the OLT Principle will make life better for your team and help them spend their time on what's most important. As Stephen Covey says, "First things first."

I was once delivering a training course to senior-level executives at the Center for Creative Leadership. Chuckling, my co-trainer and I remarked that as soon as we gave them as much as a five-minute break, the executives were immediately pacing around the halls with their phones glued to their ears or staring intently at their e-mail. "Oh, these poor people!" my co-trainer said. "They have so much on their plates. It must be so hard to get away for five whole days."

Remembering Jim Downey's wise preference for "lazy" people, I looked at her and deadpanned, "Clearly, they're either bad at prioritizing or they're total control freaks."

She laughed. "Touché!"

BANKABLE ACTIONS

Understand the Law of Diminishing Returns

✔ Make it your team's goal to work in the simplest, most efficient manner possible.

✔ Reward results rather than time or effort invested.

Focus It

✔ Have no more than three to five goals to guide the efforts of your team, and use these goals as a daily barometer to focus its activity and energy.

✔ Constantly assess whether "good enough" is enough, balancing the time required for perfection with the diminishing improvement you will probably see. This will allow you the energy to make your most important tasks or projects perfect because you won't be wasting energy elsewhere.

Delegate It

✔ Especially when they're stressed or overloaded, help your team members identify tasks that other people or groups can accomplish.

✔ Coach your employees to provide clear instructions about the end result, to hand over projects in their entirety to capable employees, and to help the person who got the project stay on track as it progresses.

Stop Doing It

✔ Stay aware of changing priorities, and be vigilant about what tasks or projects your team could stop doing entirely so they can focus their energy on what's most important.

✔ Have the courage to challenge assumptions about how your team should spend its time as business conditions change.

CHAPTER 13

FOR GOD'S SAKE . . . LOOSEN UP!

Natalie Roper felt sick.

She was working for the second boss in a row who seemed to delight in creating a joyless, miserable environment for her team. Natalie swore that when she became a leader, she would do whatever it took to create a positive environment for her employees.

Natalie is full of joy and downright sparkling—just being around her is a boost of positive energy. And when she was promoted to be the leader of her hospital's radiology and imaging services department, she knew that patients would be best served when employees enjoyed their work.

But, as Natalie brought this joy to her team—just by being herself—she started noticing that some of her colleagues viewed her happy-go-lucky approach as evidence that she couldn't deliver for the business. In the span of a few weeks, she had one radiologist and one hospital leader tell her that they couldn't take her seriously because she was *so positive it made her seem incompetent*.

Natalie became self-conscious about her approach, thinking maybe they were right—maybe she couldn't be lighthearted and drive serious business results. She started masking her natural cheerfulness and trying to act "more serious." But then, on a daily basis, people started asking her what was wrong! She felt like she was living a lie and noticed that her team was becoming unhappy and demotivated.

After a few months of this, she started wondering, *Why should I change because of two people's opinions?* Natalie realized that she should have trusted herself more; her previous approach must have been working, because when she changed it, everything started going downhill! She realized that she had to be herself and that her positivity was actually a differentiator for her as a leader.

So Natalie brought back her vivacity, eventually finding an organization where she was able to be herself. One of her first decisions in her new role was to convene a group of employees and challenge them to bring her a list of suggestion for how to bring more fun into the department. They proposed that, to get to know one another better, Natalie's departments should each host an open house—with a theme! Natalie enthusiastically endorsed their proposal, and the employees made it happen.

Lo and behold, it worked like a charm: Her employees were happier, which made them work harder, which drove results. For example, the MRI group enthusiastically dove into their open house, choosing a luau theme. They gave out leis, baked pineapple upside-down cakes, and made virgin piña coladas. And shortly thereafter, the MRI department's employee-engagement scores went from average to 100 percent of employees reporting they were engaged. In another department, the hospital's Breast Center, Natalie's employees were able to shave seven minutes off the time patients spent in the waiting room. She did this by putting her more engaged employees in the waiting room; because they worked so well with each other, they became more efficient.

Natalie's ability to inject fun is certainly a rarity. For the rest of us, when did work become such, well, *work*? Organizations are operating in a leaner and meaner fashion since the Great Recession, and most leaders have become more and more obsessed with the productivity of their teams. They assume that fun and productivity are mutually exclusive.

Yet almost everyone has heard stories about the dot-com era, and how companies like Google, Yahoo, and Amazon invest in employee fun. Perks at Google include ping-pong, foosball, billiards, air hockey, and even kayaks. The company reportedly spends $72 million per year simply on food for employees.[1]

I see leaders in more established organizations believe that only start-ups or tech companies—the ones that supposedly fly by the seat of their pants—can apply these approaches and that serious organizations need to be serious.

And perhaps as a result, things have become phenomenally dreary for most employees. Many operate under the assumption that weekdays are for "work" and weekends are for "fun." I have a friend who calls Sunday afternoons "the long dark teatime of the soul." The first time I heard this, it struck me as equal parts sad and funny—and completely true for most people. If work were truly enjoyable, your team would enter the office on Monday morning with the same level of excitement they leave with on Friday afternoons.

I hope this doesn't shock you, but when employees are having fun, they are happier and more productive. According to David Abramis, fun guru and Cal State–Long Beach professor, fun improves communication and enhances team spirit. It also reduces boredom, conflict, and absenteeism.[2]

Because of its business value, fun is a necessity. It is also an employee need. In the mid-twentieth century, psychologist Abraham Maslow first proposed a human hierarchy of needs.[3] He argued that we must fulfill more basic needs like food, water, safety before higher-order ones like status, fulfillment, and self-actualization. In 1994, psychologist William Glasser proposed a hierarchy of needs for the workplace.[4] Glasser puts the need to have fun at the top, meaning that it is our highest-order need—and the most challenging—to meet at work. Glasser's research suggests that many people see the workplace as a place where the need for fun cannot be met at all! What a bummer, right?

Regardless of company size or industry, organizations who take fun seriously almost always reap the rewards. For example, every year the Great Places to Work Institute surveys more than ten million employees around the world about what it's like to work at their companies. The result is the highly coveted "100 Best Companies to Work For" list. An average of 81 percent of employees at these companies report working in a fun environment. Only 61 percent of employees in other companies say the same.

Most leaders have difficulty fostering fun at work. For some, it can feel like the last thing they have time for given their stresses and demands. For others, it feels fluffy or frivolous. Still others want to catalyze it, but don't know how.

But Bankable Leaders take fun seriously, and you don't have to spend $72 million on food for your employees to do it.

At New Belgium Brewing Company, the third-largest craft brewer in the United States (you've probably heard of their best-selling beer, Fat Tire), fun is serious business. Before husband-and-wife team Kim Jordan and Jeff Lebesch founded the company in 1991, they took a hike in Rocky Mountain National Park and penned their initial set of Core Values: To brew world-class beers, to promote beer culture, to be environmental stewards, to have fun. Later they refined these into their current vision ("To operate a profitable brewery which makes our love and talent manifest") and top ten values (fun made the list). At New Belgium Brewing, this value isn't just something plastered on the website; it is truly embedded in the company's DNA.

So how does New Belgium Brewing create a fun environment? Kim, the company's CEO, believes it is a series of choices, large and small. For example, when the company was building more space in its facility around 2000, Kim decided it might be fun to build a slide for the employees. So when she asked the builder to help her find a slide, they came back with an estimate for a $100,000 adult slide. Fearing that this was too costly, Kim was able to find a less expensive one online, and her employees got the slide. Naturally, fun ensued.

"At the end of the day," Kim observes, "we spend a lot of time at this thing called work—if it doesn't feel joyful, it's a big investment of a life. You have to make space for levity and laughing. That takes time." In this chapter, I'll review how Bankable Leaders create an enjoyable workplace where employees are also productive. We'll start by discovering how you can find joy in what you do and help your team do the same. We'll end the chapter with tips on getting on track by getting slightly *off* track—in other words, even though it feels insane to take time out of being productive to be *more* productive, that's often what's required.

FIND THE JOY IN WHAT YOU DO

According to Kim Cameron, when employees feel positive emotions, they are more productive, creative, and committed to the organization. And companies with happy employees see more satisfied customers and even larger profits.[5]

Emotional contagion is a term used to describe the way we actually "catch" the emotions of those around us.[6] As a leader, when you find joy in what you do, it's contagious: Your team will be more likely to do the same.

Bob Chapman, whom we first met in chapter 1, has always wrestled with the "no pain, no gain," approach to work. "How is it a career if it's not fun?" he wonders. When I asked Bob about the feeling of dread that many people feel on Sunday evenings, he looked at me quizzically. Bob goes to work almost every day saying, "Are you kidding me? They pay me to do this?" I've worked with Bob's team for a while now, and I can attest to the impact this attitude has had on them. They laugh, they joke, they get things done, and above all, they love what they do. Let's review a few tips to help you bring a little joy to your team.

Help Your Employees Be Who They Are

Have you ever been in an environment where you couldn't really be yourself? The energy you probably spent on contorting to fit that environment no doubt stifled most of your fun. What a waste! Bankable Leaders, in contrast, let their team members be who they are at work.

And like many other concepts we've reviewed, it has to start with you. In his exceptional book *True North*, Bill George discusses the concept of Authentic Leadership, which means knowing—and being—who you truly are as a leader.[7] This journey takes courage, and starts and ends with two questions:

1. Can I be the same person at work as I can at home?

2. If not, what is stopping me?

About a year ago, I was talking to my mentor, Ray Vigil—the one who learned about the importance of love in chapter 4—and he said something that was so strange that at first I thought I'd misheard him: "You should think about the way you dress." At first I was shocked, then full of curiosity about what had prompted him to say such a thing. As we learned in my dress code incident in chapter 6, it wasn't as if I ever dressed inappropriately. "Do you think the way you dress in a professional setting is a good representation of your personality?" he continued.

I was dumbstruck. In a flash, I remembered my first office job. I was much younger than everyone else, so I'd gone out and bought a bunch of pantsuits.

Even though it wasn't the way I wanted to dress, I felt like I had to do that to be taken seriously. So I kept adding suits to my closet—blue suits, brown suits, black suits, gray suits. On workdays, I was always buttoned up, literally and figuratively. On days I wasn't working, I would dress like myself: casual, funky clothes, interesting jewelry, fun shoes.

Here was the epiphany I had, thanks to Ray's question: I was hiding behind the very clothes I had initially chosen to be taken seriously. I was an informal Millennial trapped in a suit. I wasn't being who I was.

The more I thought about it, the more I realized that my clothes were just the tip of the iceberg. My clients often comment that their first impression of me wasn't consistent with the personality they later uncovered once we got to know each other. I was acting *overly* professionally when I first met them, which quite frankly, is boring and forgettable—the opposite impression I'm told I create when I open my mouth (not always in a good way!).

After this uncomfortable yet profound realization, I decided to wake up every day and choose to show my true personality at work. To make my outside match my inside, I'd try to wear interesting shoes or a funky necklace or a mismatched jacket. Breaking those old patterns and habits was tougher than I had anticipated. But on days where I succeed in breaking down that barrier, it's so freeing—I feel like people can really see me. And when I feel free, I feel joy. And as we've discussed, that joy is contagious.

Once you build this foundation of being yourself, you can help your employees do the same. One great example is Stephen Ladek. He and his team have a weekly meeting that always ends with what they call the "Song of the Week." One member of the team pushes play on his or her iPod and the team listens to that song. Not only has Stephen gotten to hear some new music (he brags that he knew about "Gangnam Style" six weeks before everyone else), but the team also gets a chance to show each other exactly who they are.

Help Your Team Have a Laugh

The benefits of laughter are no joke. One survey by Hodge-Cronin & Associates of more than seven hundred CEOs reveals that people with a sense of humor are more successful at their jobs.[8] What's more, Oxford evolutionary psychologist

Robin Dunbar and her team recently discovered something comedians have known all along: Laughter really is the best medicine.[9] When we laugh, our bodies release endorphins, nature's mood-boosting pain relievers.

The ability to inspire laughter is a Bankable Leader's secret weapon. Companies like Southwest Airlines and Ben & Jerry's credit their use of humor to employees' levels of commitment, teamwork, and performance. A research team led by Washington University professor Bruce Avolio empirically tested this hypothesis, examining teams at a large Canadian financial organization.[10] They asked whether the employees' leaders used humor at work—things like telling funny stories to tone down stress, helping the team laugh at themselves when they get too serious, or using laughter to build relationships.

One year later, researchers assessed the team's results. They found that the more a leader's team reported them using humor, the better each employee—and even their business unit—performed. This doesn't mean you have to take a comedy class at your local improv theater to be a good leader. A few small changes will likely suffice.

First, accept the fact that your employees will need to blow off steam from time to time. Goofing off and joking around is part of human nature. Kim Jordan of New Belgium Brewing points out that when most leaders walk by and see this happening, they might make inferences about employees' productivity—or lack thereof. But it's important, she notes, not to put too much weight on these isolated incidents when judging their performance; you have to get the backstory. For example, if you see two employees loitering by the watercooler, ask yourself what's going on in their lives before you march them down to human resources. Maybe they've worked fifty hours so far that week and need to take ten minutes to blow off a little steam before going back to being productive.

And, as it turns out, time at the watercooler is actually a business imperative. MIT professor Sandy Pentland and his team studied call-center employees at Bank of America and found that those who were given time to informally visit with each other finished customer calls faster (results) and were less stressed (people).[11] The call center was so excited about these results that they changed employees' breaks to coincide with one another—the result was *$15 million in productivity improvements*! All because of a little chitchat.

HOW **EXECUTIVES** CAN LOOSEN UP . . . BUT NOT *TOO MUCH*

You know the type. The gray-suited, quiet, serious, just-get-the-work-done executive. Well, chances are there's a fun person inside that starched suit, just waiting to come out. We keep reading about fun at work and how it can help, but how can executives participate?

1. **TAKE OFF THE TIE SOMETIMES:** Fun can take many forms—having a costume day, or getting employees together for community projects, funny photo caption contests, or skits. According to *Entertainment Business Newsweekly,* some top corporations are encouraging employees to make music together, and executives are playing in bands with company employees. Realize that it is okay for your employees to see you having fun. In fact, not only is it okay—it's advisable.

2. **CONSULT YOUR COMMUNICATIONS AND/OR HR DEPARTMENT:** If you have the internal expertise, it is perfectly reasonable to ask the communications or HR department for help creating fun. Ask for their ideas on how you can play a role in livening things up in your company. They will be in a great position to advise you based on the specifics of your personality and the organization.

3. **DON'T FORGET YOUR IMAGE:** Of course, you are the face of your organization, so don't take the fun-having too far. If you're worried about your image or are in a public setting, try subtle things: Smile, take a more informal tone when addressing employees, do something fun in meetings. Sometimes the sum total of some of these smaller changes can be huge.

A second technique to bring humor to work is through self-deprecating humor on your part. This is a powerful tool because it also involves a little self-disclosure, which, as we know from chapter 1, builds trust. By showing your team that you're willing to laugh at yourself, you become more human and the environment becomes more fun.

So how can you take yourself a little less seriously? People love to hear about anything embarrassing or ridiculous that's happened to you. Mine your life for stories that are embarrassing or funny and find opportunities to make light of yourself. Or you can try the "turning the tables" approach: I once worked at a company that would have its leaders wash their employees' cars every year—it was a hilarious and wonderful way to help liven things up.

BE A CATALYST FOR FUN

Robert Ford and his colleagues surveyed more than five hundred human resources professionals about fun at work. A whopping 75 percent reported that their workplace was less fun than it should be.[12] And not to knock my colleagues in HR, but usually, they aren't exactly party animals.

Now hear this: Creating a fun environment isn't something you can delegate to human resources—it has to start with you. There are two ways to make your team's world just a bit more entertaining. You can inject levity into activities normally lacking it, or you can introduce new activities that are designed specifically to foster fun. Let's look at both methods.

Boring Things Don't Have to Be Boring

Bankable Leaders blur the line between "productive time" and "fun time." The advantage of introducing fun into day-to-day activities is that it doesn't require any more time or energy than you might have devoted otherwise.

For example, two of Stephen Ladek's International Solutions Group employees had been in Iraq for an eighteen-month evaluation assignment. They were coming to the end of the project, at which point they'd need to put together a report on their findings. Stephen realized that there was no reason for them to stay in Iraq to complete the report. Instead, he decided to fly them out to San

José, Costa Rica, where he lives. "Be in paradise, not a war zone" was his logic. So the two employees holed up for two weeks and cranked out the report. Stephen did invest in two plane tickets, but the report his team created exceeded his wildest expectations. And you can bet they had a good time putting it together.

You can also fold fun into existing meeting time. I was once facilitating a meeting with a VP and her team at a utility company. The meeting had been challenging—they were reorganizing their department and the choices were tough. Toward the end of a very long day, the leader stood up and said, "That's it. We need sugar." She called her assistant, who bounded in to find the team chanting, "We want ice cream! We want ice cream!"

You should have seen how happy they were when her assistant returned, arms full of packaged ice cream cones. Perhaps it was the sugar, but the team found a new store of energy and ended the day on a productive note. The moral of this story is that sometimes, you just need to send out for ice cream.

Here are some suggestions to liven up *your* day-to-day operations:

- Food is usually a slam dunk. Especially if you have to hold your employees hostage in a long meeting, buy them food! Take note of allergies and diets, but get creative—maybe something more than the classic and tedious choice of sandwiches. Or make it a potluck.

- In team meetings, make it a commitment to do something fun. Whether it's an icebreaker or just informal time to catch up over a cup of coffee, carve out this time—it's important. I once worked with a team that created an elaborate game of *Family Feud* for their annual leadership meeting—it was pure genius.

- In the course of your day-to-day work, if you don't laugh at least once an hour when interacting with your team, ask yourself, "Do we need to lighten up a little?"

- Turn normal activities into a game. *Gamification* is the use of games to engage people in activities not traditionally thought of as games. Simple examples of gamification are the "achievement badges" used on sites like Foursquare, or the process of collecting frequent-flyer miles. What if you

INTROVERTED LEADERS CAN HAVE FUN TOO!

Humor and fun at work can feel especially difficult for leaders who are inclined to keep to themselves. A study of engineers found that in certain situations, extroverted engineers are likely to use humor more than introverted ones. Introverted leaders, who often recharge by being alone, may just need to make a more concerted effort to liven things up.

1. **"BORING" FUN IS FINE:** You don't have to take your team to a karaoke bar to have a little fun. Sometimes something as simple as a lunch can go a long way. Remember to find the "low-hanging fun fruit," like celebrating hiring anniversaries or a job well done on a tough project. These do not have to be extravagant celebrations—so take the pressure off yourself!

2. **KEEP THINGS STRUCTURED:** If the very idea of attending a seemingly endless happy hour causes you stress, think about organizing more structured events: Try starting up a company-sponsored volleyball team or bowling team. If you find that your employees are making health-related resolutions, ask them how they'd feel about starting a running team. Or find a volunteering opportunity in the community. These activities can be great for introverts because there's very little small talk required!

3. **SHARE THE RESPONSIBILITY:** As your team bonds, pass them the responsibility for planning these events. Make it a rotating assignment among your team members, or ask for volunteers. Don't make it additional work; it should be something people want to do. But whatever you do, don't try to do it all yourself.

held a contest for the person who generates the most ideas in a brainstorming session and then bought the winner lunch at the restaurant of their choosing?

- By all means, if fun doesn't come naturally, get help. Find your most fun team member and have them help you perform a "fun audit." Make it a development opportunity!

Think Like a Camp Counselor

Except for my ill-fated few weeks at performing arts camp in sixth grade, I never went to summer camp. But both of my younger sisters did. Starting at the ripe old age of about eight, it became an integral part of their lives—I often joke that it was like they joined a cult. Eventually, they both became counselors and would regale me with tales of what it was like to entertain their campers twenty-four hours a day. Ever the Type A workaholic older sister, I would think, *Really? That's all they did all day? How silly! Why don't they get* real *jobs?* I now realize that instead, I should have said, "Wow—most leaders could learn a lot from you."

A camp counselor's job is to make things fun. And even though a leader's ultimate job is to get things done, making time for fun will help your team get there. Obviously, a leader in an organization can't coordinate the same activities as a summer camp, but you can certainly be inspired by them. What if you threw a barbecue at your house? Formed a department flag football team? Volunteered together in the community?

Camp counselors also let their campers blow off steam when needed. And if you assume your team members are hardworking, capable professionals, *they* should be deciding how to spend their time—as long as they're getting their work done—and should be allowed to step away from their duties for a while each day. (That said, if you walk by on ten separate occasions and each time the same employees are playing poker, you might want to speak with them.)

Extra credit goes to Bankable Leaders who *help* their employees blow off steam rather than simply tolerating it when it happens. For example, at New Belgium Brewing, the team plays volleyball every Thursday. The company provides bicycles and encourages employees to take them out if they need a break or some fresh air. They even built a climbing wall for their employees!

Here are a few "campy" ideas to get you started:

- **Arts and crafts**: One of my clients, a senior leader in the energy industry, was absolutely insistent that I help him arrange a trip with his team to a local pottery-painting shop. I jokingly mocked him for a while, thinking it was too frivolous, but finally decided to go with it and helped arrange the trip. Months later, I could see that this trip had been a pivotal moment for the team. For example, one team member had a pattern of cantankerous behavior. But at the pottery shop, his armor came off—the team saw his childlike joy as he carefully glazed a serving platter. The whole team had time to laugh and joke around. It was a slam dunk.

- **Mountaineering**: Another leader I know carves out one day every two months for his team to travel to the Rocky Mountains, hike, and meditate. And often, when the day approaches, the team hems and haws, saying they don't have time to leave the office. But afterward they always say, "This was amazing. Look what it did for us. We have to make more time for this the next time we come up here!"

- **Field trips**: At New Belgium Brewing, employees who have been with the company for five years receive an all-expense-paid trip to Belgium with Kim Jordan and other senior leaders. "We share in the culture of the beer that made our company famous, ride some bikes, and have some laughs," says Kim. Especially for employees who haven't had the chance to travel to Europe, this is truly the trip of a lifetime.

The list could go on, but the point here is to understand that carving out time to have fun *just for the sake of fun* will help your team be more cohesive and productive. And *you* might even like coming to work a little more, too!

BANKABLE ACTIONS

Find the Joy in What You Do

✔ Ask yourself whether you are the same person at work and outside work (or you can ask someone who knows you in both settings). If that's not the case, it's time to dig deeper into the reasons this might be and to start breaking down that wall (see chapter 1 for more on this).

✔ Don't be afraid to laugh. If you're not laughing at least once an hour with your team, it might be time to bring out an icebreaker or two (just Google "icebreakers" for plenty of options—it's not rocket science). Self-deprecating humor is also a great option; it makes you more human.

Be a Catalyst for Fun

✔ Realize that your team will need to goof off from time to time. If you walk by and see this happening, don't jump to the conclusion that the employee is lazy or unproductive. Ask questions and learn the pattern first.

✔ Blur the line between work and fun by making day-to-day tasks or meetings more enjoyable. Order in lunch for your team. Bring them doughnuts. Carve out meeting time for games or contests (remember *Family Feud*!).

✔ Turn otherwise-average tasks into games. For example, if your sales team makes its quota, take everyone on a field trip outside the office—say, to a baseball game.

✔ Understand that carving out "unproductive" fun time (where you're not directly working on your team's tasks) will help drive productivity and improve morale. Think like a camp counselor and bring out your (and their) inner child. By all means, start that flag football team!

BANKABLE LEADERSHIP HAPPENS DAY BY DAY

About three years ago, I decided that I wanted to learn Spanish. *I speak French,* I thought. *How hard could it be?*

So I started traveling to Spanish-speaking countries and listening carefully. I downloaded an iPhone app to help with vocabulary. I delighted my friends with my toddler-like proficiency, pointing to a dog, *perro*, or a cat, *gato*. I engaged in this strategy for years, fueled by the futile hope that I would learn the language through osmosis.

My delusion continued until I took a vacation to Mexico with two of my friends. From the moment I stepped off the plane, I was unable to communicate with, well, anyone.

But much to my surprise, my friend, whom to the best of my knowledge had never spoken the language in her life, started rattling off Spanish to everyone: the customs agent, the cab driver, the bellman. In complete shock, I stammered, "When did you learn Spanish?"

"Oh, it's been a few months. I know someone who's fluent and we practice for thirty minutes every day."

It hit me like a ton of bricks: I had been engaging in Delusional Development. Delusional Development is the futile hope that just by wanting to get better at something and knowing just enough to be dangerous, you will show improvement. But as the saying goes, hope is not a plan.

Thankfully, I came to my senses: I am now taking weekly Spanish lessons (taught by my little sister, Alex) and practicing daily. It's not always fun, but I learned more Spanish in my first two lessons than I learned in three years of Delusional Development!

Even though my goal in this book was to help you become bankable by understanding and balancing the four tensions all leaders face, you might be feeling slightly overwhelmed by the sheer amount of information and suggestions. As you continue your journey, the important thing to remember is that real leaders improve incrementally. Incremental improvement is achieved by intently focusing on what you want to improve and relentlessly practicing it every day.

For hundreds of years, exceptional skill and performance have been thought of as inborn, unalterable gifts. Scientists used to think that superior athletes were caused by biological differences in lung capacity or muscle fibers. But recent research shows that experts acquire their skills not from natural born talent, but from deliberate practice. The best marathon runners, for example, don't show physiological differences in lungs or muscle. The differences lie in how much each runner trains in the weeks leading up to the marathon.

People with average talent have achieved extraordinary things with sustained focus and commitment. After reviewing studies of grand masters of chess, scientists, authors, poets, and even radiologists, a research team led by Florida State University professor K. Anders Ericsson concluded that it takes ten years—or ten thousand hours—to become an expert. This thinking was later popularized by Malcolm Gladwell in *Outliers*[1] and by Daniel Coyle in *The Talent Code*[2]

The same is true for exceptional leaders. This is why I never accept the excuse that "I just wasn't born to be a leader." A person may not *want* to be a leader, which is entirely different, but anyone can become a more effective leader with focus and deliberate practice.

The journey to Bankable Leadership is like learning a violin concerto. You first have to learn the concepts (like reading music) and behaviors (like playing the violin). Then you practice over and over to turn that knowledge into a beautiful piece of music. Bankable Leaders must acquire the concepts (the tension between people and results) and behaviors (trust, transparency, etc.).

To be successful in this endeavor, you must first *make a plan* for what you want to improve. Second, you have to *engage in deliberate practice*. Let's review some strategies for each of these important steps.

MAKE A PLAN

There is an often-repeated joke in my profession: How many psychologists does it take to change a lightbulb? It depends—does the lightbulb want to change? Learning to lead means committing to change: It requires you to look at your own demons, insecurities, and fears. The first step toward Bankable Leadership is looking in the mirror and saying: "It can be done. And I will do it."

In modern organizations, there is little built-in time for self-reflection. For most leaders, simply getting through the day and clearing out your inbox can feel like a minor miracle. So I encourage you to start making time to reflect on your development—away from your team, your boss, or even your family if necessary. Spend time thinking about what you've learned in this book and from other leadership sources. Where do you think you have the biggest opportunity to improve?

Sometimes we don't improve because we simply feel we have too many improvements to make—so we set too many priorities for ourselves. It is absolutely critical to focus and set fewer goals. Practice the OLT Principle: Don't set more development goals than you can reasonably handle. It is far better to make progress in one or two areas than to make little or no improvement in five areas!

For an honest snapshot of your leadership effectiveness, complete the online Bankable Leadership 360 assessment available at www.BankableLeadership .com. Not only will this assessment give you information on your self-perceived "Duplicate" and "Deviate" opportunities—behaviors you should keep doing or stop doing—but you can also invite your boss, peers, or team to complete the assessment for additional feedback. (To help you digest your results, consider rereading the sections of the book pertaining to what the assessment identifies as your "Deviate" opportunities.)

Choose one or two behaviors to focus on: These will become your Bankable Actions. How do you choose which two? Well, which behaviors are most important to your success right now? Which are most important to your long-term success? And where did others spot weaknesses you didn't know you had? Once you feel you've really improved in one or two areas—that you've developed new habits and behaviors—move on to other areas of improvement.

ENGAGE IN DELIBERATE PRACTICE

You might be saying, "I've had a development plan before—it just gathers dust in my desk." Trust me, I know how it is—I see it happen a lot. But in cases where leaders have development plans in place but don't see improvements in their effectiveness, it's not usually because they *can't* get better. It's typically because they're not focusing on one action at a time, practicing it daily, or getting feedback.

The amount and quality of deliberate practice you choose will be proportionate to the level of improvement you see. Period. Remember, learning to be a leader is no different from learning to play the violin. That's why many leaders who go to training classes don't show measurable improvement: The training content loses its glow and becomes one of the new skills that's gathering cobwebs in their brain.

Instead, pick one action and commit to practicing it each day. Every day you'll have opportunities, and every day you'll learn something. Remember that 70 percent of leadership is learned. This book is your shortcut, but you have to practice to turn learning into improvement.

One common thread researchers have identified in young adults who excel at a particular skill was the presence of a coach or mentor. The impact of one-on-one attention is incredible. Benjamin Samuel Bloom, a renowned educational psychologist, once compared students who received one-on-one tutoring with students in a classroom setting.[3] Those who were tutored, on average, performed better than 98 percent of the students in the classroom setting, likely due to the one-on-one attention.

Coaches and mentors do many things to improve performance. They make sure you continue your commitment and practice, they teach you how to improve, and they believe in your ability. That's why many leaders have executive coaches. Having a trusted expert advisor can therefore mean the difference between improvement and Delusional Development.

There is no reason you can't have a mentor or coach. Start with your boss and share your thoughts on how you want to improve. Ask for feedback in those areas. Or scan your network—within or outside your organization—for people who demonstrate the skills you'd like to build. Identify someone and use this as an opportunity to build your relationship: Ask them if they would be willing to serve as your mentor. If you don't know the person you'd like to ask, request an introduction from a trusted advisor. Another option is to consider working with an executive coach. Meet with your coach or mentor at least once a month. Your mentor can provide you with advice, help you talk through problems, or challenge your thinking when necessary.

Finally, feedback is one of the most valuable gifts a coach or mentor can provide. Much as the difference between a good violinist and an exceptional one is artistry and interpretation, there is an art to the way excellent leaders translate their behaviors to fit their environment. Remember when I said that the Bankable Leadership model will get you 80 to 90 percent of the way to being a great leader. The final 10 to 20 percent of leadership effectiveness is the ability to correctly translate your skills to fit the situation. The differences across industries and organizations can be vast, which is why many leaders in large corporations who change industries fail. Often, a coach or mentor has the objectivity to give you feedback on what you're failing to see, as well as inside knowledge on the needs of your industry and organization.

■   ■   ■

Even though the behaviors of Bankable Leadership are simple, they are not easy: self-awareness, a commitment to results, and a sense of heart. The resolve to practice and improve every day. This book, no matter how good it is, cannot make you a great leader overnight. What it *has* focused on is helping you understand the behaviors of successful leaders, what areas you might need to focus on, and how you can practice daily. And if that's your approach, you will get better as a leader every day. It might be incremental improvement, but it will add up quickly.

Rajesh Setty had known Naveen Lakkur for years. Not only were they good friends; Rajesh was also an investor and serves on the board of a company where Naveen serves as CEO. Several years ago, Naveen suffered an accident. He was bedridden for eighteen months and over the course of twelve eye operations lost 97 percent of his eyesight. Yet through the ordeal, he displayed consistently remarkable strength.

One day, Rajesh suggested that Naveen write a book about his harrowing experience. "I can barely read now," Naveen scoffed. "How can I write a book?" Rajesh could see that his friend had many books in his heart but wasn't quite ready to write them yet—and he, Rajesh, was determined to help him.

"Why don't we start a blog, then?" Rajesh began innocently. So, over a period of months, Naveen started composing and posting short pieces online. Soon, people started to read the blog. Rajesh convinced Naveen to write more frequently, and over a period of months, he did. Next, Naveen started giving speeches about his experience. One day, Rajesh pointed out that Naveen could have his talks recorded and transcribed, so he did. Once the first speech was transcribed, he had his first full article.

This went on for a long time. After seven years, Naveen published an acclaimed three-hundred-page book, *Inseparable Twins*. During a launch party for the book, Rajesh saw Naveen talking to someone who'd been deeply moved by his story. The person said, "I don't know how you did this!" Having only seen the book—and not the seven years of grueling work behind it—this person thought Naveen had achieved overnight success.

Isn't that how most of us feel when looking at other leaders who have been successful? *How could this person be such a good leader?* we think. *It must come naturally.* What we don't see are the countless days and years of learning, mistakes, and incremental improvement.

Rajesh calls this alchemy. I call it Bankable Leadership. And in my own life, whenever I'm feeling overwhelmed, it helps to remember my favorite quote in the universe, by German poet Johann Wolfgang von Goethe: "Whatever you can do, or dream you can, begin it. Boldness has genius, power and magic in it."

So begin it, and go get 'em! Here's to your professional prosperity.

NOTES

Introduction

1 Jack Zenger, Joe Folkman, and Scott Edinger, "How Extraordinary Leaders Double Profits," *Chief Learning Officer*, June 28, 2009, http://www.clomedia.com/articles/view /how_extraordinary_leaders_double_profits.

2 Richard Arvey, Maria Rotundo, Wendy Johnson, Zhen Zhang, and Matt McGue, "The Determinants of Leadership Role Occupancy: Genetic and Personality Factors," *The Leadership Quarterly* 17 (2006): 1–20.

Part I

1 Pete Weaver and Simon Mitchell, "Leadership Lessons from the People Who Matter," *Development Dimensions International*, 2011, http://www.ddiworld.com/thought-leadership/research /trend-research/lessons-for-leaders-from-the-people-who-matter.

2 Michael Romano, "Best Boss? Cable Mogul Bill Daniels Drives Hard Bargain with a Soft Touch," *Rocky Mountain News*, September 18, 1988.

3 Daniels Foundation, *Relentless: The Life and Legacy of Bill Daniels*, 45.

4 Romano, "Best Boss? Cable Mogul Bill Daniels Drives Hard Bargain With a Soft Touch."

5 Daniels Foundation, *Relentless*, 38.

6 Ibid.

Chapter 1

1 Kurt Dirks, "Trust in Leadership and Team Performance: Evidence from NCAA Basketball," *Journal of Applied Psychology* 85, no. 6 (2000): 1004-1012.

2 Matt Twyman, Nigel Harvey, and Clare Harries, "Trust in Motives, Trust in Competence: Separate Factors Determining the Effectiveness of Risk Communication," *Judgment and Decision Making* 3, no. 1 (2008): 111–120.

3 Satyanarayana Parayitam and Robert S. Dooley, "Is Too Much Cognitive Conflict in Strategic Decision-Making Teams Too Bad?" *International Journal of Conflict Management* 22, no. 4 (2001): 342–357.

4 It's worth noting that in 1997, this approach was fairly novel for an HR person, but has become common practice since.

5 Patrick Müller, Rainer Greifeneder, Dagmar Stahlberg, Kees Van den bos, and Herbert Bless, "The Role of Procedural Fairness in Trust and Trustful Behavior," *Sonderforschungsbereich* 504 Publications 08-21 (2008) Universität Mannheim.

6 David Rock, "SCARF: A Brain-Based Model for Collaborating with and Influencing Others," *NeuroLeadership Journal*, 2008, www.your-brain-at-work.com/files/NLJ_SCARFUS.pdf.

7 Maureen Ambrose, Mark Seabright, and Marshall Schminke, "Sabotage in the Workplace: The Role of Organizational Injustice," *Organizational Behavior and Human Decision Processes* 89, no. 1 (2002): 947–965.

8 Jerald Greenberg and Jason Colquitt, *Handbook of Organizational Justice* (Mahwah, New Jersey: Lawrence Erlbaum Associates, 2005).

9 Bill George and Peter Sims, *True North: Discover Your Authentic Leadership* (San Francisco: Jossey-Bass/John Wiley & Sons, 2007).

10 American Psychological Association, *American Psychological Association Ethical Principles of Psychologists and Code of Conduct*, 2009, http://www.apa.org/ethics/code2002.html.

Chapter 2

1 Charlene Li, *Open Leadership: How Social Technology Can Transform the Way You Lead* (San Francisco: Jossey-Bass, 2010), xxii.

2 Nicholas DiFonzo and Prashant Bordia, "How Top PR Professionals Handle Hearsay: Corporate Rumors, Their Effects, and Strategies to Manage Them," *Public Relations Review* 26 (2000): 173–190.

3 Gordon Allport and Leo Postman, *The Psychology of Rumor* (New York: Holt, Rinehart & Winston, 1947).

4 Prashant Bordia, Elizabeth Jones, Cindy Gallois, Victor Callan, and Nicholas DiFonzo, "Managers Are Aliens! Rumors and Stress During Organizational Change," *Group and Organization Management* 31 (2006): 601–621.

5 Patrick Lencioni, *The Five Dysfunctions of a Team: A Leadership Fable* (San Francisco: Jossey-Bass, 2002).

6 Jacob Eskildsen and Kai Kristensen, "Customer Satisfaction—The Role of Transparency," *Total Quality Management & Business Excellence* 18, no. 1–2 (2007): 39–47.

7 Paul Meyer, "The Truth About Transparency," *ASAE Executive Update*, 2003, www.asaecenter.org/Resources/EUarticle.cfm?itemnumber=11786.

Chapter 3

1 Richard Ronay, Katharine Greenaway, Eric Anicich, and Adam Galinsky, "The Path to Glory Is Paved with Hierarchy: When Hierarchical Differentiation Increases Group Effectiveness," *Psychological Science* 23, no. 6 (2012): 669–677.

2 Wolfram Schultz, "Explicit Neural Signals Reflecting Reward Uncertainty," *Philosophical Transactions of the Royal Society* 363 (2008): 3801–3811.

3 Sabine Sonnentag and Michael Frese, "Stress in Organizations," in *Comprehensive Handbook of Psychology, vol. 12: Industrial and Organizational Psychology,* eds. Walter Borman, Dan Ilgen, and Rich Klimoski (New York: Wiley, 2003): 453–491.

4 Robert Wood, Anthony Mento, and Edwin Locke, "Task Complexity as a Moderator of Goal Effects: A Meta-Analysis," *Journal of Applied Psychology* 72 (1987): 416–425.

5 Xander Bezuijen, Peter van den Berg, Karen van Dam, and Henk Thierry, "Pygmalion and Employee Learning: The Role of Leader Behaviors," *Journal of Management* 35 (2009): 1248–1267.

6 George Doran, "There's a S.M.A.R.T. Way to Write Management's Goals and Objectives," *Management Review* 70, no. 11 (1981): 35–36.

7 James Collins, *Good to Great: Why Some Companies Make the Leap—And Others Don't* (New York: HarperBusiness, 2001).

8 John Donovan, "Work Motivation," *Handbook of Industrial, Work, & Organizational Psychology, Volume 2,* eds. Neil Anderson, Deniz Ones, Hadan Sinangil, and Chockalingham Viswesvaran (Thousand Oaks, CA: SAGE, 2001): 53–76.

9 Carol Dweck, "Motivational Processes Affecting Learning," *American Psychologist* 41 (1986): 1040–1048.

Chapter 4

1 William Gentry, Todd Weber, and Golnaz Sadri, "Empathy in the Workplace: A Tool for Effective Leadership," Center for Creative Leadership White Paper, 2007. www.ccl.org/leadership/pdf/research/EmpathyInTheWorkplace.pdf.

2 Douglas Noll, "Peacemaking," 2004, www.nollassociates.com/Columns/Peace60.html.

3 Martha Stout, *The Sociopath Next Door: The Ruthless vs. the Rest of Us* (New York: Broadway Books, 2005).

4 Giacomo Rizzolatti and Laila Craighero, "The Mirror-Neuron System," *Annual Review of Neuroscience* 27 (2004): 169–192.

5 Johanna Shapiro, Elizabeth Morrison, and John Boker, "Teaching Empathy to First Year Medical Students: Evaluation of an Elective Literature and Medicine Course," *Education for Health* 17, no. 1 (2004): 73–84.

6 Michael Krasner, Ronald Epstein, Howard Beckman, Anthony Suchman, Benjamin Chapman, Christopher Mooney, and Timothy Quill, "Association of an Educational Program in Mindful Communication with Burnout, Empathy and Attitudes Among Primary Care Physicians," *Journal of the American Medical Association* 32, no. 12 (2009): 1284–1293.

7 Adam Galinsky, Joe Magee, M. Ena Inesi, and Deborah Gruenfeld, "Power and Perspectives Not Taken," *Psychological Science* 17, no. 12 (2006): 1068–1074.

8 Harold Feldman, "The Problem of Personal Names as a Universal Element in Culture," *American Imago* 16 (1959): 237–250.

9 Kare Anderson, "What Captures Your Attention Controls Your Life," *Harvard Business Review* blog, http://blogs.hbr.org/cs/2012/06/what_captures_your_attention_c.html.

10 Matthew Lieberman, Naomi Eisenberger, Molly Crockett, Sabrina Tom, Jennifer Pfeifer, and Baldwin Way, "Putting Feelings into Words: Affect Labeling Disrupts Amygdala Activity in Response to Affective Stimuli," *Psychological Science* 18, no. 5 (2007) 421–428.

Part II

1 Douglas McGregor, *The Human Side of Enterprise* (New York: McGraw-Hill, 1960).

2 Elton Mayo, *The Human Problems of an Industrial Civilization* (New York: Macmillan, 1933); T.N. Whitehead, *The Industrial Worker: A Statistical Study of Human Relations in a Group of Manual Workers* (London: Oxford University Press, 1938).

3 Lawrence Lindhal, "What Makes a Good Job?" *Personnel* 25 (1949): 263–266; Kenneth Kovach, "Employee Motivation: Addressing a Crucial Factor in Your Organization's Performance," *Employment Relations Today* 22, no. 2 (1995): 93–107; Kenneth Kovach, "What Motivates Employees? Workers and Supervisors Give Different Answers," *Business Horizons* 30, no. 5 (1987): 58-66; Kenneth Kovach, "Why Motivational Theories Don't Work," *Advanced Management Journal* 45, no. 2 (1980): 54–60.

4 Daniel Pink, *Drive: The Surprising Truth About What Motivates Us* (New York: Riverhead Books, 2009).

Chapter 5

1 Robert Spector and Patrick McCarthy, *The Nordstrom Way to Customer Service Excellence: A Handbook for Implementing Great Service in Your Organization* (New York: John Wiley & Sons, 2005).

2 Christopher Hann, "Leadership Lessons from the Top of the Org Chart," *Entrepreneur Magazine*, February 22, 2012, www.entrepreneur.com/article/222797.

3 Robert Rosenthal and K. L. Fode, "The Effect of Experimenter Bias on Performance of the Albino Rat," *Behavioral Science* 8 (1963): 183–189.

4 Robert Rosenthal and Lenore Jacobson, "Teachers' Expectancies: Determinants of Pupils' IQ Gains," *Psychology Reports* 19 (1966): 115–118; Robert Rosenthal and Lenore Jacobson, *Pygmalion in the Classroom: Teacher Expectation and Pupils' Intellectual Development* (New York: Holt, Rinehart & Winston, 1968).

5 Dov Eden and Abraham Shani, "Pygmalion Goes to Boot Camp: Expectancy, Leadership, and Trainee Performance," *Journal of Applied Psychology* 67, no. 2 (1986): 194–199.

6 I thank my colleague, partner, and friend, Scott Haskins, for first introducing me to this phrase.

7 Collins, *Good to Great*, 2001.

8 Dean Crutchfield, "Meet the Gang of Four Who Make Every Decision," *Forbes Online*, March 30, 2012, http://www.forbes.com/sites/deancrutchfield/2012/03/30 /meet-the-gang-of-four-who-make-every-decision/.

9 James O'Toole and Warren Bennis, "What's Needed Next: A Culture of Candor," *Harvard Business Review*, June 2009: 54–58.

10 Peter Shankman, "Tweet Joke Leads to Morton's Surprise Steak Dinner at Newark Airport," *Huffington Post*, August 18, 2011, www.huffingtonpost.com/2011/08/18/peter-shankman-mortons-steak-tweet_n_930744.html.

11 Morten T. Hansen, Herminia Ibarra, and Urs Preyer, "The 100 Best-Performing CEOs in the World," *Harvard Business Review Online*, January/February 2013, http://hbr.org/2013/01 /the-best-performing-ceos-in-the-world/ar/1.

12 Devindra Hardawar, "How Jeff Bezos' Long-Term Thinking Paid Off Big for Amazon," Venturebeat. com, September 9, 2011, http://venturebeat.com/2011/09/09/jeff-bezos-long-term-amazon/.

13 Muammer Ozer, "A Moderated Mediation Model for the Relationship between Organizational Citizenship Behaviors and Job Performance," *Journal of Applied Psychology* 96, no. 6 (2011): 1328–1336.

14 Nancy Dodd and Daniel Ganster, "The Interactive Effects of Variety, Autonomy, and Feedback on Attitudes and Performance," *Journal of Organizational Behavior*, 17 (1996): 329–347.

15 Gary Sherman, J. J. Lee, A. J. C. Cuddy, Jonathan Renshon, Christopher Oveis, James Gross, and Jennifer Lerner, "Leadership Is Associated with Lower Levels of Stress," *Proceedings of the National Academy of Sciences 2012*; published ahead of print September 24, 2012, doi:10.1073 /pnas.1207042109.

16 "The WorldBlu List 2012: HCL Technologies," WorldBlu, http://worldblu.com/awardee-profiles /2012.php.

17 Joe Reynolds, "Give Your Employees Unlimited Vacation Days," Inc.com, January 5, 2012, http://www.inc.com/joe-reynolds/give-your-employees-unlimited-vacation-time.html.

18 Edward Shepard III, Thomas Clifton, and Douglas Kruse, "Flexible Work Hours and Productivity: Some Evidence from the Pharmaceutical Industry," *Industrial Relations* 35, no. 1 (1996): 123–139.

Chapter 6

1 We now know the former Camp Cooke and Cooke AFB as Vandenberg Air Force Base, home to much of the US military space program.

2 John F. Kennedy, excerpt from an address before a joint session of Congress, May 25, 1961, http://www.jfklibrary.org/Asset-Viewer/xzw1gaeeTES6khED14P1Iw.aspx.

3   Kim Cameron, *Positive Leadership: Strategies for Extraordinary Performance* (San Francisco: Berrett-Koehler Publishers, 2008), 67.

4   Richard Hackman and Edward Lawler, "Employee Reactions to Job Characteristics," *Journal of Applied Psychology* 55 (1971): 263.

5   I thank my colleague Dr. Wayne Cascio for first telling me his story about how a janitor at a pharmaceutical client of his actually said this. Amazing.

6   For another excellent discussion on how to impart meaning, see Kim Cameron's *Positive Leadership*, 2008.

7   Yochi Cohen-Charash and Paul Spector, "The Role of Justice in Organizations: A Meta-Analysis," *Organizational Behavior and Human Decision Processes* 86 (2001): 278–321.

8   Kristin Laurin, Aaron Kay, and Gavan Fitzsimons, "Reactance Versus Rationalization: Divergent Responses to Policies that Constrain Freedom," *Psychological Science* 23, no. 2 (2012): 205–209.

9   Guylaine Landry and Christian Vandenberghe, "Relational Commitments in Employee–Supervisor Dyads and Employee Job Performance," *The Leadership Quarterly* 23, no. 3 (2012): 293–308.

10 Wayne Boss, "Team Building and the Problem of Regression: The Personal Management Interview as an Intervention," *Journal of Applied Behavioral Science* 19 (1983): 67–83.

Chapter 7

1   Paul Lawrence and Nitin Nohria, *Driven: How Human Nature Shapes Our Choices* (San Francisco: Jossey-Bass, 2002), 107.

2   Anders Dysvik and Bård Kuvaas, "The Relationship Between Perceived Training Opportunities, Work Motivation and Employee Outcomes," *International Journal of Training and Development* 12, no. 3 (2008): 138–157.

3   Lawrence and Nohria, *Driven*, 2002.

4   Tom Rath, *StrengthsFinder 2.0* (New York: Gallup Press, 2007).

5   Donald Clifton and James Harter, *Investing In Strengths* (San Francisco: Berrett-Koehler Publishers, 2003).

6   Cameron, *Positive Leadership*, 2008.

7   Peter F. Drucker, "Managing Oneself," *Harvard Business Review* 77 (1999): 4.

8   If you don't know about the Macbeth thing, it's bad luck to utter the word "Macbeth" in a theater. Theater people go to great lengths to say "The Scottish Play" instead, lest they curse the production they're currently in.

9   Diana Tamir and Jason Mitchell, "Disclosing Information About the Self Is Intrinsically Rewarding," *Proceedings of the National Academy of Science* 109, no. 21 (2012): 8038–43.

10 I'd like to thank Jenny Rogers and her book *Coaching Skills: A Handbook* for first inspiring me to come up with magic coaching questions for leaders.

11 Nathanael Fast and Serena Chen, "When the Boss Feels Inadequate: Power, Competence, Aggression," *Psychological Science* 20 (2009): 1406–1413.

12 Laurence Peter and Raymond Hull, *The Peter Principle: Why Things Always Go Wrong* (New York: William Morrow and Company, 1969).

Part III

1   Anthony Robbins, *Unlimited Power: The New Science of Personal Achievement* (New York: Free Press, 1994), 373.

Chapter 8

1   "More Than Money Motivates Employees," June 1, 2005, www.shrm.org/hrdisciplines /compensation/Articles/Pages/CMS_013033.aspx.

2   Albert Bandura, "Self-Efficacy: Toward a Unifying Theory of Behavioral Change," *Psychological Review* 84, no. 2 (1977): 191–215.

3   Timothy Judge and Joyce Bono, "Relationship of Core Self-Evaluations Traits—Self-Esteem, Generalized Self-Efficacy, Locus of Control, and Emotional Stability—with Job Satisfaction and Job Performance: A Meta-Analysis," *Journal of Applied Psychology* 86 (2001): 80–92.

4   Joyce Bono and Timothy Judge, "Self-Concordance at Work: Toward Understanding the Motivational Effects of Transformational Leaders," *Academy of Management Journal* 46 (2003): 554-571.

5   Josh A. Arnold, Sharon Arad, Jonathan Rhoades, and Fritz Drasgow, "The Empowering Leadership Questionnaire: The Construction and Validation of a New Scale for Measuring Leader Behaviors," *Journal of Organizational Behavior* 21 (2000): 249–269.

6   Bezuijen, van den Berg, van Dam, and Thierry, "Pygmalion and Employee Learning" (2009).

7   Bob Nelson and Dean Spitzer, *The 1001 Rewards & Recognition Fieldbook: The Complete Guide* (New York: Workman Publishing Company, 2002).

8   John Norcross, Marci Mrykalo, and Matthew Blagys, "*Auld Lang Syne*: Success Predictors, Change Processes, and Self-Reported Outcomes of New Year's Resolvers and Nonresolvers," *Journal of Clinical Psychology* 58, no. 4, (2002): 397–405.

9   Shawn Achor, "Positive Intelligence: Three Ways Individuals Can Cultivate Their Own Sense of Well-Being and Set Themselves Up to Succeed," *Harvard Business Review* 90, no. 1/2, (2012): 100–102.

10 Stephen Covey, *The 7 Habits of Highly Effective People: Restoring the Character Ethic* (New York: Free Press, 1989).

11 Robert Emmons and Michael McCullough, "Counting Blessings vs. Burdens: An Experimental Investigation of Gratitude and Subjective Well-Being in Daily Life," *Journal of Personality and Social Psychology,* 84 (2003): 377–389.

12 Paul Harvey and Kenneth Harris, "Frustration Based Outcomes of Entitlement and the Influence of Supervisor Communication," *Human Relations,* 63 (2010): 1639–1660.

13 B. F. Skinner, *The Behavior of Organisms: An Experimental Analysis* (New York: Appleton-Century, 1938).

Chapter 9

1   Pete Weaver and Simon Mitchell, "Lessons for Leaders from the People Who Matter: How Employees Around the World View Their Leaders," Development Dimensions International, 2011: www.ddiworld.com/thought-leadership/research/trend-research /lessons-for-leaders-from-the-people-who-matter.

2   Avraham Kluge and Angelo DeNisi, "The Effects of Feedback Interventions on Performance: A Historical Review, a Meta-Analysis, and a Preliminary Feedback Intervention Theory," *Psychological Bulletin* 119 (1996): 254–284.

3   I want to thank my colleagues at the Center for Creative Leadership for this learning.

4   Jing Zhou, "Feedback Valence, Feedback Style, Task Autonomy, and Achievement Orientation: Interactive Effects on Creative Performance," *Journal of Applied Psychology* 74 (1998): 580–590.

5   Ralph N. Pampino Jr., Jennifer E. MacDonald, Jill E. Mullin, and David A. Wilder, "Weekly Feedback vs. Daily Feedback," *Journal of Organizational Behavior Management* 23, no. 2–3 (2004): 21–43.

6   Robert Chapman, "Attitude Toward Performance Appraisal: The Concepts of Expectancy and Trust," unpublished thesis, Canisius College (2007).

7   Joseph Folkman, "Are You Creating Disgruntled Employees?" HBR Blog Network, July 23, 2012, http://blogs.hbr.org/cs/2012/07/are_you_creating_disgruntled_e.html?awid=6327518778022674349-3271.

Chapter 10

1   Judith Hicks Stiehm and Nicholas W. Townsend, *The U.S. Army War College: Military Education in a Democracy* (Philadelphia: Temple University Press, 2002).

2   I'd like to thank my colleague Tom Turney for reminding me of this amazing study. G. R. Stephenson, "Cultural Acquisition of a Specific Learned Response Among Rhesus Monkeys," *Progress in Primatology*, eds. D. Starek, R. Schneider and H. J. Kuhn (Stuttgart: Fischer, 1967): 279–288.

3   Mark Hughes, "Do 70 Percent of All Organizational Change Initiatives Really Fail?" *Journal of Change Management* 11, no. 4 (2011): 451–464. Note: this Mark Hughes is not the same as the Mark Hughes from previous chapters—just a coincidence!

4   Martin E. Smith, "Implementing Organizational Change: Correlates of Success and Failure," *Performance Improvement Quarterly* 15, no. 1 (2008): 67-83

5   George Daniels and Ann Hollifield, "Time of Turmoil: Short- and Long-Term Effects of Organizational Change on Newsroom Employees," *Journalism & Mass Communication Quarterly* 79, no. 3 (2002): 661–680.

6   Atul Gawande, *The Checklist Manifesto: How to Get Things Right* (New York: Metropolitan Books, 2010).

Part VI

1   Jamal Muhammad, "Relationship of Job Stress and Type-A Behavior to Employees' Job Satisfaction, Organizational Commitment, Psychosomatic Health Problems and Turnover Motivation," *Human Relations* 43, no. 8 (1990): 727–738.

2   Mihaly Csikszentmihalyi, *Beyond Boredom and Anxiety: Experiencing Flow in Work and Play* (San Francisco: Jossey-Bass, 1975).

3   "This Day in History: Ford Factory Workers Get 40-Hour Week," History Channel website, http://www.history.com/this-day-in-history/ford-factory-workers-get-40-hour-week.

Chapter 11

1   Ed Frauenheim, "Today's Workforce—Pressed and Stressed," *Workforce Magazine,* December 16, 2011, www.workforce.com/article/20111216/NEWS02/111219976/todays-workforce-pressed-and-stressed.

2   *The Loyalty Deficit: The Impact of Recession on Engagement,* The Hay Group, 2008: www.haygroup.com/uk/downloads/details.aspx?id=28490.

3   Marianna Virtanen, Archana Singh-Manoux, Jane Ferrie, David Gimeno, Michael Marmot, Marko Elovainio, Markus Jokela, Jussi Vahtera, and Mika Kivimaki, "Long Working Hours and Cognitive Function," *American Journal of Epidemiology* 169 (2009): 596–605.

4 Tony Schwartz, "More Vacation Is the Secret Sauce," HBR Blog Network, September 6, 2012, http://blogs.hbr.org/schwartz/2012/09/more-vacation-is-the-secret-sa.html.

5 Elaine Eaker, Joan Pinsky, and William Castelli, "Myocardial Infarction and Coronary Death Among Women: Psychosocial Predictors from a 20-Year Follow Up of Women in the Framingham Study," *American Journal of Epidemiology* 135, no. 8 (1992): 854–864.

6 "Job Burnout: How to Spot It and Take Action," The Mayo Clinic, December 8, 2012, www.mayoclinic.com/health/burnout/WL00062.

7 Joe Robinson, "Overworked and Underplayed: The Incredible Shrinking Vacation," *The Huffington Post,* May 31, 2011, http://www.huffingtonpost.com/joe-robinson/vacation-time_b_868655.html.

8 Ibid.

9 "American Workers' Time Off Survey," Adecco Group, December 2012, http://www.adeccousa.com/articles/American-Workers%E2%80%99-Time-Off-Survey.html?id=208&url=/pressroom/pressreleases/pages/forms/allitems.aspx&templateurl=/AboutUs/pressroom/Pages/Press-release.aspx.

10 Ibid.

11 Robinson, "Overworked and Underplayed."

12 Dalia Etziona, "Annual Vacation: Duration of Relief from Job Stressors and Burnout," *Anxiety, Stress & Coping: An International Journal* 16 (2003): 213–226.

13 Jessica de Bloom, Sabine Geurts, and Michiel Kompier, "Effects of Short Vacations, Vacation Activities and Experiences on Employee Health and Well-Being," *Stress and Health* 28, no. 4 (2012): 305–318.

14 Atsunori Ariga and Alejandro Lleras, "Brief and Rare Mental 'Breaks' Keep You Focused: Deactivation and Reactivation of Task Goals Preempt Vigilance Decrements," *Cognition* 118, no. 3 (2011): 439–443.

15 Rainer Maria Rilke, *Letters to a Young Poet* (New York: Norton, 1934).

Chapter 12
1 Timothy Ferriss, *The 4-Hour Workweek: Escape the 9–5, Live Anywhere, and Join the New Rich* (New York: Crown Publishing, 2009).

2 Paul Leinwand and Cesare Mainardi, *The Essential Advantage: How to Win with a Capabilities-Driven Strategy* (Boston: Harvard Business Press Books, 2010).

3 Covey, *The 7 Habits of Highly Successful People.*

Chapter 13
1 "Google Spends $72 Million on Free Employee Food Per Year," *Huffington Post*, May 1, 2008, www.huffingtonpost.com/2008/04/23/google-spends-72-million_n_98255.html.

2 David Abramis, "Play in Work: Childish Hedonism or Adult Enthusiasm?" *American Behavioral Scientist* 33, no. 3 (1990): 353–373.

3 Abraham Maslow, "A Theory of Human Motivation," *Psychological Review* 50, no. 4 (1943): 370–96.

4 William Glasser, *The Control Theory Manager* (New York: HarperBusiness, 1994).

5 Kim Cameron, "Organizational Virtuousness and Performance," *Positive Organizational Scholarship*, eds. Kim Cameron, Jane Dutton, and Robert Quinn (San Francisco: Berrett-Koehler Publishers, 2003), 48–65.

6 Gerald Schoenewolf, "Emotional Contagion: Behavioral Induction in Individuals and Groups," *Modern Psychoanalysis* 15 (1990): 49–61.

7 Bill George and Peter Sims, *True North: Discover Your Authentic Leadership* (San Francisco: Jossey-Bass/John Wiley & Sons, 2007).

8 Pamela Sherrod, "Execs Smile On Those Who Can Tell a Joke," *Chicago Tribune*, July 29, 1986, http://articles.chicagotribune.com/1986-07-29/business/8602240480_1_ humor-new-perspective-survey.

9 Robin Dunbar, Rebecca Baron, Anna Frangou, Eiluned Pearce, Edwin van Leeuwen, Julie Stowe, Giselle Partridge, Ian McDonald, Vincent Barra, and Mark can Vuht, "Social Laughter Is Correlated with an Elevated Pain Threshold," *Proceedings of the Royal Society of Biological Sciences* 279, no. 1731 (2012): 1161–1167.

10 Bruce J. Avolio, Jane M. Howell, and John J. Sosik, "A Funny Thing Happened on the Way to the Bottom Line: Humor as a Moderator of Leadership Style Effects," *The Academy of Management Journal* 42, no. 2 (1999), 219–227.

11 Martha Mangelsdorf, "The Surprising Benefits of Office Chitchat," *MIT Sloan Management Review*, August 27, 2010, http://sloanreview.mit.edu/improvisations/2010/08/27/ the-surprising-benefits-of-office-chitchat/.

12 Robert C. Ford, John W. Newstrom, and Frank S. McLaughlin, "Making Workplace Fun More Functional," *Industrial and Commercial Training* 36, no. 3 (2004): 117–120.

Conclusion

1 Malcolm Gladwell, *Outliers: The Story of Success* (New York: Back Bay Books, 2011).

2 Daniel Coyle, *The Talent Code: Greatness Isn't Born. It's Grown. Here's How.* (New York: Bantam, 2009).

3 Benjamin Bloom, "The 2 Sigma Problem: The Search for Methods of Group Instruction as Effective as One-to-One Tutoring," *Educational Researcher* 13, no. 6 (1984): 4–16.

INDEX

WANT TO HARNESS THE POWER OF YOUR COMPANY'S LEADERS?

Keynote Speaking

Dr. Tasha Eurich meticulously customizes her keynotes, seminars, and workshops to fit her clients (not the other way around). Her approach is never, ever to bring a "motivational speech in a box." Instead, she learns her clients' objectives (e.g., drive market share, revenue targets, employee engagement) and creates a custom learning event to achieve them.

Dr. Eurich has successfully served clients in many industries, including finance and banking, cable and telecommunications, education, electronics, engineering and construction, energy, financial services, food and beverage, government, healthcare, legal, nonprofit, pharmaceuticals, professional services, technology, and transportation.

The Eurich Group—Building Inspired Leaders and Effective Teams

What We Do

The Eurich Group helps organizations succeed by improving the effectiveness of their leaders and teams. We help our clients:

- **Learn.** We are thought leaders who connect business leaders and HR professionals with the latest research and practices in leadership, teams, employee engagement, and organizational culture and strategy.

- **Adapt.** We help leaders embrace change and ambiguity, successfully transition into new roles, let go of old patterns derailing their success, and harness experience as a powerful development tool.

- **Lead.** We catalyze organizational performance by enhancing leaders' skills in setting strategy, leading and engaging employees and teams, emotional intelligence, self-awareness, mindfulness, and abundance.

How We Do It

We practice in organizations of all sizes and industries and specialize in:

- Leadership training and development programs.
- High potential identification and development.
- Executive coaching and new leader integration.
- Team development and alignment.
- Executive retreats and meeting facilitation.
- Employee performance, engagement and retention.
- Culture assessment and transformation.

How We're Different

We are a credible business partner. Whether we are working with executives to understand their business' complex needs, simplifying complicated research models for leaders or dispelling HR jargon, our clients note that we are different from other consultants because we are business people first.

We build our solutions around your needs, not the other way around. While many consultants like to put your company's logo on their materials or push their approach, we create truly customized solutions. Rather than focusing on activities or inputs, we begin with the business results you want to achieve (e.g., increasing sales effectiveness, market share) and build solutions that produce them. You will never be passed off to an account manager or feel like the meter is running; we bill on a flat fee basis. We also know you work in a 24/7 world, so we make ourselves available whenever you need us.

We care as much about practical solutions as we do about cutting-edge science. Having been dubbed "Thoughtful Pragmatists" by a client, our wealth of internal organizational experience tells us that it doesn't matter if an organization has the "fanciest" process or strategy available—the rubber meets the road when you implement it and make it stick. The ultimate measure of success is whether our clients are successful after we have left!

We have an unquenchable energy and belief in the potential of people. Our energy and passion are often noted as key factors in the success of our work. We approach people problems from a place of abundance. In our experience (and scientific researchers agree), leaders and organizations realize the strongest results when we find and unlock potential.

For more information, please visit www.theeurichgroup.com.

ABOUT THE AUTHOR

Dr. Tasha Eurich is a leadership expert, speaker, author, and principal of the Eurich Group. Her life's work is to help organizations succeed by improving the effectiveness of their leaders and teams.

With a contagious passion and energy, Dr. T (as her clients call her) pairs a scientific grounding in human behavior with a practical approach to solving business challenges. Her ten-plus-year career has spanned roles as an external consultant and a direct report to both CEOs and human resources executives. The majority of Dr. Eurich's work has been with executives in large Fortune 500 organizations, recently including CH2M HILL, Xcel Energy, Western Union, Newmont Mining, Centura Health, CoBiz Financial, the City of Cincinnati, and HCA.

Dr. Eurich is a frequent speaker with organizations, conferences, and associations, and her expertise has been highlighted in outlets like the *New York Times, Forbes*, and Denver's 9NEWS business segment with Gregg Moss. In 2013, Dr. Eurich was honored as one of *Denver Business Journal's* "40 under 40" based on her achievements in business and involvement in the community.

In addition to *Bankable Leadership*, she has published articles in *Chief Learning Officer, The Journal of Business and Psychology, Oil & Gas Monitor, The Psychologist-Manager Journal*, and *The Work Style Magazine*.

With a PhD in industrial-organizational psychology from Colorado State University and BAs in theater and psychology from Middlebury College, Dr. Eurich serves on the faculty at the Center for Creative Leadership, one of the top ten executive development institutions in the world. She has also lectured at Colorado State University and the University of Denver's business schools. Her research on generations at work has been showcased around the world.

Dr. Eurich serves on the board of Rocky Mountain HR People & Strategy and the Sensory Processing Disorder Foundation. She also delivers pro bono consulting to nonprofit organizations. In her spare time, she enjoys traveling, cycling (especially the National Multiple Sclerosis Society's annual 150-mile bike ride, which she does in honor of her stepdad), and spending time with her husband and their three rambunctious dogs.